T0355630

JAN PAŘEZ
HEDVIKA KUCHAŘOVÁ

THE IRISH FRANCISCANS
IN PRAGUE 1629-1786
HISTORY OF THE FRANCISCAN COLLEGE OF THE IMMACULATE CONCEPTION OF THE VIRGIN MARY IN PRAGUE

CHARLES UNIVERSITY IN PRAGUE
KAROLINUM PRESS 2016

Reviewed by: doc. PhDr. Ivana Čornejová, CSc.
            Dr Joseph MacMahon, OFM
            PhDr. Jiří Mikulec, CSc.
            doc. Ondřej Pilný, PhD.

The Cataloging-in-Publication Data is available from the National Library
of the Czech Republic

ISBN 978-80-246-2676-5
ISBN 978-80-246-2709-0 (online: pdf)

CONTENTS

ILLUSTRATIONS

FIGURES

PHOTOS

Jan Pařez (1–9, 12–20, 22–25, 28–34), Národní archiv (10–11), Národní knihovna (26), Národní památkový ústav (21, 27, 35)

COVER

A view of the Irish Franciscan church and college in Prague. Coloured engraving by Johann Balzer and Joseph Anton Scotti, 1781 (SK). Photo Jan Pařez.

The publication of this book has been supported by the Department of Foreign Affairs and Trade, Ireland; the Franciscan Province of Ireland; and the Centre for Irish Studies, Charles University, Prague.

Sincere gratitude is due to the Embassy of Ireland in Prague, and in particular to H.E. Richard Ryan, for ongoing support of the English-language translation of the present volume.

AUTHORS' ACKNOWLEDGEMENTS

We would like to thank in particular:

Ivana Čornejová of the Institute of History of Charles University in Prague for many valuable comments,

Jiří Mikulec of the Historical Institute of the Academy of Science of the Czech Republic likewise for his valuable suggestions and for his information concerning documents on the Fraternity of St. Patrick,

also

Thomas O'Connor of the Department of History of the National University of Ireland, Maynooth, for enabling us to obtain literature from Ireland,

Mícheál MacCraith of the National University of Ireland, Galway, and St. Isidore's College, Rome, for providing written version of his conference speech from autumn 2000 in Maynooth,

Dáibhí Ó Cróinín of the National University of Ireland, Galway, for providing literature,

Harriett Fennell for important assistance in mediating contacts,

Helga Robinson-Hammerstein of Trinity College, Dublin, for much photocopying and advice,

Jaroslava Kašparová of the National Museum Library for drawing our attention to certain prints from the "Hibernian" library in the National Library and to the related bibliographical data,

Helena Klímová and other officials at the First Department of the National Archives in Prague for the extraordinary willingness with which they bore our often time-consuming requests,

Zlatuše Kukánová for the provision of data from the book of ordinands by Šimon Brož,

Anthony Lynch for providing literature,

Petr Maťa of the Institute of Advanced Study, Central European University, Budapest for data from the "Martinic Testament" (scenes from the Old Testament in the Martinic Palace in Prague),

the Strahov librarian, Father Evermod G. Šidlovský OPraem, for the provision of normally inaccessible literature from Rome and for permission to reproduce the Strahov materials,

the Embassy of Ireland in Prague for the loan of literature,

Ignatius Fennessy OFM of the Franciscan Library, Killiney for his very kind reception and for providing invaluable assistance and literature,

Ladislav Zápařka for the provision of historical documents,

Zdeněk Kalvach, who was in at the beginning of everything,

Jana and Michael Stoddart for translating this book into English,

Father Joseph MacMahon of the Franciscan Friary in Dublin for reviewing the text and for many valuable suggestions,

Linda Jayne Turner for copy editing,

and, finally, Ondřej Pilný, Director of the Centre for Irish Studies at the Department of Anglophone Literatures and Cultures, Faculty of Arts, Charles University, Prague, for all his assistance, language support and making this English edition possible by coordinating the translation.

TRANSLATORS' ACKNOWLEDGEMENTS

We must express our grateful thanks to Father Joseph MacMahon of the Franciscan Friary, 4 Merchant's Quay, Dublin, for his resolution of many knotty problems and for his great enthusiasm for the project.

INTRODUCTION

When Queen Elizabeth of England banished the Franciscans from Ireland at the very end of the sixteenth century, she very clearly had no idea that she was indirectly responsible for one of the most intensive contacts between two small European lands – Ireland and Bohemia. Apart from the activities of the Irish Franciscans, who in Bohemia were called "hyberni" after the Latin name of their homeland, the Irish significantly affected Bohemian history in two further areas; in the less fortunate instance, this concerned the Irish officers who participated in the murder of Albrecht Valdštejn in Cheb and their successors who served in the Imperial forces, and in the happier instance, this concerned the Irish students and, above all, teachers of medicine who worked at Prague University and in Bohemia generally.

This study is an attempt based primarily on archive sources to define the place which the College of the Immaculate Conception of the Virgin Mary of the Irish Franciscans of the Stricter Observance in Prague occupied in Bohemian history and to document the activity of its members. Because we were dealing with a hitherto largely neglected theme, we concentrated mainly on domestic sources. We believe that it is only after the wealth of material present in the Czech archives has received appropriate attention that research should address the material in archives abroad.

As is evident from the survey of sources and literature and ultimately from the further text, too, it was extremely difficult to present the history of the college in the form of a simple chronological description of events. On the one hand, we had at our disposal a wealth of material relating to the period of the blossoming of the college in the second half of the seventeenth century as well as documents connected with its dissolution. On the other hand, there are long periods in the eighteenth century for which there are no written records. Some periods cannot be revealed without a study of personalities such as Anthony Bruodin or events such as the dispute about tuition at the archiepiscopal seminary, but this would lead to a serious imbalance in our study. We therefore decided that we would present the history of the Franciscan college in the form of research into various time periods. To those we have added the necessary accounts of a biographical, prosopographical and political nature.

Chapter 1 with its survey of sources and literature is followed by a summary essay on the Irish in Bohemian society, and then a chapter describing the Irish province of the Franciscans of the Stricter Observance, and the founding and first years of the college. This is linked with a section on the most famous period of the college after the middle of the seventeenth century, then a chapter describing the withdrawal of the Irish Franciscans from public life. The sixth part is a look at the ranks of the turbulent community in 1737. The final chapter deals with the dissolution of the Irish Franciscan college and the secularisation of the buildings and property in the 1780s.

Finally, a list of all the known members of the college and of the guardians is appended.

Strahov, 1 October 2001
The authors

INTRODUCTION
TO THE ENGLISH EDITION

When we set about preparing the English edition about eleven years after publishing our monograph on the Irish Franciscans in Prague, we faced a difficult set of issues. These concerned, not only the current developments in research, but also decisions pertaining to translation or adaptation. To begin with, we had to consider our recent work that has focused on documents related to the dissolution of the friary and the departure of the members of its community, since this information needed to be added to the English edition. As regards new publications by Czech historians, these have centred mainly on the artistic heritage of the Irish Franciscans, the legacy left by renowned artists working both in Prague and other parts of Bohemia in the seventeenth century in particular. Similarly, the excellent edition of the diaries of the Prague Archbishop Ernst Adalbert, Cardinal Harrach, as well as recently published studies dedicated to the ecclesiastical history of mid-seventeenth century Bohemia gave us more specific or marginal information, but nothing of major import.

The extensive historiographical literature in English that had been published during those eleven years meant more difficult decisions for us. Works like the magisterial *The Irish Franciscans 1534–1990*, edited by Edel Bhreathnach, Joseph MacMahon and John McCafferty (2009) placed the Prague convent in an eminently mobile and flexible Irish Franciscan community that moved across the continent from Louvain to Rome. For the members of this community, Prague, the capital of the Kingdom of Bohemia, was one of the hubs of a dense network connecting their insular homeland with Catholic centres in continental Europe and with other emigrants who had settled on the mainland. Many an important personality passed through the Prague college. This permanent state of flux of the community, the nature of life in exile and on a mission might be surprising, not only for the general reader, but also for many a Central European historian. However, we felt that the intended Anglophone audience of the present volume would be sufficiently familiar with this perspective, and also able to readily access these remarkable studies in English.

The same holds for more recent interpretations of the history of Ireland in the seventeenth and eighteenth century. We are acutely aware that our coverage of the area is sketchy, and is based only on the sources available to us in the 1990s. Therefore, we must beg the reader for indulgence: the primary aim of having our history of the Prague college of the Irish Franciscans translated has always been to make the copious and invaluable material from Czech and Central European archives available in English. Adapting the Czech text so that it organically incorporated the recent research of Irish historians would essentially have meant to write a new book, and address issues such as the current debates pertaining to Irish history for which we lack the expertise. The present volume thus includes updated information pertaining to discoveries made in local archives but, as regards international research from the same period, limits itself to merely referencing the most important essays by way of pointers. It is our modest hope that our work will still be found useful, and will help to fill the gaps relating to what is known internationally about the Irish Franciscans in Prague.

Strahov, 10 May 2014
The authors

TRANSLATORS' NOTE
ON TERMINOLOGY

The Czech original, when referring to the Irish Franciscan institution in Prague, uses the words "klášter," "konvent" and "kolej." Based on present-day usage and taking into account Benignus Millett's comments on nomenclature,[1] we have adopted "college" wherever the reference is to the Prague institution in accord with, for example, St. Isidore's College in Rome, "friary" where appropriate for other Franciscan institutions and "monastery" where appropriate for other, non-mendicant, orders.

Also, as pointed out by the authors, the word "hybern," from the Latin "Hybernia" (or "Hibernia") meaning Ireland and thus "Hybernus" (or "Hibernus") meaning an Irishman, was used by the Czechs to denote primarily (if not exclusively) an Irish Franciscan. However, to use this word in English did not seem appropriate as the word is rarely used today in English, nor does it have such a specific, relevant historical meaning. Therefore, we have translated the original title, "Hyberni v Praze," as "The Irish Franciscans in Prague" and "Hyberni" usually as "the Irish Franciscans."

---

1   Benignus Millett, *The Irish Franciscans 1651–1665* (Rome: Gregorian University Press, 1964) 66.

TRANSLATORS' NOTES ON NAMES

The above indicates the difficulties the authors laboured under in deciding the forms in which names should be shown. In translating the text into English, we decided to render the Christian or order names into the usual English form. With the various families of the nobility, with reference to as many sources as possible, whenever we found the German form of the name widely used, we used this, otherwise we retained the Czech form. With other nationalities, we have used the original names where it has been possible to determine them. Here, too, there are exceptions where a common English form exists for well-known historical figures, for example, John Huss or John Amos Comenius.

Our main reference tool in terms of names has been Benignus Millett's *The Irish Franciscans 1651–1665*, whose example in terms of vocabulary and usage we have largely, but not slavishly, followed.

1. THE IRISH AND BOHEMIAN SOCIETY – AN IRISH ISLAND IN A BOHEMIAN SEA

THE ROAD TO EMIGRATION

The Irish began to arrive in Bohemia in greater numbers in the first half of the seventeenth century. They had left their native land primarily for religious reasons, because their Catholicism had exposed them to repression since the period of the Tudor dynasty, whose famous representative Henry VIII had begun to enforce a local form of the Reformation. Hand in hand with the suppression of the Catholic faith went the attempt by the English to bring the whole of Ireland under their control. At that time, Ireland was divided into three power-political-ethnic areas: the area around Dublin under direct English rule, known as the Pale; then that controlled by the "Anglo-Irish rebels," local long-term English settlers who had mixed feelings about the English occupation; and that of the original Celtic (Gaelic) inhabitants who lived in a significantly different social order (laws, institutions, traditions and language). The latter were regarded by the English as enemies. Feuds were typical, not only between all the groups, but also within individual units, particularly among the Irish, for whom – in their own words – this trait is allegedly almost a national attribute.

During the sixteenth and seventeenth centuries, the Irish, under pressure of an increasing consolidation of English power, rose up in a series of greater or lesser rebellions, all of which were unsuccessful and always worsened the existing conditions. The rebellion by Hugh O'Neill and his Ulster allies in the late sixteenth and early seventeenth century ended in the Battle of Kinsale, the "Flight of the Earls" and the definitive subjection of Ireland by the English. Then came the confiscation of land held by Catholics and the Plantation of Ulster by Protestant Englishmen and especially Scots. Another rebellion instigated by Sir Phelim O'Neill at the end of the reign of Charles I was brutally ended by Oliver Cromwell after Charles's execution and was followed by further confiscations and a wave of emigration. Confiscated property passed into the hands of Protestants. After the fall of the English Republic, during the Restoration, some returned hoping for religious freedom and the restitution of their property, but of the original three-fifths of agricultural land which had been in the hands of Catholics before 1641, only one-fifth was restored.

Although in practice it was, to a certain degree, tolerated, Catholicism hovered on the brink of illegality, and representatives of the Church were often persecuted, imprisoned and executed. After the Catholic James II ascended to the throne, the situation began to change. The first Earl and Duke of Tyrconnell, Richard Talbot, James's confidant and also a Catholic, was named the Irish Viceroy and during his rule his fellow Catholics quickly began to enter government administration. However, their imminent return to the Irish Parliament was thwarted by another coup d'état in England which led to the succession of William of Orange, James's Protestant son-in-law. James then escaped to Ireland, where he summoned the Irish Parliament which proclaimed its independence from the English Parliament. William of Orange however, landed in Ireland and, after a psychologically important defeat of James at the Battle of the Boyne in 1690, marched triumphantly through the country. Even though Catholics enjoyed limited religious tolerance and the confiscation of their property was not too extensive, after the Treaty of Limerick the following year, a great many Irish left the country and it was clear that the Catholic side had suffered a severe defeat. This soon manifested itself in practice in the Penal Laws, which turned Catholics into second-class citizens. Under the Penal Laws, they were excluded from Parliament, forbidden to hold government office, practise law or serve as officers in the army, and forbidden to buy land or rent it for over thirty-one years. Further indignities were imposed, in particular a prohibition on education at home or abroad. In much the same way as it was necessary to swear an "immaculate oath" on the Immaculate Conception of the Virgin Mary so as to be allowed to study at university in Bohemia, in order to study in Ireland, students were obliged to publicly deny transubstantiation and renounce certain Catholic dogma as idolatry. Despite the law of 1697 exiling the Catholic clergy and a repression lasting three quarters of a century, from 1778 onwards, the Catholics gradually managed to limit discrimination.

The previous three paragraphs show that the Irish emigrated in many waves over almost two centuries. The reasons were various; Irish soldiers were threatened with execution for rebellion, the clergy were forced to train in the more peaceful setting of a country with religious tolerance or one where Catholicism was the state religion, and Catholic students had no other choice but to study at universities on the continent.

The greatest paradox of the arrival of the Irish Franciscans in Bohemia therefore remains the fact that, despite their own experience of cruel religious and social persecution in their own country, they arrived here in order, albeit indirectly, to participate in a parallel oppression, but this time in the name of "the one true faith."

Fig. 1 The assassination of Albrecht of Valdštejn in Cheb (Eger). Engraving by Matthäus Merian, 1639 (SK).

THE IRISH FRANCISCANS AND SOLDIERS

Irish emigrants who had been forced to leave their own country for the above-mentioned reasons were welcomed in, among other places, Bohemia.[1] Among the first to arrive were the Franciscans in 1629, but the beginnings of their college were enshrouded in the bloody atmosphere of the Saxon invasion. Immediately afterwards, Irish soldiers intervened in Czech history with the murder in Cheb of Albrecht of Valdštejn (Fig. 1). The Imperial officers who had participated in the conspiracy against the "generalissimus" and in his death were richly rewarded by the Emperor: Colonel Walter Buttler,[2] Lieutenant-Colonel Robert Geraldin,[3] Captain Walter Deveroux, Captain Edmund Burke and others. In times of war, monetary rewards were converted into

---

1   For an extensive but not exhaustive list, see Ludvík Schmid, "Irská emigrace do střední Evropy v 17. a 18. století" [Irish Emigration to Central Europe in the Seventeenth and Eighteenth Centuries], *SH* 32 (1985): 189–254; *SH* 33 (1986): 247–293.
2   Walter Buttler of Ballinakill Castle, Roscrea belonged to the Butler family – the Earls of Ormond. His life, piety and charity were mentioned as early as 1639 by Thomas Carve in *Itinerarium R. D. Thomae Carve Tripperariensis … cum Historia facti Butleri, Gordon, Lesly & aliorum…*, Moguntiae 1639 (SK, EV VII 64), especially pages 57–59.
3   Josef Janáček, *Valdštejnova smrt* [*The Death of Valdštejn*] (Praha: Mladá fronta, 1970); 315 gives an incorrect first name, Walter.

estates,[4] which gradually became one of the reasons why some of Valdštejn's murderers settled in Bohemia. From the beginning, there were clearly close contacts between the Franciscan college and the Imperial officers, who not only had themselves buried in the church but also left the Franciscans sums of money or Mass endowments. Among the first known contributors appear the names of the Cheb conspirators, whose wills eloquently testify to the extensive friendly relations which prevailed among the Irish soldiers.

After the Thirty Years' War, a great number of the Irish nobility settled in Bohemia and, because only the high-born could serve as officers in the army, it was mainly from this group that Imperial soldiers were recruited. Apart from the families of the murderers of Valdštejn, that is, Buttler-Clonebough,[5] Deveroux and Gall,[6] there were also the D'Alton,[7] O'Brien,[8] MacCaffry,[9] MacBrady,[10] O'Donell,[11] MacEnnis,[12] Lodgman,[13] MacAwley,[14] Maquire,[15] Nugent,[16] Kavanagh,[17] O'Reilly,[18] Watlet,[19] Wallis[20] and Taaffe families.[21] The members of some Irish families sometimes intervened significantly in Czech history, while others played only an episodic role, such as the O'Hegerty[22] or Browne families.[23] Only six of these families still lived in Bohemia in 1918.[24]

---

4   See Tomáš Bílek, *Dějiny konfiskací v Čechách po r. 1618. Část druhá* [*The History of Confiscations in Bohemia after 1618. Second Part*] (Praha: František Řivnáč 1883) 762.

5   *Die Wappen des böhmischen Adels. J. Siebmacher's grosses Wappenbuch. Band 30* (Neustadt a.d. Aisch: Bauer und Raspe, 1979) 110 + table 59. (Further quoted as *Siebmacher*).

6   Miroslav Baroch and Ludvík Schmid, "Irská a skotská emigrace do střední Evropy" [Irish and Scottish Emigration to Central Europe], *Heraldická minucí* 1987-88 (1988): 16-17.

7   Ibid., 12-13.

8   Ibid., 46-47.

9   Ibid., 34-35.

10   Ibid., 32-33.

11   Ibid., 48-49.

12   *Siebmacher*, 58-59 + table 41.

13   Baroch and Schmid, "Irská a skotská emigrace do střední Evropy," 26-27.

14   *Siebmacher*, 145-146 + table 68. Michael Adam Franck von Franckenstein wrote a genealogical work on the family, *Origines Magawlyanae*, Pragae 1736 (SK, AO II 26). The Irish Franciscan and theologian James Griffin participated as editor. See Miroslav Baroch, "Magawly Cerati," *HaG* 16.4 (1983): 220-226.

15   Baroch and Schmid, "Irská a skotská emigrace do střední Evropy," 40-41.

16   Ibid., 44-45.

17   *Siebmacher*, 129 + table 64.

18   Ibid., 153 + table 70.

19   Ibid., 96 + table 55.

20   Ibid., 186 + table 79.

21   Ibid., 175-176 + table 77.

22   Miroslav Baroch and Ludvík Schmid, "Rod O'Hegerty" [The O'Hegerty Family], *HaG* 23.1 (1990): 3-16.

23   Maxmilian Ulysses Browne, Baronet of Camus and Mountany, was fatally wounded in the battle with the Saxons near Prague in 1757, see Miroslav Baroch, "Irové v Čechách" [Irishmen in Bohemia], *HaG* 16.3 (1983): 188-190.

24   Schmid, "Irská emigrace do střední Evropy," 194, lists the houses of Browne, Ennis, MacCaffry, O'Donell, Taaffe and Wallis. The links of these houses with Ireland were, however, strong even

We will try to establish how the Irish officers in particular left traces in the college archive, how they attempted to safeguard the Irish Franciscan college at the time, and what their attitude was towards the Bohemian side. We will also note other Irishmen who were involved with the college, although their occupation remains unknown. The wills which enabled the Irish Franciscans to make claims, whether they were successful or not, have been preserved in the original or as a copy in the archive.

The first will to be mentioned is that of Edmund Burke, written less than a year after Valdštejn's murder, in which he bequeathed the Irish Franciscans a hundred thalers.[25] If the Imperial debt for the Cheb "service" were paid (which was more than the single reward of one thousand thalers that the murderers received immediately after the deed), an additional two thousand florins would go to the college.[26] One of the other conspirators, Walter Deveroux, who according to his will dated 1639 asked to be buried in the Church of the Irish Franciscans by St. Ambrose, bequeathed them 8,000 florins (Fig. 2).[27] Walter Buttler had died childless on Christmas 1634[28] and so over the matter of the division of his property a dispute arose which lasted many decades, known as "causa buttleriana." It concerned not only the newly acquired money and estates in Bohemia but also estates in Germany and Belgium. Buttler's heirs from his family gradually handed over power of attorney for the settlement of their share into the hands of their relative, Edmund O'Kennedy, court chaplain in Vienna. The first to do this was Richard Buttler (Fig. 3),[29]

---

centuries later. For example, in the first half of the nineteenth century, the Taaffes built a romantic imitation of their old manor in Ballymote on their estate in Nalžovy, Bohemia. Edward Taaffe became prime minister in the last decade of the nineteenth century. In the 1930s, the last member of the house emigrated back to Ireland.

25 NA, ŘHyb Praha, no. 18, 23.1.1635, Visenstecke? The will of Edmund Burke (Boorke) [de Burgo]. As his Colonel, he mentions Walter Deveroux and Captain Denis MacDaniel and, amongst other friends, Buttler, Stephenson, Purcell and Geraldin. To compare the value of money bequeathed with present currency is virtually impossible. To give a general idea how much it was worth, annual living expenses for one who studied at the archiepiscopal seminary were 93 florins and 20 kreuzers. One thaler was approximately two florins.

26 Ibid., "Item quod mihi imperator propter servitium Egraneum largitus est, inter colonellos Gal, Deverox et Geraldinum aequaliter distribuendum reliquo sub hac tamen conditione, si id aequisiverint collegio Pragensi duo millia florenorum solvant, et tria millia florenorum vexillifero meo Joanni Casey." [Item, what the Emperor owes me for my service in Cheb I bequeath to be distributed evenly among Colonels Gal, Deveroux and Geraldin on the condition that they pay two thousand florins to the Prague college...].

27 Ibid., nos. 31, 32, 28.12.1639, Praha. The will of Walter Deveroux.

28 Brendan Jennings ed., *Documents of the Irish Franciscans College at Prague. I*, Archivium Hibernicum or Irish Historical Records. Volume IX, Maynooth 1942, 171–294. On the front page and in the contents of the volume it is quoted incorrectly *Irish Franciscan Documents: Prague, I*, (further quoted as *IFD*). See no. 76, 10.1635, Praha. Gerald Geraldin tells Luke Wadding, amongst other things, that "our noble patron Coronell [!] Walter Butler ... die in the land of Vittemberg upon Christmas holidayes...," after being ill for 11 days.

29 Ibid., no. 34, 10.5.1641, Opava. The will of Richard Buttler. Ibid., no. 38. There is the last will of

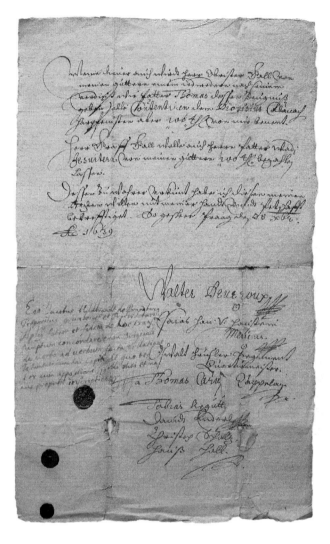

Fig. 2 The last page of Walter Deveroux's last will, 28 December 1639 (NA).

then later his brother, Thomas Theobald.[30] The attempt to settle Walter Deveroux's will is clear from the fact that in 1650 his widow gave the Irish Franciscans
1,650 florins,[31] and twelve years later bequeathed the college 16,000 florins.[32]
Although in his will of 1674 Edmund O'Kennedy, already protonotary apos-

---

Richard Buttler dated 21 November 1642 in Prague. In it he identifies himself as Captain (*Haubt-
mann*). The will was witnessed by Jeremiah O'Donovan who will be mentioned later.

30   Ibid., no. 65, 15.4.1653, Regensburg. Power of Attorney for Fr. Edmund O'Kennedy from Thomas
Theobald Buttler. For more about the Buttlers, see Schmid, "Irská emigrace do střední Evropy,"
207–209.

31   Ibid., no. 55, 1.8.1650, Praha. Johann Hartwig, Count Nostitz in Falknov, etc. as curator confirmed
that the Irish Franciscans by St. Ambrose had received a donation of 100 florins from Countess
Anne Mary Buttler.

32   Benignus Millett, *The Irish Franciscans 1651–1665* (Rome: Gregorian University Press, 1964) 147.

Fig. 3 The last page of Richard Buttler's last will, 21 November 1642 (NA).

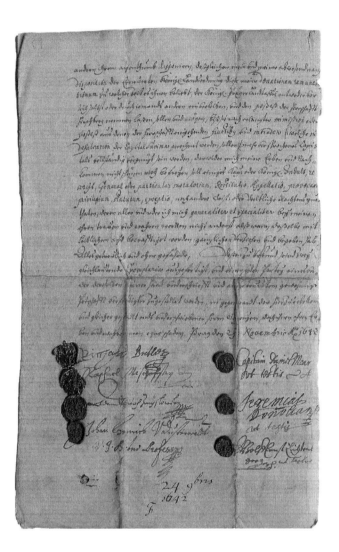

tolic at the time, made the Irish Franciscans in Prague his universal heirs[33] (the then guardian, Bernardine Clancy, was incidentally a relative of his) and passed on to them the debts owed to him by Walter Gall, Walter Deveroux and Edmund Buttler it is not clear how much the Irish college in Prague actually received. We only know that O'Kennedy died the following year.[34] According

---

33 NA, ŘHyb Praha, no. 119. 22.11.1674, Wien. The will of Edmund O'Kennedy, an apostolic protonotary and court chaplain at the Imperial court Further, from Edmund Buttler's 2,000 florins debt, he ordered 300 florins to be paid to the Irish Franciscans without delay and from the remaining debt of 1,000 florins, when the money was available, 600 florins would again be paid to the Irish Franciscans "and to my brother's grandson, Thaddeus O'Kennedy, 400 florins."

34 Ibid., no. 120, 9.1.1675, [Wien]. The Augustinian, Marek Forstall, announced to the Irish Franciscans that Edmund O'Kennedy had died.

to Hammerschmid, Buttler even bequeathed the Irish 30,000 florins, which was mostly to go towards the building of a church and a college.[35] This claim, however, seems exaggerated to us, mainly because "*causa buttleriana*" dragged on for many years afterwards.

Another member of the Buttler family who supported the Irish Franciscans in Prague was James.[36] As early as 1632, the commentaries on Aristotle by Pietro Tartareto were either donated by him or bought for the emerging college library with his money, as is evidenced by the postscript "*Ad usum fratrum Hybernorum collegii Pragensis ex dono illustrissimi domini Jacobi Butleri Hiberni 1632.*"[37]

Another Irish officer who expressed a wish to be buried in the Irish church was the commander of the imperial guard, John de Barry, who devoted 200 thalers to this purpose.[38]

Also noteworthy from the same year is the will of Captain Jeremiah O'Donovan and the relationships which ensued. Besides the wish to be buried with his wife Judita in the chapel of the Irish Franciscan church in Prague, he included in his will a bequest to the Irish Franciscans of 1,000 florins and the material for the provision of antependia for the church.[39] His stepson, Thaddeus, son of the deceased commander of the guards, James O'Meary,[40] and his relative James O'Hea, a citizen of Prague's Lesser Town, were named as his heirs. Admittedly, until he came of age, Thaddeus's guardian was to be Šimon Hesselius, notary public and syndic of Prague's Lesser Town, but on all matters he had to consult with the Irish Franciscans, Bernardine Clancy and Bonaventure Bruodin. Among the friends remembered in the will are also the names of Walter Deveroux, two members of the Geraldin family,[41] Edmund MacGranna and John O'Mulraynne.[42] O'Donovan also deposited in the Irish Franciscan archive (!) a great gold chain, saying that it was to be

---

35 Jan Florian Hammerschmid, *Prodromus gloriae Pragenae*, Vetero-Pragae 1717, 302. This information has not been confirmed by any other sources or literature.
36 Possibly it refers to Baronet James Buttler, who died in 1634 as a high-ranking officer in the battle of Schorndorf, although it could also be James Christian Buttler, commander and owner of a regiment established in 1630, with headquarters in Silesia, see Schmid, "Irská emigrace [Irish Emigration]", 208.
37 *Clarissima singularisque totius philosophie necnon methaphisice Aristotelis magistri Petri Tatareti expositio*, [Lyon] 1503, SK, JB III 36. Translation of the note: "For the use of the Hibernian friars of the Prague college by way of donation from the most illustrious Sir Jacob Butler, Irishman, 1632."
38 NA, ŘHyb Praha, no. 70, 30.9.1653, Praha. The will of commander John de Barry.
39 Ibid., nos. 66, 67, 68, 11.9.1653. Jinočany (?). The will of Jeremiah O'Donovan. No. 66 is a German version, no. 67 a Latin excerpt and no. 68 a Latin version.
40 In the Latin version *privignus*, in the German one *Stieffsohn*; see Schmid, "Irská emigrace [Irish Emigration]", 260, introduces him as early as 1653 as a burgher of Prague's Lesser Town.
41 The members in question were Robert and another called in the document "Heraldus," possibly a younger member of the family.
42 Mentioned as a field captain (*capitaneus campestris*).

Fig. 4 Jeremy O'Donovan's letter asking for restoration of the golden chain, late 1680s (NA).

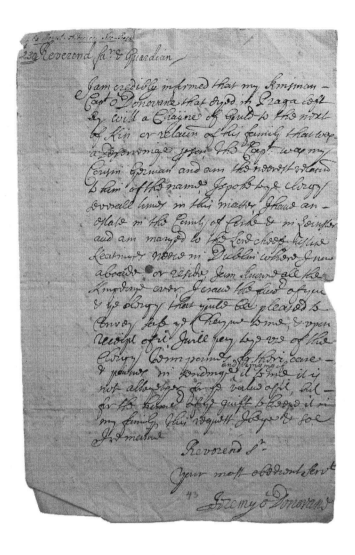

given to his nearest relative.[43] To demonstrate how strong the contacts were between the Irish homeland and the emigrants even within the Irish community in Prague, let us look here at the fate of that gold chain. As shown from the letter written in 1663 by Clancy's widow, Maria Ursula (née Baroness of Strahlendorf, to the archbishop, Bernardine Clancy entrusted this chain for a certain time to his nephew Daniel (*"de Clancy"*). Daniel gave it to his wife, Maria Ursula, before he left for England. Shortly afterwards, the executor of Jeremiah's will ascertained the fate of the chain, whereupon Maria

---

43   "Catenam auream magnam in archivio reverendorum patrum Hybernorum deponendam ordinat et constituit illustrissimo domino domino O'Donovan ipsi data occasione dandam aut transmitendam."

Ursula had the chain taken away from her and it was returned to the Irish Franciscans (Fig. 4). In the letter, Maria asked for the chain to be returned to her.[44] An undated copy of the letter in English which Daniel O'Donovan of Banelahan, resident in Dublin, sent to the guardian of the Prague college, informing the custodian of the chain of the close relationship of the writer (his own cousin) with Jeremiah O'Donovan and, as his closest relative, identified her as the rightful heir.[45] Daniel O'Donovan sent the letter by the Franciscan, Eugene McCarthy of Munster, to whom he also gave power of attorney in the matter of collecting the chain.[46] Whether the chain was collected or not, we do not know, but a hundred years later no such item is to be found in the list of valuables in the college.

As the last written item connected with the wills of the Irish officers from the Irish Franciscan archive we would like to mention an undated extract from the last will of Colonel Geraldin. He bequeathed 3,000 florins to the Irish Franciscans in Prague.[47]

As far as we know, the Kavanagh family, which, in the person of Maurice Kavanagh, senior officer in the Austrian army, had been elevated to the ranks of the Bohemian nobility in 1728, settled in Bohemia in the eighteenth century.[48] In the list of fifty-three Mass endowments of the Irish Franciscan church in Prague from 1787 there is, among several of Irish origin, also a Kavanagh endowment, but we cannot be certain that it originated from this decidedly military family,[49] although we do know that in 1784 the outstanding debts owed to General Kavanagh by the state were passed on to the Irish Franciscans.[50] Ludvík Schmid mentions other Irish soldiers, but we have no information about their links to the Irish Franciscans.[51]

---

44   NA, APA, carton no. 2100.
45   NA, ŘHyb Praha, s.a., s.l., unnumbered. A letter from Daniel O'Donovan to the guardian of the Prague college of the Irish Franciscans. His origin, discussed also with Brother Farrell, and his claim is mentioned at the beginning of the text: "I am credibly informed that my kinsman capt. O'Donovane that dyed in Praga left by will a chayne of guld to the next of kin or relative of his family that was a defending of him. The capt. was my cousine german and am the neerest relative to him of the name. I spoke bye clergy Farrell linies in this matter. I have an estate in the County of Corke & in Leinster and am maryed to the Lae [?] chief justise Keatinges neew in Dublin where I now aboarde or reside…"
46   Ibid., no. 136, 11.6.1687, Ireland? Daniel O'Donovan alias Donovan of Banelahan in the County of Cork, empowered the Franciscan, Eugene McCarthy from the province of Munster, to collect a golden chain which had been kept for him, as the chief of the family, in the Prague College of the Irish Franciscans ("Chief of the family of the Donovans").
47   Ibid., no. 214.
48   *Siebmacher*, 129 + table 64.
49   NA, ČG Publ, 1786–1795, 145/111/1786-7, carton no. 2729, 5.8.1787. List of Mass endowments.
50   Schmid and Polišenský, "Irové ve střední Evropě a Universita Karlova" [The Irish in Central Europe and Charles University], *AUC-HUCP* 16.2 (1976): 53–66.
51   Ludvík Schmid, "Robert Smith Mac Gavan of Balroe, Commander of the Invalid's [sic] House in Prague," *The Irish Sword* 14.56 (1981): 256–257; ibid., "Robert Smith Mac Gavan of Balroe, velitel

THE IRISH FRANCISCANS AND DOCTORS

We have mentioned above the relations between the Irish officers in Imperial service and the Irish Franciscan community. Their ties were quite close, in particular at the beginning of the college's existence. Gradually, however, there was a loosening of those ties and we can attribute the waning interest of the officers and nobles in the college in the eighteenth century to the decrease in its importance and the much reduced settlement of Irish nobility in Bohemia. Towards the end of the seventeenth century, however, there began an influx of Irish students, which understandably increased after the Penal Laws were introduced in Ireland. They were mainly students of medicine, from whose ranks important academic dignitaries of Prague University were recruited over the course of time. Some of them even managed to combine medicine and soldiering, such as the member of another noble family settled in Bohemia, Terence Brady, who was Chief Field Physician of the Imperial Army and who received *incolatus*, i.e. was incorporated into the Bohemian nobility in 1758.[52] A survey of Irish doctors in Bohemia is to be found in the life-long work of Ludvík Schmid.[53] Recently, two exhibitions have been devoted to this theme: *A Bohemian Refuge: Irish Students in Prague in the eighteenth century*[54] in Dublin in the Long Hall of Trinity College Library and *Irové na pražské lékařské fakultě a v českých zemích v 17.–18. století* [*The Irish*

---

pražské invalidovny" [Robert Smith Mac Gavan of Balroe, Commander of the Veterans' Hospital in Prague], *Vojenské zdravotnické listy* 51 (1982): 154–155; ibid.: "Irští námořníci v rakouských službách" [Irish Sailors in Austrian Service], *HaG* 25.2 (1992): 133–140.

52 *Siebmacher*, 55 + table 60.

53 It is not only the above-mentioned "Irská emigrace," but mainly his key work *Irští lékaři v Čechách* [*Irish Doctors in Bohemia*] (Praha: Univerzita Karlova, 1968); also the already quoted article published with J. Polišenský, "Irové ve střední Evropě a Universita Karlova" and the lesser works: "Irish Doctors in Bohemia," *Irish Journal of Medical Science* 1 (1968): 497–504; "Irský lékař Eugen Mac Mahon v Českých Budějovicích" [The Irish Doctor Eugen Mac Mahon in České Budějovice], *JSH* 38 (1969): 15–19; "Jacobus Smith de Balroe," *Časopis lékařů českých* 108 (1969): 928–931; "Wilhelm Mac Neven O'Kelly ab Aughrim, profesor lékařské fakulty pražské university" [William MacNeven O'Kelly of Aughrim, Professor of the Faculty of Medicine at Prague University], *Zprávy Archivu UK* 2 (1977): 4–30; "Irští lékaři a naše lázně" [Irish Doctors and our Spas], *Fyziatricko-reumatologický věstník* 56 (1978): 179–183; "Lékařská rodina O'Hehirů v Praze" [The O'Hehir Family of Doctors in Prague], *Zprávy Archivu UK* 3 (1980): 85–90; "Theobald Held a potomci irských emigrantů v Praze" [Theobald Held and the Descendants of Irish Emigrants in Prague], *Praktický lékař* 62 (1982): 61–63; "Ke vzniku Komenského Ianua linguarum" [On the Creation of Comenius's Ianua linguarum], *Studia Comeniana et historica* 14.27 (1984): 65–69; "Invalidovna" [The Veterans' Hospital], *Praktický lékař* 67 (1987): 277–278; articles, published with Miroslav Baroch: "Rod Leslie" [The Leslie Family] and "Rod O'Hegerty" in *HaG* 22.2 (1989) and 23.1 (1990). Apart from Schmid's articles, it is also possible to mention an article by Karel Pletzer, "Irští lékaři Daniel O'Karin a Eugen Mac Mahon v Českých Budějovicích" [The Irish Doctors Daniel O'Karin and Eugen Mac Mahon in České Budějovice], *Kulturní kalendář* (November 1975): 26–27.

54 The exhibition took place from December 1997 to May 1998. An explanatory text (not a catalogue) by Prof. Helga Robinson-Hammerstein related to the exhibition was published in 1997.

at Prague's Faculty of Medicine and in the Bohemian Crown Lands in the Seventeenth and Eighteenth Centuries][55] in the Carolinum in Prague. On the former occasion, the above-mentioned *Migrating Scholars* was published, containing five studies of Czech-Irish relations.

Let us, therefore, at least mention two of the most important Irishmen at the Prague Faculty of Medicine. The first of them was James Smith of Balroe (c. 1695-1744). After studying medicine from 1714 to 1719, he became one of the personal physicians to Charles VI, then in 1726 he became a professor at the faculty, ten years later the dean, and from 1743 to 1744 he was even the rector of the university. This resulted in his elevation to the nobility, along with his brothers, Thomas and Robert. The latter was one of the first directors of Prague's Invalidovna[56] (a veterans' hospital). He was involved (as censor) in the publication of the first Bohemian pharmacopoeia, *Dispensatorium medico-therapeuticum Pragense*.[57] His descendants also entered the medical profession. James Smith himself supported penniless students, especially Irish ones.[58]

The second important figure of Irish origin at the university was William MacNeven (1719-1787). After graduating in Prague, he became Professor of Medicine at the Faculty of Medicine and personal physician to Empress Maria Theresa. In 1754, he was named the first director of medical studies at the university. In 1750, he had been adopted by his uncle, William MacNeven O'Kelly of Aughrim who lived in Vienna and elevated to the nobility in 1753.[59] During his directorate, the faculty underwent important changes, his approach reflected that of enlightenment science promoted by Gerard van Swieten.

What primarily interests us here, however, is the relationship of the Irish medical students, doctors and university teachers to the college of the Irish Franciscans. The financial situation of all doctors was clearly not as good as that of members of the nobility, so there is less documentation on financial support or pious bequests from the doctors' side. It should also be borne in mind that the academic community, of which the teachers and students of Irish origin were already an integral part, was to a certain degree a comity of a special kind, in which the barriers between nationalities could be easily dissolved and the isolation of the Irish emigrants in Prague could be broken.

---

55   Zdeněk Kalvach and Jan Pařez, *Irové na pražské lékařské fakultě a v českých zemích v 17.–18. století. Katalog výstavy v Karolinu 25.9. – 16.10.1998* [*The Irish at Prague's Faculty of Medicine and in the Czech Lands in the Seventeenth and Eighteenth Centuries. Catalogue of the Exhibition in the Carolinum, 25 September to 16 October 1998*], Praha: Strahovská knihovna, 1998.

56   See Schmid, "Robert Smith Mac Gavan of Balroe."

57   *Dispensatorium medico-therapeuticum Pragense*, Vetero-Pragae 1739, SK, CY I 26.

58   The protection provided by director MacNeven to his countrymen during their studies at the university became a reason for the criticism of him, see Polišenský and Schmid, "Irové ve střední Evropě a Universita Karlova," 64.

59   See *Siebmacher*, 78 + table 48.

We know, however, that the relationship of the Irish clergy with the Irish doctors was just as intense as their relationship with the other groups of emigrants. This is shown, for example, by the fact that, in 1772 in Týn Cathedral, the guardian of the Irish Franciscans, Michael Tipper, gave away Klára, the daughter of the Irish doctor, Silvester O'Hehir, to the doctor, Josef Mikan,[60] or that Marie, the wife of William MacNeven, although she had died in the town of Zruč, was buried in the Irish Franciscan church.[61] The last will, written in German in 1671, of Johanna Plündergastin indicates the complicated interrelations.[62] She wished to be buried in the Irish Franciscan church, to which end she contributed the sum of 100 florins. There were other bequests for the Irish: Plündergastin left twenty Imperial florins to Cornelius Horan, and among the legatees was Edmund Buttler, Count of Clonebough. The will was witnessed by John Duigenan, Master of Philosophy and Candidate of Medicine, famous in the scholarly literature as the first Irishman to be registered at the Faculty of Medicine at Prague University.[63]

In the archive of the College of the Immaculate Conception of the Virgin Mary is the original inheritance inventory from 1714 of the deceased Michael de Boyne, MD. We can only surmise that it was deposited there in connection with a bequest.[64]

Overall it can be said that although the intricate contacts between the Irish Franciscans and the doctors have been demonstrated, their intensity, at least on the financial side, cannot be compared with the relationship of the Franciscans to the Irish nobles and soldiers. The solidarity among all the Irish groups in Bohemia was, however, widely known, whether it concerned the said protective hand of the Irish teachers over their compatriot students, scholarships for young Irish soldiers endowed by wealthy officers serving in the Austrian army (O'Brien, Browne, MacCarthy, etc.),[65] or support provided by other aristocrats (Kavanagh and Taaffe) to students of other subjects (theology and law) as shown by the dedications of students defending their university thesis.[66]

---

60 Schmid, "Lékařská rodina O'Hehirů," 85ff. Although Klara was half Czech, not to mention Mikan, this was done because the Irish Franciscans did not have their own parish, so that the guardian, Tipper, had to be asked to conduct the ceremony in Týn.
61 Schmid, *Irští lékaři v Čechách*, 31. William MacNeven himself was buried elsewhere because the Irish Franciscan college had been dissolved.
62 NA, ŘHyb Praha, no. 107, 23.2.1671, The will of Johanna Plündergastin. Her contacts made us think that her surname was in reality Irish and the correct spelling was Pendergast.
63 Polišenský and Schmid, "Irové ve střední Evropě a Universita Karlova," 59. John Duigenan from Leitrim enrolled on 21.2.1668.
64 NA, ŘHyb Praha, nos. 149 (Latin) and 150 (German), 27.3.1714, Praha. Inventory of Dr. Michael de Boyne's estate. Published in Czech by Schmid, *Irští lékaři v Čechách*, 40–42.
65 Polišenský and Schmid, "Irové ve střední Evropě a Universita Karlova," 64.
66 See the dedication by the chairman, O'Brien to Thomas Kavanagh, Baron of Elleringstown, in *Theses ex universa philosophia, ad mentem Doctoris subtilis … quas praeside P. F. Antonio ô Brien … De-*

THE IRISH FRANCISCANS AND OTHER IRISHMEN

Besides the above groups of Irish emigrants, there were other Irish people living in Prague whose relationship to the Irish Franciscans was by all accounts
more or less neutral. The best known of these was William MacNeven O'Kelly
of Aughrim, the above-mentioned adoptive father of the doctor, William
MacNeven. This member of an old Irish aristocratic family left with James
II for the Continent in 1690, lived for a time in Prague and then settled in
Vienna. He was accepted, in comparison with his fellow Irish soldiers, with
relatively open arms by the Bohemian nobility. The reason for this seems to
be his heraldic interests. In 1705, he wrote the work *Speculum heraldicum* and,
besides this, published several celebratory pieces on aristocratic Bohemian
families.[67] He was also named Imperial Palatine (*comes palatinus*) and Privy
Counsellor.[68]

Other important figures of Irish origin, about whose relations with the
Irish Franciscans we have no further information, were Charles Michael
O'Lynch, originally a professor at the Royal Academy in Lignica, Silesia, who
later became a professor in the Department of History and Auxiliary Historical Sciences at the Law Faculty about the middle of the eighteenth century,[69]
and John Robert Wallis (1636–1683), who taught at the Faculty of Arts and
then the Faculty of Theology in Prague, and later at the Faculty of Theology in
Olomouc.[70] Equally, we have no more detailed information about the contacts
of Peter Wadding, an Irish Jesuit, who was a friend of one of Valdštejn's murderers, Walter Deveroux.[71] We were also unable to document any contacts
with the Irish Franciscans by Bernard Farrell of Balligarow, who defended a

---

fendendas susceperunt P.F. Stephanus Wyse, F. Eugenius Hanly, ejusdem religionis, collegii, et nationis
alumni, Vetero-Pragae 1750, SK, AF XIV 99; the dedication by a law student who was "ex comitatu
Longfordiae Hibernus" to Count Theobald Taaffe in [Farrellus de Balligarow, B.:] *Theses canonico-*
civiles de jure-jurando, Pragae 1666, SK, CK V 21/21.

67 See Hedvika Kuchařová and Jan Pařez, "On the trail of Irish émigrés in the collections of the
Strahov Abbey Library in Prague," *The Ulster Earls and Baroque Europe. Refashioning Irish Identi-*
ties, 1600–1800, eds. Thomas O'Connor and Mary Ann Lyons (Dublin: Four Courts Press, 2010)
212–213.

68 *Siebmacher*, 78.

69 I. Čornejová ed., *Dějiny Univerzity Karlovy II, 1622–1802* [*The History of Charles University II, 1622–*
1802] (Praha: Univerzita Karlova, 1996) 101, 143–144.

70 Ivana Čornejová and Anna Fechtnerová, *Životopisný slovník pražské univerzity. Filosofická a theo-*
logická fakulta 1654–1773 [*A Bibliographic Dictionary of Prague University: Philosophical and Theo-*
logical Faculties 1654–1773] (Praha: Univerzita Karlova, 1986). In 1664, he graduated in theology,
see Josef Tříška, *Disertace pražské univerzity 16.–18. století* [*The Dissertations of Prague University in*
the Sixteenth to Eighteenth Centuries] (Praha: Univerzita Karlova, 1977) 40.

71 As will be noted later in the text, Peter Wadding was a relative of Luke Wadding and his source
of information about the Prague environment. His relation to the Franciscans was very positive
and some of them were certainly his friends; however, there are no detailed reports.

thesis in not one but two faculties of Prague University and whose Christian name would suggest close contact with the Irish Franciscans.[72]

However, another Irish priest, Hugh Molloy, maintained close contacts with the college until his death. This is not surprising as he was a secular priest, private chaplain to the provost of the Vyšehrad Chapter, Benno, Count of Martinice. In addition, Molloy was a Franciscan tertiary. In his will dated 1657, he expressed the wish to be buried in the Irish Franciscan church. He also bequeathed the Franciscans table mats, maps and some items for the infirmary. He left his personal effects to the Franciscan, Edmund MacGranna as well as twenty florins to the above-mentioned Edmund O'Kennedy. The Franciscan Francis Magennis was entrusted with the settlement of the will.[73]

Thus, the Irish Franciscan college also acted somewhat as an intermediary between the various members of the Irish community in Bohemia. For instance, in 1676, through the Irish Franciscans, Elisabeth Farrell collected fifty florins which she had received from Francis Taaffe, Count of Carlingford, Viscount of Corin, Baronet of Ballymote, Imperial Chamberlain and senior commander of the Imperial Lorraine Regiment.[74] When John Louis O'Devlin, a soldier in the Austrian army wrote his last will in 1729, he left fifty florins for de la Motte of Sicherhoff which were saved at the Irish Franciscan college in Prague. He also bequeathed one thousand florins to the college for Masses and prayers.[75] We can also find written evidence of other Irish, for example, a letter of discharge which Otto Christoph von Dittlen drew up for the Irishman Thaddeus Edmond Chasy.[76] In Tesmar in Lower Hungary, Count John Taaffe, the Captain of Kavanagh's Regiment of Dragoons, had another document drawn up for the recruiting clerk (*Musterschreiber*), John Tongan, born near Dublin. This discharge paper released the latter from service and made him a free man.[77] The explanation offered is entry into the Prague college of the Irish Franciscans; however, we have been unable to find proof that

---

72   Tříška, *Disertace pražské university*, 42 (*Theses canonico-civiles de iure iurando … 1666*), 46 (*Theses iuridicae canonico-civiles de contractibus et quasi … 1670*).

73   NA, ŘHyb Praha, no. 76, 19.2.1657, Praha. The will of Hugh Molloy. He possibly had relatives there; he bequeathed a clock which did not chime and a ring to Mr Arthur Molloy and his brother Charles.

74   Ibid., no. 123, 13.4.1676, Praha. However, the Irish Franciscans also provided similar services to the Bohemians, as witnessed in ibid., nos. 101, 102 and 103, 7.9.1667, Prague. The surviving relatives of Kryštof, Baronet Karel of Svárov, i.e. Kryštof Karel of Svárov (3/4) and Anna Ekerstorfová (1/4), represented by Ignác Tan, requested back from the Irish Franciscans the box with the inheritance, including an inventory, which had been left by the baronet.

75   Anselm Ó Fachtna, "The last will of John Louis O Devlin (1729)," *Journal of the South Derry Historical Society*, 1.4 (1983–84): 348–356.

76   NA, ŘHyb Praha, no. 85, 13.2.1660, Praha.

77   Ibid., no. 128, 30.10.1679, Tesmar, Lower Hungary.

these two men did in fact become members of the college. Similarly, there is a passport drawn up by Ferdinand III for Denis Kavanagh's journey to Ireland.[78]

THE IRISH FRANCISCANS AND THE NOBILITY

Relationships between the local nobility and the Irish Franciscans were quite extensive. From as early as 1640, the last will of Gerhard, Baronet of Wachtendung, has been preserved. Although this nobleman wished his body to be buried in the Irish church *"sine magna pompa atque apparatu"*[79], at the same time he left the not insignificant sum of 2,000 Imperial florins for the funeral and the prayers.[80]

In 1672, Maria Mechtilde de Dieten, née de Bois, made a will. This was of particular interest to the Irish Franciscans for several reasons. First of all, she expressed the wish to be buried in the Irish Franciscan church by her husband in the Chapel of the Virgin Mary which she had had built at her own expense. She bestowed 600 florins on the Irish Franciscans for Masses, the money to be paid from the income of her estate.[81] She also had an eternal lamp installed in the same chapel, bequeathed 400 florins for the lamp and the oil, and gave the chapel a white chasuble. She also endowed the church foundation with 1,000 florins for a High Mass on the anniversary of her death.

Finally, she left the Seminary of St. Wenceslas 100 florins on condition that Bernard Connor would be supported in his studies for five years or, in the event of his death, his brother. She also bequeathed Bernard Connor fifty florins for clothing.

In 1679, the guardian of the college, Thaddeus Fallon, issued a receipt that he had received 1,000 florins as money for the endowment with a return of sixty florins over two years from Kateřina, the widowed Countess of Martinice.[82] The activity here was almost entirely on her side: when the college was dissolved, there were fifty-three Mass endowments. As far as we can tell, of these only six had been established by Irishmen (O'Byrn, O'Farrell, Kavanagh, Plunkett, Hamilton and Taaffe).

---

78 Ibid., no. 49, 3.8.1650, Wien.
79 "Without great pomp or preparations."
80 Ibid., no. 33, 17.1.1640, Praha.
81 Ibid., no. 112, 20.7.1672, Praha. On the de Bois family, see Olga Fejtová, "Zahraniční literatura v měšťanských knihovnách na Novém Městě pražském v 17. století. Knihovna rodiny de Bois" [Foreign Literature in the Libraries of the Burghers in Prague's New Town in the Seventeenth Century. The Library of the de Bois Family], *K výzkumu zámeckých, měšťanských a církevních knihoven*, ed. J. Radimská, (České Budějovice: Jihočeská univerzita, 2000) 323–337. In the copy of the last will, the names are distorted into de Ditting and de Boye.
82 NA, ŘHyb Praha, no. 126, 8.3.1679, Praha.

Fig. 5 Franz Anton, Count Sporck with a depiction of his own architectural foundations as well as his father's military victories. A copperplate from *Gladius spiritus*, a book by Francis O'Devlin, Prague 1698 (SK).

Let us introduce at least one example from a later date: in 1747, a certain von Gastheim devoted to the Irish Franciscans the income from his Vršovice annuities for the brewing of beer.[83]

Pavel Preiss has already written about the relations between Count Sporck and the Irish Franciscans.[84] When Franz Anton, Count Sporck was studying at the Jesuit school, the Irish Franciscan Francis O'Devlin acted as his tutor. Preiss connects some of Sporck's ideas and attitudes with the Scotist interpretations of the Irish Franciscan circle. In addition, we know that Sporck's patronage was aimed at the Irish Franciscan college, as is evidenced not only by the printed thesis of Louis Ryan from 1698 (Fig. 5) with a dedication to F. A. Sporck[85] but also by the dedication to the four Sporck brothers

---

83   Ibid., no. 163, 12.1.1747, Bechyně.

84   Pavel Preiss, *František Antonín Špork a barokní kultura v Čechách* [*Franz Anton Sporck and Baroque Culture in Bohemia*] (Praha – Litomyšl: Paseka, 2003) 136.

85   *Gladius spiritus quod est Verbum Dei scriptum et traditum in septem controversiis, cum septem thesibus … praeside R.P.F. Francisco ô Devlin, ord: min: strict: observ: SS. Theologiae ac Verbi Dei lectore. Defendendum assumpsit P.F. Ludovicus Ryan ejusdem ord: et nationis, Vetero-Pragae 1698.* SK, BCh IX 65.

in the introduction to O'Devlin's 1710 work, *Philosophia scoto-aristotelica*.[86] Doubtless the fact that the Sporck palace and the College of the Immaculate Conception were neighbours played a role; indeed, in 1699, the palace and the oratory of the church were joined by a suspension corridor.[87] One of the witnesses who signed the contract for the installation of this corridor was Václav Vojtěch, Count of Šternberk, who was a spiritual father (*geistlicher Vater*) – or officially the apostolic syndic of the convent. Two years later, he was involved in the creation of the college library and later even a part of his private book collection ended up there.[88] The Šternberk family had generally close contacts with the Irish community in Prague, the above-mentioned William MacNeven O'Kelly dedicated the detailed, celebratory publication *Chrám slávy*[89] to the family, and the most famous Prague Scotist, Anthony Bruodin, dedicated his work *Propugnaculum catholicae veritatis* to them as a New Year gift for 1669.

Preiss mentions the almost fashionable character of the Irish Franciscan college and corroborates this with reference to the nobility's endowments during the refurbishment of the church. Members of the leading families of the Bohemian nobility commissioned pictures from Karel Škréta for the chapels in the Irish church which they had founded: in particular, the brothers Jan Norbert, Václav Vojtěch and Ignác Karel, Counts of Šternberk for the Chapel of St. Francis and its altar (the altarpiece *The Stigmatisation of St. Francis*,[90] *The Baptism of Christ*, *The Conversion of St. Paul*, *St. Anthony of Padua* and *The Crucifixion*).[91] Possibly at the wish of Johann Anton, Count Losy of Losinthal, *The Immaculate Conception of the Virgin Mary* appeared on the

86 *Philosophia Scoto-Aristotelico universa ... authore P. F. Francisco ô Devlin, ... Tomus primus logicam et physicam complectens*, Norimbergae 1710. SK, AF XII 2.

87 NA, ČG Publ, 1786–1795, 145/111/1786-7, carton no. 2729. A copy of the agreement dated 4.5.1699 between Franz Anton, Count Sporck and the Irish Franciscans about the building alterations is added to the material from 9.9.1786 in which Johann Franz, Count of Sweerts-Sporck, talks about the "Hibernian infirmary" (*Krankenhaus*), a room inside it and the oratory of the church with a corridor.

88 The editions of some documents are in Alžběta Birnbaumová, "Příspěvky k dějinám umění XVII. stol. z archivu Šternbersko-Manderscheidského" [Contributions to the History of the Art of the Seventeenth Century from the Šternberk-Manderscheid Archive], *PA* 34 (1925): 496ff.; for the history of the library, see Kevin MacGrath, "The Irish Franciscan Library at Prague," *Franciscan College Annual 1951*, (Multyfarnham 1951). For the fate of two books from the of Šternberk library which appeared in the college library, see Kuchařová and Pařez, "On the trail of Irish émigrés," 195.

89 *Templum gloriae in monte stellari extructum et ... familiae Sternbergicae consecratum...*, Neo-Pragae, 1697. SK, AB VIII 44/43, BP VI 51/79, BQ II 189/5.

90 Jaromír Neumann et al., *Karel Škréta 1610–1674. Katalog výstavy NG v Praze* [*Karel Škréta 1610–1674. Catalogue of the Exhibition in the National Gallery in Prague*] (Praha: Národní galerie, 1974) 259ff.; Hammerschmid, *Prodromus gloriae Pragenae*, 303.

91 Neumann, *Karel Škréta*, 109–112, 218ff.

Fig. 6 A true image of St. Peter of Alcantara dedicated to Zuzana Polyxena, countess of Martinice by Anthony Bruodin. Engraving by Daniel Wussin, Prague after 1669 (SK).

main altar.[92] Also, the Vyšehrad provost, Benno, Count of Martinice, had the main altar furnished and columns installed in the church and chapel. Among others who participated in the building, decoration and furnishing of the church were the above-mentioned Franz Anton, Count Sporck, Jan of Talmberk the Elder, Vilém Václav František Michna of Vacínov and Humprecht Jan, Count Černín of Chudenice.[93]

The leading Bohemian aristocrats' patronage of the Irish Franciscan college and generally their close relationship to its members is evidenced by three other facts: the dedications of authors from the Irish Franciscan intel-

---

92   Ibid., 220.
93   Hammerschmid, *Prodromus gloriae Pragenae*, 220ff.

lectual circle to the Bohemian nobles as patrons, the support of Irish students of theology by the Bohemian nobility, and that the Irish Franciscans acted as domestic tutors to young aristocrats.

With regard to the first instance, we might mention in particular the writings of Anthony Bruodin (Fig. 6). In 1663, he dedicated his *Oecodonomia* to Ferdinand Vilém, Count Slavata, the above-mentioned *Propugnaculum* (1669) to the Šternberk family, his hagiography of St. Pedro de Alcántara (1669) to Humprecht Jan, Count Černín of Chudenice, and *Armamentarium* (1676) to Jan Jáchym, Count Slavata, and to Ernst Josef, Count of Valdštejn. William MacNeven O'Kelly dedicated to the Hrzán of Harasov family the whole of his celebratory work *Rubra domus* (1700), as well as his *Philosophia aulica* (1700). His description of Ireland, published three years later in Vienna, he dedicated to the two brothers, Jiří Adam and Maxmilián, Counts of Martinice. O'Devlin's dedication to Sporck has already been dealt with.

Among the abundant examples of printed theses by Irish students there are many inscriptions to Bohemian aristocrats, by which the defenders thanked them as patrons. Here we can find dedications to Jan Kryštof Kager, Count of Štampach (1723), Václav Kašpar Bechyně of Lažany (1727), Josef František, Count of Vrbno (1732), Joachim Joseph, Count Des Fours (1735), František Michael Bořita, Count of Martinice (1736), Václav Josef Údrčský of Údrč (1738), Jan Ludvík, Count of Žerotín (1741), Josef Jáchym Vančura of Řehnice (1752) and Joseph Wilhelm, Count of Nostitz (1756).[94]

The tutoring by Francis O'Devlin at Count Sporck's has already been referred to. That this was no accident in the case of the later guardian is also evidenced by the list of friars drawn up about 12 September 1786, that is, when the college was being dissolved. Of thirty-seven brothers, three were working as tutors or chaplains in aristocratic families.[95] The question of the tuition of exceptional students is connected to the fact that these students defended their theses in the Irish college: one example might be the preserved printed thesis of such a disputation, where the defender was František Ferdinand Gorgonius, Count Novohradský of Kolovraty.[96]

The close relations between the Irish Franciscans and Bohemian aristocratic families is also documented by the certificate of authenticity for the lock of hair of the Virgin Mary and the fragments of bone of the apostles,

---

94   More detailed information about some of the documents and theses in the last two paragraphs can be found later in the text; their precise bibliographical citations are provided in Kuchařová and Pařez, "On the trail of Irish émigrés."

95   NA, ČG Publ, 1786–1795, 145/111/1786-7, 12.9.1786, carton no. 2729. Anthony Coskran was tutor at the house of Prince Lobkowitz, Francis Connelly, tutor at the house of the Baron Hildebrand and John Commins was tutor at the house of Earl Peter von Morzin of Zeitlang.

96   *Cursus philosophicus ... adjunctis ex universa philosophia thesibus, et disputationi expositis ... sub praesidio A. V. F. Petri Arcedeckne*, Pragae 1732. SK, JA V 35.

James the Great and James the Less, which the guardian, Patrick O'Kelly, had drawn up in 1727 for Juliana, Countess Malovcová.[97] That the Irish Franciscan church was still popular with the nobility at the beginning of the eighteenth century is evidenced by the fact that it still served as a place of burial.[98]

THE IRISH FRANCISCANS AND THEIR PRAGUE NEIGHBOURS

The subject about which there is the least information is the relationship of the inhabitants of the Prague towns, in particular the New Town, with the Irish Franciscans. This appears to be because the Irish Franciscans did not have their own parish, since they were not allowed to run a parish in Europe,[99] and, apart from some later exceptions, they were not allowed to collect alms. The language barrier also played a role: the newly arrived Irish in particular did not speak Czech, at best they spoke German. Otherwise, of course, the linguistic potential of these, to some extent, world travellers was very good, as shown by the two lists of confessors published by Benignus Millett.

Immediately after their arrival in Prague, the Irish Franciscans gained little sympathy with the compulsory purchase of the houses adjacent to the half-demolished Church of St. Ambrose.[100] Later, their newly built church created a fairly exclusive impression and served in particular the needs of certain aristocratic circles and some of their own countrymen.

There are only two items from the Irish Franciscan archive which illustrate their general coexistence with their neighbours. The first, which is difficult to date, comes from the period 1637 to 1657. It is a copy of a complaint, written in Czech, from the Irish Franciscan college and its guardian, addressed to the royal officials which claimed that Philip, Count Magni had assumed the right to forbid them to build a higher wall but himself wanted

97 Issued by Simone Gritti, Bishop of Ferentino on 12.4.1727 in Ferentino for Patrick O'Kelly who, according to his own note on the reverse, dedicated it to the above-mentioned noblewoman on 7.5.1728. The original is in the private collection of Mr Ladislav Zápařka of Prague.
98 See Jan Beckovský, *Poselkyně starých příběhův českých. Díl druhý (od roku 1526–1715). Sv. třetí (L. 1625–1715 i s dodatky)* [*Messenger of Old Bohemian Stories. Vol 2 (1526–1715). Part 3 (1625–1715 with appendices)*], ed. Antonín Rezek (Praha: Dědictví sv. Prokopa, 1880), where there is a report about the burial of Sir Benedict Kacius in "a cellar of the same Kacius family close to his parents…" in "…the church of the Irish Franciscans" in 1704 (23). In April 1752, funeral rites for Count Vršovec, killed in a duel, see Václav Mentberger, "Z deníku Jana Josefa hraběte z Vrtby" [From the Diary of Jan Josef Joseph, Count of Vrtba], *XXI. Ročenka Národopisného musea Plzeňska* (Plzeň: Národopisné muzeum Plzeňska, 1940) 15.
99 Anthony Bruodin, *Corolla oecodomiae … sive pars altera manualis summae totius theologiae speculativae*, Pragae 1664, 275.
100 Luboš Lancinger, "Z místopisu Nového Města pražského v 15.–19. století – Hybernská ulice I" [On the Topography of Prague's New Town in the Fifteenth to Nineteenth Centuries – Hybernian Street I], *PSH* 20 (1987): 173–179.

"to break through it for windows looking into the college and our garden [!] and some building done to our detriment." How the matter ended, we do not know.[101] The second item is a police matter and concerns fire regulations. In 1691, the captain (the official with police competence) of Prague's New Town admonished the Irish Franciscans in Czech and warned them, after a shed had burnt down, to be more watchful and to be careful with fires.[102]

We can mention at least the wills which were made in favour of the Irish Franciscans by two women who, we may assume, were from Prague, or were at least Bohemian townswomen. In the first will, written in German in Brandýs nad Labem in 1679, Anna Marie Kratochvílová left the Irish friars thirty florins for Masses.[103] In the second will, a year later, on her estate two miles from Prague, Anna Polexina M. Palečková bequeathed 2,000 florins for statues of Jesus, Mary, Joseph and St. Anne to be erected on the altar of the church, with St. Anne to be on the top of the altar, flanked by St. Barbara and St. Polexina.[104]

Initially, relations with the Franciscans of the Bohemian province were good. After their arrival in Prague, the Irish friars stayed at the Friary of Our Lady of the Snows and assisted with the teaching of philosophy and theology there. Louis Cooney took part in the renewal of theological studies. The Bohemian province assisted the Irish Franciscan college when they had internal problems. As will be described below in more detail, in the 1650s, friars who had had to leave their own houses temporarily due to internal disputes lived there. Apart from such temporary departures, there were also transfers from the Irish to the Bohemian province, which were most likely regarded as permanent (although circumstances forced Anthony Bruodin to return to the Irish friars – and which were indisputably enriching for the Bohemian province.

Friendly relations ended when open rivalry began, but this problem between the Franciscans of the Irish and Bohemian provinces only became acute once, when the Irish friars attempted to establish a house in Namslav in Silesia. The local Franciscans took this as a dangerous precedent and resisted the enterprise with such determination that no such attempts were made again from the Irish side. Admittedly, the dispute about precedence in public processions dragged on for many years, but it never became open antagonism.[105] Written sources refer to problems rather than to mutually

---

101 NA, ŘHyb Praha, no. 167, 1637–1657. (Dated by the years of reign of Emperor Ferdinand III).

102 Ibid., no. 141, 29.1.1691, Praha.

103 Ibid., no. 127, 31.8.1679, Brandýs nad Labem.

104 Ibid., no. 129, 26.5.1680, Praha. We have not been able to identify the location of the estate.

105 More attention will be paid to the above-mentioned persons and events in the chapter *The Irish Franciscans in the Service of the Archbishops of Prague (1639–1692)*. In 1671 and, later, in 1675, priests from Our Lady of the Snows requested to be able to walk in front of the guardians of the Irish

good relations and, with regard to the lack of material referring to problems, it is possible to assume that good relations prevailed.

Relationships with other orders were clearly more intensive, when the Irish friars were teaching at the archiepiscopal seminary and were in daily contact with their colleagues from the houses of other orders. They also assisted in the teaching of theology for other orders, as is illustrated by Bernardine Higgins, who taught for thirteen years in the Cistercian monastery in Plasy and James Coghlan who taught the Benedictines in Kladruby. These contacts extended even beyond the borders of the Bohemian Crown Lands, because Peter Marian Murry and Francis O'Devlin taught in the Cistercian monastery in Waldsassen in Bavaria.[106] A certain bitterness was caused by the circumstances surrounding the departure of Irish friars from the seminary and their attempts to return. The friars were among the popular preachers at the two great festivals of the Irish community: on the Feast of the Immaculate Conception of the Virgin Mary, it was mainly Jesuits, Minorites, Augustinians, Premonstratensians and Piarists who preached; on the feast of St. Patrick the preachers included Premonstratensians, Dominicans, Minorites, Piarists and Carmelites. Secular priests were also invited to these occasions, often those who were involved with the archiepiscopal seminary.[107] Of the numerous sermons, one that is particularly worth mentioning (for its author rather than its content) is the panegyric to St. Patrick delivered in 1751 in the Church of the Immaculate Conception of the Virgin Mary by Gelasius Dobner (1719–1790), a Piarist and the first modern historian of Bohemia.[108]

With relation to parish administration, there sometimes arose disputes over jurisdiction, that is, the Irish friars tended to appropriate rights which were not theirs. In 1643, Ambrose Barducius, Carmelite and administrator of the Parish of St. Gall, conducted a dispute before the consistory because, without his knowledge and against his will, they had buried the Irish Captain William Farrell, a parishioner of St. Gall's, in their own church.[109] In 1712, a

---

Franciscans during public processions because the Irish Franciscans walk "sub cruce nostra" only as guests and not as representatives of an independent house of a religious order. This purely formal question, decided in 1646 in favour of the Bohemian province, was only resolved in 1681, see ŘF, carton no. 22.

106 *Quartum quod incedit feliciter seu numerus quaternarius, celeberrimo collegio archi-episcopali Pragensi, felix, faustus, et fortunatus, discursu panegyrico deductus*, Pragae 1697, no pagination.

107 Antonín Podlaha, "Učení o neposkvrněném početí Panny Marie v Čechách před prohlášením učení toho za dogma" [The Doctrine of the Immaculate Conception of the Virgin Mary in Bohemia before the Declaration of the Teaching as Dogma], *ČKD* 45.7–8, 9, 10 (1904): 472–494, 553–569, 638–642 and *ČKD* 46.1, 2 (1905): 39–45, 135–144.

108 Gelasius Dobner, *Panegyricus divo Patricio Hiberniae apostolo ... dictus*, Pragae 1751, SK, CQ VIII 8/19. The author concentrated mainly on the saint's missionary work in Ireland.

109 According to his own testimony on 23 May 1643, Barducius was asked to come to the house called The Three Crowns to grant the last rites to the captain. When he arrived, he found two Irish Franciscans there. When the captain died the following day, Barducius asked the Irish Francis-

request that the procession on the feast of Corpus Christi take place within the walls of the college was taken as a violation of local custom. Matěj Václav Jelínek, curate of the Parish of St. Henry, stated that no other monastery in Prague did such a thing.[110]

It is clear that the relations of the Irish Franciscans to the Bohemian Franciscans of Our Lady of the Snows were close even in the period of the dissolution of the college. At that time, two lay brothers moved to the Bohemian friary.[111]

To conclude, we will add one interesting detail. Attached to the Irish college was a garden where they grew potatoes, which had up until that time been regarded in Bohemia as ornamental plants.[112]

These were the relations which connected the Irish community in Bohemia with the local inhabitants at all social levels and those which prevailed amongst themselves. From the above, it is clear that there always existed, in its own way, a closed world, and evidently not even a deep Christian feeling could conceal the original Celtic tribal archetypes with all their negative (frequent disputes) and positive (solidarity) features.

It is possible to follow the overall development of the relations of the Irish college to its surroundings, from the strong original links of the first generation of Irish officers and soldiers of fortune and support from the Emperor, the Archbishop of Prague and the Catholic wing of the Bohemian nobility, through the gradual loosening of ties, especially on the part of the head of state and the head of the Church in Bohemia, to the gradual extinction of a community isolated from the world outside because of the impossibility of teaching in the archiepiscopal seminary. It was precisely at that time that two of the college's greatest patrons, Count Sporck and Count Šternberk, decided to support it and by their patronage elevated the Irish friars to an exceptional position, that of tutors in aristocratic families. They continued to maintain relations with their fellow countrymen, in particular, doctors and soldiers from families settled in the monarchy, though more in terms of social life than that of financial support.

---

cans not to take the body away to be buried until the rights of the parish priest had been satisfied. The Irish Franciscans told him that they wanted to wait until other military dignitaries came and that then they would provide for his funeral. However, they broke this promise by secretly taking the deceased captain and burying him. The Irish claimed that the captain was not a parishioner at St. Gall's and they defended themselves by means of his last will. Barducius, however, accused them of tampering with the will. APA, carton no. 2100.

110 NA, APA, carton no. 2100.
111 NA, ČG Publ, 1786–1795, 145/111/1786-7, carton no. 2729, 21.10.1786.
112 Josef Polišenský, *Tisíciletá Praha očima cizinců* [*The Thousand-Year History of Prague through the Eyes of Foreigners*] (Praha: Academia, 1999) 63.

2. BETWEEN THE EMPEROR AND THE ARCHBISHOP (1629–1636)

THE IRISH PROVINCE OF THE ORDER OF FRANCISCANS OF THE STRICTER OBSERVANCE: FROM THE ATLANTIC TO THE MEDITERRANEAN AND THE BALTIC

Who exactly were the Franciscans who were called Hibernians (hyberni) by the people of Prague? In 1517, after more than three hundred years of the existence of the Order of Friars Minor, founded in 1209 by St. Francis of Assisi, it was divided into two separate orders – Conventuals and Observants. One of the Observant provinces, which was subordinated only to the general of the order and his definitorium, was the Irish province. From the 1580s, the Irish Franciscans were outlawed and persecuted by Queen Elizabeth. Admittedly, for many of them, this did not mean that they had to leave Ireland, but for many years they were forced to hide and at times minister under very difficult conditions. Oppression on the part of the English occurred in several waves in the seventeenth century, the worst of which was the Cromwellian settlement of Ireland. At the beginning of the century, some of the Franciscans went abroad to establish a more peaceful environment, not only for the education of their own friars and fellow countrymen, but also for the training of missionaries who were sent back to Ireland, particularly during the Cromwellian repression. In this way, several colleges gradually appeared outside their homeland, among them the college in Prague; these teaching institutions remained part of the Irish province. The Irish Franciscans, or rather some of them, then returned home as missionaries, for many of whom this meant death or imprisonment.

In order to better understand the purpose of the colleges of the Irish Franciscans, we must give a survey of the structure of the Irish province and the powers of its institutions and organs.[1]

The basic community was the friary, of which there were sixty-four in total in Ireland, divided among the four traditional provinces as follows: twenty-two in Munster, twenty in Leinster, thirteen in Connaught and nine

---

1   The content of this part is based mainly on the quoted work by Benignus Millett which represents an important contribution to the interpretation of the Irish Franciscan sources of the seventeenth century.

in Ulster. As has been mentioned above, some friaries had been dispersed and their members were hiding in forests and caves. As elsewhere in the order, at the head stood the provincial, who also often had to conceal where he was living.[2] Several communities of Poor Clares and Sisters of the Third Order of St. Francis also fell within the Irish Franciscan province. (The first Poor Clare convent in Ireland was established in Dublin in 1629 and there is no clear evidence of Franciscan nuns before this.)

The basic assembly, the provincial chapter, took place every three years, chaired by a special delegate of the general of the order. The chairman was usually a friar appointed by the general council. He was called a commissary visitator and before a meeting of the chapter would lead a canonical visitation. The main purpose of the provincial chapter was to elect the provincial and his definitory. In times of danger and if the chapter could not meet, the provincial and the superiors of the province were appointed by the general of the order or by the Holy See. The provincial chapter was the highest source of power in the province. It had the right to create regulations. Its highest representatives were the provincial, the custos and four definitors. All of these were elected. There were also differences between the rest of the order and the Irish province: for example, only two former provincials or *patres provinciae* could be admitted to the definitory of the Irish province. Apart from this, an interim chapter (*congregatio intermedia*) could be arranged. It mostly took place in the second year of the provincial's three-year office, and it was the provincial who presided. It was not intended for the election of a new provincial but as a meeting of the provincial, the definitory and the *patres provinciae*, or former provincials. Local representatives did not participate. Interim chapters did not have the right to create regulations or constitutions, but they were able to regulate essential business in the administration of the province by means of decrees. If a seat became vacant, they could appoint a representative, replace the current guardian or praeses and confer diplomas on preachers and confessors. Interim chapters were very important, because during them the list of four candidates, members of the province, was drawn up and submitted to the general of the order. He named one of them commissary visitator and president of the next chapter. The Irish province received the privilege of presenting the proposed names in 1612, and it was confirmed in 1651. The Irish Francisans were awarded the privilege as a result of the bitter persecution in Ireland. Although there is no word of interim chapters, it is clear that this was done in connection with them because in this period of

---

2   NA, ŘHyb Praha, no. 113, 3.3.1673. Bernard Kelly, the provincial of the Irish Province, sent a priest, Anthony Flynn, and a cleric teacher, Francis Hanly to the Prague college. The place of publication is not known. It is only stated that it is "a place of our refuge" (*datum loco nostri refugii*). The provincial, Kelly, wanted to avoid betrayal in case the letter issued by him fell into the hands of the English authorities.

repression there was a huge time lag in communication between the provincial and the curia of the order and therefore lengthy preparation was needed.

Religious persecution, as has been mentioned, forced some of the Franciscans to emigrate. Before the Cromwellian repressions, they had founded four colleges or teaching institutions for the training and preparation of new members of the order on the Continent, and two more were gradually added. This, in its own way, influenced the reorganisation, development and structure of the Irish province for many years. The first continental foundation, St. Anthony's College in Louvain, appeared as early as 1607, to provide the persecuted Irish province with missionaries and friars. It later supplied other European Franciscan centres with lectors in theology and philosophy. It was financed primarily by Irish soldiers serving in Europe. Otherwise, the Irish Franciscans in the college were so poor that if they wanted money for a journey to Ireland they were forced to beg for alms from door to door.

Fifty years after it was founded, the Franciscans' college in Louvain was famous for its scholarship, not only in theology, but also in the Irish language, hagiography and history. Mainly, however, it acted as a refuge for friars who had escaped (especially during the Cromwellian oppression), but the number of those arriving became excessive and so those who had taken vows were sent to the colleges in Rome or Prague. The head of the college was the guardian, who, under normal circumstances, was appointed from Ireland. Because of its geographical position, the college was granted quasi-provincial or extra powers normally reserved for the provincial (1626); it could order members of the order to return to Ireland, accept novices, accept professions, and perform priestly and lesser ordinations. In 1655, the commissary *pro natio Germano-Belgica* issued a proclamation requiring all those who had arrived without a permanent place of residence and whom he had sent to St. Anthony's College or those who had arrived with "letters of obedience" from the prelates of their orders to subordinate themselves to a representative of the college and behave according to the college's regulations.

In 1625, with the help of Pope Urban VIII and the general of the order, Benigno da Genova, Fr. Luke Wadding founded St. Isidore's College in Rome. Although this was part of the Irish province, its guardian was appointed by the general. St. Isidore's College became the centre of a revived Scotism and functioned primarily as an establishment for the training of missionaries and was intended for the teaching of theology and Church affairs. It became essentially a storehouse for lectors in philosophy and theology, who dispersed into various European provinces of the order.

The third institution of Irish Franciscans outside the province was the College of the Immaculate Conception of the Virgin Mary in Prague (1629) and the fourth was the Friary of the Annunciation of the Virgin Mary in Wieluń in Poland (1645), from which, however, the Irish had already been expelled in 1653. In the same year, a residence (a small house of the order) was established in Paris and, in 1656, the Friary of Our Lady of the Plain was founded in Capranica in the province of Viterbo in Italy. The latter served as a novitiate.[3]

Commissaries and others at the same level of authority helped to improve, develop and speed up relationships between the closer and more distant provinces and the centre of the order, as well as the specifically built houses of the order outside the Irish province itself.

Because they are of such extraordinary importance for the Prague college, here is a survey of these. The first of them was the commissary general for the *natio Germano-Belgica*. In 1526, the general congregation of the order decreed that the transalpine Franciscans were to be divided into three "nations": German, Spanish and French. Although the Scots and the English belonged to the German "nation," the Irish Franciscans became part of the Spanish "nation;" the Irish province may have been "part" of this but it is uncertain, though there were close links possibly thanks to the important cultural and trade contacts between the Irish and the Spanish and ultimately to their geographical position, which enabled speedy links by sea. Later, after the extinction of the Spanish and French "nations," the Irish province, probably because of the location of the Louvain college, was attached to the German "nation" (first mentioned in 1630), which was soon renamed *natio Germano-Belgica*. The division into "nations" relates mainly to the Recollect movement within the Observants. Each "nation" had a different experience: the German-Belgian absorbed the other Observants, the French existed side by side with the Observants, each enjoying autonomy, while the Spanish Recollects remained under the jurisdiction of the Observants. The "nations" experienced near extinction at the time of the French Revolution. The extensive powers of the commissary for the *natio Germano-Belgica* were a result of the fact that most of the provinces were contaminated by the Lutheran and English "heresies." In the years 1636 to 1837, the *natio Germano-Belgica* had its own agent – a *sollicitator* – in the curia.

Over time, the office of the Irish commissary gained in importance for the Irish Franciscan college. After the Prague college was destroyed in 1631 during the Saxon invasion, the Irish friars returned but were met with the opposition of the Austrian Franciscans and the Bohemian Capuchins. In 1633, the affair ended up before the general chapter in Toledo: the general of the order, Juan de Campaña, placed the college directly under his authority and

---

3   For the period when colleges were founded, see Mary Ann Lyons, "The role of St Anthony's College, Louvain in establishing the Irish Franciscan college network, 1607–60," *The Irish Franciscans 1534–1990*, eds. E. Bhreathnach, H. MacMahon, OFM and J. McCafferty (Dublin: Four Courts Press, 2009) 77–84. Older literature was reprinted in *Mícheál Ó Cléirigh, His Associates and St Anthony's College, Louvain*, ed. Nollaig Ó Muraíle (Dublin: Four Courts Press, 2008).

named the Irishman, Hugh Burke, his special delegate, with the authority and powers of a commissary general, to oversee the affairs of the college. In 1634, Burke was confirmed in office and his authority extended to Louvain, but several years of setbacks were to follow.

The commissary for the *natio Germano-Belgica* was made superior to the commissary for the colleges, but it is not clear what authority he had in the case of the Prague college, which actually lay outside his area.

When attempts were made in 1648 to remove the colleges in Prague and Wieluń from the Irish province, into which they had been incorporated by the general of the order, and amalgamate them under the authority of the commissary general for Upper Germany, Italian Father Maxentius ab Arco, the vicar general, Daniel a Dongo, announced two years later that the students belonged to the Irish province and temporarily placed them under his own jurisdiction. It showed, however, that the colleges, which were far from the centre and outside the area of the province, could not be administered because the order's bureaucracy was too slow.

After the chapter in 1650, John Colgan was appointed the new commissary for the order's houses in Louvain, Prague and Wieluń, and their members had to swear obedience to him. Squabbles and jealousy afflicted the colleges, whose members began to divide into groups according to whether they supported the greater or lesser dependence of the colleges on the centre. Finally in 1653, the general of the order, Pedro Manero, intervened. He very severely reproached the Louvain Franciscans for their discord, disunity and inability to accept the Rule, the visitator, etc. and threatened the direst of punishments. He confirmed Daly, Colgan's successor, in office and, under the threat of excommunication, he compelled the Louvain friars, who had most strongly resisted the influence of the Irish commissary for the college, to an oath of obedience.

Daly also took action that same year. In a long letter to the Cardinals, he explained the importance of the seminaries and colleges abroad for the support of the Irish missionaries and intellectuals. His efforts finally led to Pope Alexander II, at a general assembly of the sacred congregation *De propaganda fide*, issuing a decree by which all Irish Franciscan houses, in whichever country they might be, came under the administration of the Irish province.

In 1661, however, further adjustments were made to the standing of the colleges, which returned them to the situation which had applied prior to Daniel a Dongo's ruling of 1650. The authority of the Irish provincial was limited, which meant he could only select the Louvain guardian. Nevertheless, the college in Prague also came within his authority because it was part of the Irish province. The guardian was appointed by the general of the order, who could, however, only select one person out of four who had been nominated by the discretorium. At that time, there was no longer any mention of a commissary for the college and the commissary for the college, Bernardine Barry, learnt from a letter that neither the provincial nor the college were asking for a commissary to be appointed. After that, the colleges were to prepare for discussions concerning the visitation of the commissary for the *natio Germano-Belgica*.

The commissary for Upper Germany, who usually resided in Vienna and to whose jurisdiction the Prague college belonged geographically, also had an influence on the fate of the college. Sometimes his authority over the college was weakened, such as in the years 1650 to 1662, thanks to the existence and activities of the commissary for the college.

The final person who was on the same level as the commissary general was the *procurator* – the representative of a province or provinces of the same language group at the courts of Europe. The procurator of the Irish province was based in Madrid.

When comparing the political situation in Bohemia and Ireland in the course of the seventeenth century, we can see two completely different pictures of the period. All that the two countries had in common was religious oppression and persecution. The forced re-Catholicisation in the Lands of the Bohemian Crown with its Renewed Land Ordinance (1627) resulted in a complete Catholic monopoly whereas, at the same time, Irish Catholics were being widely persecuted by Protestants in accordance with the Penal Laws in Ireland. However, while the process of Catholic monopolisation of the Bohemian Crown Lands was more or less continuous, Catholics in Ireland saw a succession of good and bad times.[4]

Unfortunately, also in the Irish case, it all ended badly. After the Battle of the Boyne in 1690, the Banishment Act was passed by the Parliament of Ireland in 1697 as one of a series of Penal Laws. It banished all Catholic bishops from Ireland. The next year, Irish Franciscan authorities advised the friars to leave the country. In 1699, a brand new continental refuge for Irish Franciscans was established in Boulay, Lorraine. Nevertheless, this was unable to change the overall situation. Persecution of Catholics continued in Ireland. In the Irish Franciscan province, there was a lack of original scholars like those of the mid-seventeenth century. This applied to the whole Irish Franciscan province, so it was no surprise that Joseph MacMahon called this period "the silent century."

Towards the end of the eighteenth century, a wave of adverse events affected the continental refuges of the Irish Franciscans. The College of Immaculate Conception in Prague was abolished in 1786 by Emperor Joseph II when he launched reforms of the Church in his Central European monarchy.

---

4   Raymond Gillespie, "The Irish Franciscans, 1600–1700," *The Irish Franciscans 1534–1990*, 45–76.

Boulay friary was dissolved at the beginning of the French Revolution, soon to be followed by St. Anthony's College in Louvain (1793). St. Isidore's College in Rome and the friary in Capranica were both closed in 1798, but this was only temporary since with the ultimate fall of Napoleon both institutes went back to the Irish Franciscans.[5]

As we have already seen and as we will be able to substantiate, in the course of time the two New Town Franciscan friaries, that is, the Irish Franciscan college and the Friary of Our Lady of the Snows, both cooperated and competed. The Friary of Our Lady of the Snows was also of course at the time a teaching institution for the local province, and the Irish were regarded by the Bohemian Franciscans as a foreign element. The history of the Bohemian Franciscans by Severin Vrbčanský from the middle of the eighteenth century provides no information about the Irish friars, apart from a reference to their attempt to establish their own friary in Namslav in Silesia.[6] At the same time, we know that from start to finish (which Vrbčanský understandably did not record), quite close contacts existed between the two institutions.

FALLON'S MISSION

At the beginning of 1629, travellers on the Empire's roads could observe a man in a dark brown habit with a cowl and a white cord around his waist stride steadily across the winter countryside from Louvain in the Spanish Netherlands towards his destination, the Austrian metropolis of Vienna. Like himself, his companion also had a wide shaved tonsure and walked the whole way barefoot.[7] Although the oddest travellers could be found on Central European roads in the storms of the Thirty Years' War, it would be difficult for the chance observer to judge by his simple outer appearance that this was a scholar and teacher, the brilliant theologian from the Franciscan St. Anthony's College in Louvain, Father Malachy Fallon,[8] who was hurrying to meet Emperor Ferdinand II (Fig. 7) on an important mission. Like his companion, Gerald Fitzgerald also called Geraldin, he was an Observant Franciscan who had had to leave his Irish homeland due to the religious oppression of the English.

---

5   Joseph MacMahon OFM, "The silent century, 1698–1829," *The Irish Franciscans 1534–1990*, 77–84.
6   Severin Vrbčanský, *Nucleus minoriticus*, Vetero-Pragae 1746. SK, section Hořovice, ref. no. KI 1006, 312.
7   The image of Fallon walking without shoes in the snow seems to us to be exaggerated and it is possible to attribute it to the fabulation skills of Anthony Bruodin, whose *Propugnaculum* translated by Sousedík is our source of information. It is probably true that Fallon travelled in sandals.
8   Malachy Fallon also used the surname Hanlan, see *IFD*, 173.

Fig. 7 Ferdinand II. Engraving by Balthasar Montcornet, 1630s (SK).

His intellectual ability, allied to his skills as a negotiator, led to Malachy Fallon being chosen by the superiors at his overcrowded Louvain college[9] to describe to the Emperor the fate of the Irish Catholics, to emphasise that the Irish Franciscan colleges were irreplaceable in the training of Irish priests and intellectuals and to ask him for permission to establish another such college within his Empire.

It would be an illusion to think that the first Irishman to arrive in Prague fleeing religious oppression was the founder of the Prague college himself, Malachy Fallon (Fig. 8).[10] This is refuted by a glance into the ordination register kept by the auxiliary Prague bishop, Šimon Brož for the years 1627 to

---

9   See the translation by S. Sousedík from Bruodin's *Propugnaculum* in Stanislav Sousedík, *Jan Duns Scotus. Doctor subtilis a jeho čeští žáci* [John Duns Scotus. Doctor Subtilis and His Bohemian Pupils] (Praha: Vyšehrad, 1989) 320.

10   For instance, the fates of Irish military units during their march on Prague under Bucquoy's command were described by their chaplain Henry Fitzsimon, see Josef Polišenský, *Tisíciletá Praha očima cizinců* [The Thousand-Year History of Prague through the Eyes of Foreigners] (Praha: Academia, 1999) 63.

Fig. 8 A Franciscan of stricter observance. Engraving by Christoph Weigel, Nuremberg 1711 (SK).

Francifcanus de strictiori Obferuantia.

1643,[11] in which two Irishmen can be found as early as 1628: Arthur MacDonnell and Thaddeus O'Fian.[12] According to this document, from 1628 to 1643, a total of thirteen Irishmen were ordained, of whom at the very least two were members of an order (Dominican and Benedictine). The remainder, with one arguable exception, were secular priests. It cannot be ruled out that some of them later entered the Franciscan college, as in the case of Edmund Mac-

---

11   NA, APA, ref. no. C 119/2, carton no. 2100.
12   The name of the other Irishman who was ordained in 1628 is recorded by Dr. Kukánová as "Offiaei" so it is not clear what the surname was (probably O'Finn with a Latin ending); Latinised forms of the names in the book of ordinations were, however, often bizarre, as well as the Czech (for example, the Irish surname Lynch was recorded in the form of "Lynže"!).

Granna. He was ordained a secular priest in 1640, mentioned later as an Irish friar in the last will of Jeremiah O'Donovan dated 1653, and also mentioned in the will of Hugh Molloy dated 1657, according to which he received Molloy's personal effects. Hugh Molloy was, incidentally, also ordained (in 1636), his close relation to the Irish Franciscan college is clear from his will, in which he identifies himself as a Franciscan tertiary and appoints the guardian, Francis Magennis, as executor. So the Irish were already arriving in re-Catholicised Prague before the Franciscan college of their fellow countrymen was created.

Anthony Bruodin described the beginning of the college in his *Propugnaculum*, but other sources complement his account and allow us to correct it. When the Irish Franciscans decided to found a new college, they had clearly already inspected the Prague terrain, or at least knew the situation. In this respect, therefore, Bruodin's account that Fallon confided to Cardinal Harrach – affected only by his sincere welcome – his hitherto secret aim of settling in Prague after his arrival there from Vienna in 1630 seems distinctly untrustworthy and is unmistakeably marked by Bruodin's propagandist inclinations.[13]

It is possible to refute it entirely by Fallon's own letter, sent on 13 March 1629, to the guardian of the Louvain college, Hugh Warde.[14] Fallon wrote it in Vienna but not only does he mention preparing to leave for Prague, he also says that he is returning to the city (*"revertemur Praga"*). Besides this, the text also contains other evidence that the writer had already visited the capital of Bohemia. It urges the Louvain guardian, for many reasons, not to select Vienna but Prague for the new college, explains that the most suitable time for the foundation of a house in "Germania" has just come and the most appropriate place appears to be Prague with its university. Among the requests for a letter of recommendation from the congregation *De propaganda fide* for Cardinal Harrach and others, it also mentions that the Archbishop of Prague is himself uncommonly gracious and favourably disposed to the matter. It is clear from this that even before Fallon's presence in Vienna in March; someone – most probably Fallon himself – must have met with Harrach. According to the letter, Fallon was preparing to start for Prague on 14 March, where he intended to spend Easter and even possibly try to find a place for the future college.[15] Fallon indeed reached Prague before Easter and managed to meet with Archbishop Harrach and persuade him to consent in writing to the establishment of the Irish friars as early as 18 April (the Wednesday

---

13   See Benignus Millett, The Irish Franciscans 1651–1665 (Rome: Gregorian University Press, 1964) 245–248. The author also mentions that B. Jennings calls Bruodin "a first-class propagandist." The translation of the passage from Bruodin's *Propugnaculum* was by Sousedík, *Jan Duns Scotus*, 319ff.

14   *IFD*, no. 4, 176–177.

15   "Crastino die, Deo favente, proficiscimur Pragam, ut videamus statum loci, et aliquot ova colligamus pro Paschate."

Fig. 9 Archbishop Harrach invites believers to give Irish Francisans alms, 28 April 1629 (NA).

after Easter) 1629 (Fig. 9), almost nine months before Ferdinand's founding charter.[16]

Malachy Fallon then turned his steps again towards Vienna to discuss an actual course of action at the Imperial Court. His negotiations with the Emperor ended successfully, thanks to the intercession of the monarch's son, Ferdinand, and despite the opposition of some of the Emperor's counsellors. When he then hurried to Prague, he carried with him the important document on parchment. It began with the words: *"We, Ferdinand the Second, by the grace of God, Roman Emperor..."* and after a comprehensive explanation of why it had been issued, it continued: *"we grant and allow the right of the friars of the named order and nation to establish in our aforementioned Royal City [Prague] for themselves and their own a residence...".*[17] The charter was dated 19 November 1629, in Vienna (Fig. 10).

---

16   NA, ŘHyb Praha, no. 2, 18.4.1629, Praha. Cardinal Harrach, Archbishop of Prague, consents to the settlement of the Irish Franciscans.

17   A considerably damaged original is stored in NA, L 2, ŘH sv. Ambrož, no. 2, 19.11.1629, Wien: three copies are available there as well. NA, ŘHyb Praha, nos. 3, 4 and 5; the first edition was provided by Vigilius Greiderer, *Germania franciscana, seu chronicon geographo-historicum ordinis S. P. Francisci in Germania. Tomus I.*, Oeniponte 1777, 786. It is based on various sources (among others, by comparison with the no longer extant description of the history of the Prague college cited by the editor – *Monum. Collegii Pragens. Franciscan Hibernorum* – which, however, was probably not

Fig. 10 The foundation chart of the Irish Franciscan college in Prague, 29 November 1629 (NA).

In Prague, Malachy Fallon stayed at the Franciscan Friary of Our Lady of the Snows, which would provide support for the Irish friars and, despite varying relations, caused by divergent and convergent interests, and to the Irish in Bohemia was (naturally) the closest house of the order. Fallon himself chose the site for the future college. It was to be the former monastery of the Ambrosians and become the Franciscan friary by St. Ambrose in Prague's New Town. At that time, however, it lay derelict and was called, due to an implemented conversion, "Na kovárně" ("The Forge"). Malachy Fallon then

a masterwork of its kind, as is evidenced by the incorrect dating of the founding charter). For the last, not quite correct, edition of the copies, see *IFD*, no. 8, 179–180.

departed for Louvain, where he began preparations for the construction of the Prague house. Doubtless, the internal discussions were not as quick and unanimous as described by Anthony Bruodin. Not until 9 August in the following year did the provincial, Valentine Browne, appoint Hugh Warde lector in theology.[18] Not even the question of the formal subordination of the Prague college was quickly and satisfactorily resolved: it was only on 13 November that the guardian and council of St. Anthony's College in Louvain announced that the newly founded college in Prague would fall within the jurisdiction of the commissary general for Belgium.[19] In any case, we do know that the lector in theology, Patrick Fleming, who had been allegedly unanimously elected as the first guardian of the Prague college, arrived in Prague in the middle of November 1630, accompanied by Gerald Geraldin. Other friars arrived at the end of November the same year and in the following February.[20]

PATRICK FLEMING AND HIS DEATH

If it is possible to indisputably credit any one of the Irish with building, almost from nothing, the Irish Franciscan college in Prague's New Town, it would doubtless be Patrick Fleming. By his efforts (although not with his money) the purchase of the plots of land was accomplished, the work began and the first building was erected. For a long time, his violent death gave him the aura of a saint, and also in later accounts, Fleming overshadows his other contemporaries who were involved in the original activities in Prague. However, the quantity of Fleming's correspondence is much greater than that of his fellow friars and in other ways Fleming's leading position in the community is evident from this: a position to which he was clearly predestined by his noble origin.[21] Fleming wrote primarily to Robert Chamberlain, who was *lector jubilatus* in theology in Louvain, but also to two other men, the first of whom was linked with the spiritual birth of the college, the second with the diplomatic discussions connected with the Emperor's consent, that is, Luke Wadding and Malachy Fallon.

In the winter of 1631, Patrick Fleming, who bore the reputation of an able theologian and a resolute and fervent young man, was endeavouring – to the limit of his powers – to arrange the future residence. He and other Irish Franciscans continued to accept the hospitality of their Bohemian brethren

---

18 IFD, no. 9, 180–181.
19 IFD, no. 10, 13.11.1630, 181. It was understandably the commissary *pro natio Germano-Belgica*.
20 Sousedík, *Jan Duns Scotus*, 322.
21 He came from the family of the Barons of Slane, see *The Catholic Encyclopedia*. Vol. 6 (New York: Robert Appleton Company, 1909) and Richard J. Kelly, "The Irish Franciscans in Prague (1629–1786): Their literary labours," *Journal of the Royal Society of Antiquaries of Ireland* 52 (1922): 169ff.

at Our Lady of the Snows. The gloomy financial situation of the Irish friars was still complicated by a lack of knowledge of local conditions and insufficient contacts, although Bruodin asserts that there were enough sympathetic supporters.[22] Therefore, the unexpected support of the Imperial Military Counsellor, Don Martin de Hoff-Huerta[23] and the Secretary of the Bohemian Court Chancellery, the knight, Šimon Petr Oulík of Třebnice, also an Imperial Counsellor, must have seemed like manna from heaven. Both noblemen offered to build the Irish friars a house at their own expense. At the request of the Irish friars, they also accepted spiritual patronage and thus gained the title *parentes spirituales*.[24]

In the spring of 1631, Fleming began to negotiate with the owners of houses around the derelict Monastery of St. Ambrose over the purchase of their real estate. On 4 April, the first one was acquired for 126,000 Meissen groschen, the house of Kateřina Čejková, née Chotouchovská of Nebovidy, in which there had at one time been a forge.[25] From 1631 to 1634, the Irish friars bought up ten houses which were adjacent to the allocated space on which there was only rubbish.[26] The whole enterprise was supported by the highest

---

22   Sousedík, *Jan Duns Scotus*, 322.

23   Bruodin states that Hoff-Huerta was the supreme commander of the guard, as does Jan Florian Hammerschmid, *Prodromus gloriae Pragenae*, Vetero-Pragae 1717, 300.

24   It was the position of apostolic syndic, for which the above-mentioned term "pater" or "parens spiritualis (or *geistlicher Vater*) was used in Bohemia, see Anthony Bruodin, *Corolla oecodomiae ... sive pars altera manualis summae totius theologiae speculativae*, Pragae 1664, 289ff. It was usually a secular person in an important position: in the case of a more important monastery, it was a nobleman; for a smaller rustic monastery, it was also a respected citizen. The person was chosen by the provincial on behalf of the Holy See and there was supposed to be one in each monastery. Syndics had certain obligations to the religious houses (e.g. the overseeing of financial and economic matters) and, at the same time, they and their families and relatives participated in the spiritual benefits of the order.

25   See Luboš Lancinger, "Z místopisu Nového Města pražského v 15.–19. století – Hybernská ulice I" [On the Topography of Prague's New Town in the Fifteenth to Nineteenth Centuries – Hybernian Street I], *PSH* 20 (1987): 177. For the request by the Irish Franciscans to confirm the sale by the Imperial officials, see NA, SM, ref. no. H 99 1, 11.4.1631, Praha, Bohemian Chamber. It conveys a request by Patrick Fleming and Gerald Geraldin to approve the sale and purchase of the house, which was bought by three Irish Franciscans (contract dated 4 April 1631) from Kateřina Čejková, née Chotouchovská, for 126,000 Meissen groschen. The Irish Franciscans were concerned that her brother Jindřich would claim the house once he reached adulthood. Bruodin's description of the "conquering" of the forge guarded by "a giant blackened by smoke" seems to be pure artistic licence. The date 4.12.1637 is then possibly a misprint (Sousedík, *Jan Duns Scotus*, 323).

26   Lancinger, "Z místopisu Nového Města pražského," lists ten houses which were on the site of the current house no. 1037 and which he denotes A-J. However, it seems that in reality there were only eight houses, as is also confirmed by the anonymous historical record in the archive SM, ref. no. H 99 8. In brackets there is Lancinger's identification: "The Hybernian Fathers own the following houses: the House of Master Jindřich Chotouchovský (J). the House of Master Daniel Nathaniel, townsman S. M. P. (I). the House of Master Jakub Hubáček (H). the House of Master Hendrych Dendulín (F). the House of Master Pavel Polynkar, baker (E). the House of Master Jan Čáslavský, baker (D). the House of Mariána Šulcová, ropemaker (C). and the House of Master

circles and gained the Irish friars very little sympathy from the inhabitants of Prague. Particularly in the effort to acquire the house of the Mladá Boleslav's Royal Magistrate, Jakub Hubáček, the Royal officials acted unscrupulously and "in the name of the king" finally forced the owner to concede in 1634.[27]

From Fleming's pen we learn of the gradual "operation" of the Franciscan college on the building side and also of the general spiritual functioning of the community.

However, Fleming's first letter from Prague, which has been preserved, is dated 12 April 1631. Surprisingly, in this, Fleming mentions mainly the difficulties he has with the construction of the library. Among other things, he informs Robert Rochford, lector in philosophy at St. Anthony's College in Louvain that books are both scarce and expensive in Prague. In the three towns of Prague, it was apparently possible to visit only one or, at most, two booksellers. In time, this would evidently lead to him having books brought from Frankfurt.[28]

In the spring, construction was already in full flow. In the middle of May, the Irish friars appealed to the Count of Martinice, as the President of the Bohemian Chancellery, for building materials, in particular wood and planks.[29] On 7 June, Fleming informed Fallon, among other things, that a choir for thirty people had been built, plus a small chapel which stood on the site of the former forge.[30] Fleming's description of the site of the college, possibly from the summer of the same year, has been preserved.[31] A shortened version of this below gives the general impression.

The college lay near the future archiepiscopal seminary, outside the Old Town Gate on the road to Vienna, which also passed through the New Town Gate. It was where several roads met. One side of the road was continuously built up, the other side was undeveloped. At the time of origin of the report, the Irish friars had acquired four of the wooden houses, with gardens extending between them. Not far (*"duodecim circiter passus"*) from the house was the town's water main, from which it was quite easy to run a branch pipe to the college. The houses provided accommodation for about twenty friars, not counting another house in the neighbourhood which the Irish were only just thinking about acquiring. The refectory could hold thirty people, the choir above the small chapel many more. The sacristy was equipped with iron gates

---

Kašpar Belvic (AB)." Houses A and B probably formed one whole. According to Lancinger, who drew on the city records, house G was last mentioned in 1608; however, it is not mentioned in the above record.

27   NA, SM, H 99 8; Lancinger, "Z místopisu Nového Města pražského," 177.
28   *IFD*, no. 12, 12.4.1631, Praha.
29   NA, SM, H 99 4, 14.5.1631, Praha.
30   *IFD*, no. 15, 7.6.1631, Praha.
31   Ibid., no. 17, without date: Jennings included this unaddressed and undated letter in the documents dated 10 July and 6 August.

and contained a stove (*fornax*). The school, which had previously served as a stable, was far enough away from the street and lay on the side of the larger gate and was to be open during disputations. Behind the school was a garden, from which the friars already expected a crop of nuts and other produce that year. Inside, there was also a deep well with excellent water and two cellars.

On the same day that Fleming wrote Fallon the above-mentioned letter, in which he also announced his decision that he would begin begging for alms,[32] Archbishop Harrach permitted him, Gerald Geraldin and Patrick Taaffe to say fifty-five Masses at a portable altar in the newly constructed residence in the New Town.[33] Monastic life began to regularise itself. 6 June was the celebration of the inauguration of the new college, which must already have been consecrated to the Virgin Mary (the College of the Immaculate Conception of the Virgin Mary by St. Ambrose).[34] In late June and early July, First Masses were said by newly ordained priests with the Burgrave of Prague and Archbishop Harrach in attendance.[35] On 6 June, on the occasion of the start of tuition in the archiepiscopal seminary, Cardinal Harrach and representatives of state authorities joined the Mass at the college. It was explained in a Latin sermon why the Irish Franciscans had come to Prague and people were encouraged to give alms. How many friars there were at that time is not known but various references indicate that there were probably less than ten. Besides Fleming, Fitzgerald and Taaffe, Matthew Hore and Francis Magennis are known by name.

The actual institutionalisation of the college is documented by a seal bearing the date 1631, which is preserved in the Seal Collection in the National Archives. Around it is written: * SIG:[ILLUM] COLL:[EGII] PRAG:[ENSIS] IM.[MACULATAE] CONCEP.[TIONIS] AD S.[ANCTUM] AMBRO.[SIUM] FF[RATRUM] MIN:[ORUM] STRICT.[IORIS] OBS:[ERVANTIAE] PROV:[INCIAE] HIBERNIAE (The seal of the College of the Immaculate Conception by St. Ambrose of the Friars Minor of the Stricter Observance of the Irish Province) (Fig. 11).[36]

---

32 "... will begin to take upp the contribution ..."
33 NA, ŘHyb Praha, no. 9, 7.6.1631, Praha. Cardinal Harrach, Archbishop of Prague, gives permission to Brothers Fabricius [!] Fleming, Gerald Geraldin and Patrick Taaffe to serve "in cubiculo exstructo in Nova Civitate ... super altari portatili 55 missas..." [55 Masses at a portable altar ... in a room built in Prague's New Town].
34 See *IFD*, no. 28, 207–208, where such a consecration is already mentioned at the beginning of 1631.
35 Ibid., 209.
36 NA, SbT. A description by Dana Stehlíková with many mistakes (e.g. "řád hybernů [the Order of Hybernians]", "Malachiáš Fullov [Malachy Fullov]", etc.). is included in the exhibition catalogue "Rudolf II. a Praha. Císařský dvůr a rezidenční město jako kulturní a duchovní centrum střední Evropy" [Rudolf II and Prague. The Imperial Court and Residential City as the Cultural and Spiritual Centre of Central Europe], eds. Eliška Fučíková et al. (Praha: Správa pražského hradu, 1997) 470, catalogue no. V/573.

Fig. 11 The Prague college's seal matrix
of 1631 (NA).

The promising beginnings of the college, however, were plagued by new
difficulties almost from day to day. Shortly after Patrick Fleming had left for
Vienna[37] at the beginning of August, a dispute arose over the site of the newly
constructed college. That is to say, on 20 August, the Prague Capuchins –
whose relations with the Irish friars had been very good up until that point,
as evidenced by their help with the portable altar and by the Masses they had
said in the Irish Franciscan chapel – sent a complaint in which they laid claim
to the site which already belonged to the Irish college.[38] The situation was
rather difficult for the Irish and their disenchantment and indignation great,
particularly perhaps because it happened in the absence of Patrick Fleming.
Gerald Geraldin and Matthew Hore informed not only Fleming but also Luke

---

37 *IFD*, no. 18, 6.8.1631, Praha. Patrick Fleming mentions that he is planning to go to Vienna the next
day. At the beginning of the letter, there is also the news that a young Francis Magennis has arrived.

38 Ibid., no. 22, 6.8.1631, Praha. Gerald Fitzgerald [Geraldin] reports to Luke Wadding in detail what
happened: "the Capucins being present, healping us for our altar, fa. Magnus himsealf celebrat-
ing 3 or 4 tymes in our Chapple and neaver a one of them spake one woord of this business, untle
it was the 20 of August that they have sent us this supplication…".

Wadding, who had already received the news unofficially from his relative, the Jesuit, Peter Wadding, who was living in Prague at the time. The latter praised the Irish friars, saying that they were doing well in Prague and had a good reputation, only the Capuchins were causing them problems.[39]

Here it must be pointed out that the dispute over the site of the college had been going on since the very beginning. The Capuchins too had chosen a site near the Irish Franciscan college for the establishment of the Friary of St. Joseph. Therefore, in 1631, the guardian of the friary in Hradčany, Alexius Burgund, protested to Cardinal Harrach against the building of the Franciscan house. In the complaint, Burgund referred to the discussions of the previous year.[40] Although we know that Fallon had chosen the site for the college immediately after his arrival from Vienna, where he had gained the Emperor's permission, that is, in late 1629 and early 1630, and that his intention probably preceded the Capuchins' plans, Fallon only began to buy up the houses in 1631. Therefore, from the outset, it was not easy to induce the Capuchins, who did not like to be next to another friary, to concede.

When Patrick Fleming learnt what had happened in Prague, he sent letters to Robert Chamberlain in St. Anthony's College in Louvain and Luke Wadding in St. Isidore's College in Rome, while at the same time initiating diplomatic activity at court. There, of course, he found himself among a number of other supplicants and was forced into lobbying. The interests of the senior representatives of other orders, who were only concerned about minor details and far removed from both the distant reality in newly re-Catholicised Prague and the persecution of Catholics in Ireland, is nicely illustrated by the incident described by Fleming in his letter to Robert Chamberlain. Fleming met in Rome with the vicar general of the Ambrosians, who in pre-Hussite times had built their Monastery and Church of St. Ambrose on the site of the Irish college,[41] and had a verbal battle with him over how to commemorate the former Church of St. Ambrose in the name of the college. Besides this, Fleming discovered that he was not welcomed everywhere with open arms: he was even criticised by the ill-informed Austrian Franciscans, led by their provincial, Prosper Galbiato.[42] Therefore, using additional documents, he put together a concise account of how the college had been approved, founded

39   Ibid., no. 19, 12.9.1631, Praha.
40   Vavřinec Rabas, *Řád kapucínský a jeho působení v Čechách v 17. století* [*The Capuchin Order and its Activity in Bohemia in the Seventeenth Century*] (Praha: [Vydavatelstvo Časopisu katolického duchovenstva], 1937) 48.
41   On the Ambrosian monastery, see Jan Pařez, "Kláštery na Novém Městě pražském do husitských válek a jejich právní a ekonomické postavení v městském prostředí" [Monasteries in Prague's New Town before the Hussite Wars and their Legal and Economic Position in the Urban Environment], *DP* 17 (1998): 75–91, including further literature.
42   See, for example, *IFD*, no. 29, 25.10.1631, Wien. The Austrian Franciscans did not like the ambiguous position of the Irish Franciscan college, see further in the text.

and established in practice in Prague and sent it to Louvain.[43] He then appealed to Luke Wadding to intercede with the Bishop of Rome himself.[44]

The correspondence offers us a look into high Church and state politics through the eyes of an educated Catholic priest defending his people and his faith, whose fate, however, was to assert the interests of one monastic institution, one which, from the viewpoint of local political and power interests, if it was not unimportant was at least not too significant. In terms of their missionary work, the Irish friars had their own country primarily in mind, were led by their own political interests and absorbed in the fate of their own nation. They now suddenly found themselves in the middle of a maelstrom for them unknown and essentially remote, a struggle in a faraway country. In addition, it seems, they found themselves caught between two Catholic sides. Archbishop Harrach, supported by the perceptive intellect of his confessor, the Capuchin, Valeriano Magni, and no doubt significantly influenced by his advice, attempted to assert the supremacy of the Bohemian Church in the question of re-Catholicisation.[45] He was supported in this by the older orders which had been active in Bohemia for centuries, especially the Premonstratensians, Cistercians, Dominicans and Franciscans. On the other side was the coalition of the Jesuits with the ruling house and their attempt to make the process of re-Catholicisation subordinate to state control. It was based on the circle of Romano-German nobility, newly settled in Bohemia, and around it the community establishing itself from the ranks of the victorious Imperial side. The attempt by the Jesuits to attain supremacy in questions of theology by gaining a dominant position in higher education in Prague met with the opposition of Archbishop Harrach. Conversely, attempts by the archbishop for a plurality of theological interpretation were rejected. The primary dispute, however, was over, in today's terms, the "technology" of re-Catholicisation, that is, how and under whose authority it would be accomplished.[46]

So how would the Irish Franciscans have felt in Prague? They exploited the condescension of the Emperor, who had demonstrated his willingness to take the endangered Catholics under his protection and to whom they

---

43   See, for example, ibid, no. 27, 28 and in particular Fleming's defence of the new college, no. 32.

44   Ibid, no. 20, 12.9.1631, Wien.

45   Last mentioned by Stanislav Sousedík, *Valerián Magni. Kapitola z kulturních dějin Čech 17. století* [*Valeriano Magni. A Chapter from the Cultural History of Bohemia in the Seventeenth Century*] (Praha: Vyšehrad, 1983), which also includes older literature, of which let us mention at least the monograph by František Krásl, *Arnošt hrabě Harrach, kardinál sv. církve římské a kníže arcibiskup pražský* [*Ernst, Count Harrach, Cardinal of the Holy Roman Church and Prince Archbishop of Prague*] (Praha: Arcibiskupská knihtiskárna, 1886), and works by Rabas about the Bohemian Capuchins in the seventeenth century which were published in the second half of the 1930s in the magazine *Časopis katolického duchovenstva* and also as an independent print.

46   Apart from Sousedík's *Valerián Magni*, see also I. Čornejová ed., *Dějiny Univerzity Karlovy II, 1622–1802* [*The History of Charles University II, 1622–1802*] (Praha: Univerzita Karlova, 1996).

were indebted for permission to settle in Prague, and at the same time the support of the Cardinal, who saw in them theologians and teachers famed abroad and, as such, intended to exploit them for his own conception of re-Catholicisation. Thus, they found themselves somewhere in the middle, led by a strenuous endeavour to build an adequate base for religious exiles and reverse conditions in their homeland through missionary work and the training of clergy, and did not even notice that they had become a pawn in a game which was only marginally related to them. Patrick Taaffe expressed, albeit somewhat later, the position of the Irish Franciscans among the political currents in the Bohemian Church in one of his letters to Luke Wadding: "*I protest bee fore God, quod non simus Petri, nec Pauli; non Joannis nec Jacobi, sed solius Christi...*".[47]

If we consider their political and in the long run even missionary objectives in the Bohemian Crown Lands, from this point of view they were in fact modest. As soon as the Irish, in an attempt to found another college (Namslav in Silesia), encroached on the territory of the Bohemian Franciscan province, they were plainly, without hesitation or sentiment, given to realise by their otherwise welcoming and hospitable colleagues that they were overstepping their authority. Although they in no way neglected their spiritual responsibilities, they were never (and could never be) in fact given charge of a parish in the Bohemian Crown Lands. But even their role, providing primarily for the spiritual needs of the above-mentioned Romano-German community and, sooner or later, also of the gradually settling members of the Irish nobility and clearly also of students and the intelligentsia (because it was all of these who primarily provided the Franciscans with an income within the three towns of Prague, as the Irish friars were only permitted to beg for alms outside Prague), was essentially a luxury, especially from the viewpoint of a parish network with inadequate personnel.

The only missionary we know from the sources is the Irish Franciscan, Hugh (surname unknown), although we do not know exactly what his relationship with the Prague college was. In July 1635, Pope Urban VIII granted him fairly extensive powers to carry out missionary activity in Bohemia. He could confess the faithful where there was no parish priest, bishop or other person allowed to hear confessions; he could grant absolution for heresy, apostasy or schism; once grant absolution for all sins reserved by the papal bull, *Coena Domini*, to the Holy See, and for simony, if the penitents were prepared to relinquish their benefices and reimburse their emoluments; also he had permission to read heretical and forbidden books in order to refute heretical opinions; he could say Mass at a portable, damaged or desecrated

---

47   "...that we are neither Peter's, nor Paul's; neither John's, nor James's but Christ's alone...". *IFD*, no. 44, 29.7.1632, Praha. Patrick Taaffe to Luke Wadding in Rome.

altar even in the presence of those excommunicated; he could change simple vows, give dispensations against impediments of the ordained arising from secret crimes which had not been brought before the court apart from murder, simony and bigamy, and, under precisely stipulated conditions, grant full and partial indulgences.

In order to have a clearer picture of the situation of the Irish Franciscans, we must again remember their friendly contacts with the above-mentioned Jesuit, Peter Wadding. He was for them, as they were for him, a fighter in a common cause and one of the few links with the homeland. Peter Wadding's relationship with the "long monk," as the Capuchin, Valeriano Magni, was nicknamed, was extremely tense, all the more so because Wadding was the first dean of the theological faculty and later acted as chancellor of the university.[48] In addition, he enjoyed writing replies to all kinds of anti-Jesuit pamphlets and Philippics.[49] For Magni, who never missed an opportunity to attack the Jesuits, Wadding was thus the embodiment of everything that he so sincerely hated. This almost irrational aspect of Magni's character is entirely consistent with other somewhat effusive sides of his approach to the world.[50]

For that matter, Wadding made no secret of what he thought of Valeriano Magni. If we may be permitted to express it thusly, in his letter to his relative, Luke, at St. Isidore's College in Rome, in which he refers to the Capuchin, overflows with insular irony: *"I doe helpe them* [the Irish Franciscans] *the best that I can, but that troublesom Capucin hath a strange hedde, and gouverneth the cardinal, and as you knowe your selfe persuadeth mannie in the Court of Roome what he wil. He denieth to have anny part in this busins against the friars of our nation. I doe believe that the good father hath good intentions in this busins, but the pure trueth is, that he disgousteth the hole kindome, the nobilitie, the clergie, and the Emperour's courte. He calleth himself missionarius Apostolicus, and doeth nothinge in the conversion of soules, and al his reformation is to founde the cardinal his iurisdiction, with displeasure of al the world."*[51]

So perhaps Fleming did not even suspect why a seemingly petty squabble had begun over a plot of land, which six months before had been strewn with piles of rubbish and ruins, and that he had been drawn into a Bohemian game

48 Čornejová ed., *Dějiny Univerzity Karlovy II*, 251. Peter Wadding is listed as Dean of Theological Faculty in 1630; he is mentioned as Chancellor in 1632; he held this post as late as 30 August 1638 (Krásl, *Arnošt hrabě Harrach*, 385). Bibliography provided by Ludvík Schmid, "Irská emigrace do střední Evropy v 17. a 18. století" [Irish Emigration to Central Europe in the Seventeenth and Eighteenth Centuries], *SH* 33 (1986): 284.
49 See, for example, Krásl, *Arnošt hrabě Harrach*, 370.
50 See also Sousedík, *Valerián Magni*, 27; Rabas, *Řád kapucínský a jeho působení v Čechách*, 114–115; see also a letter by Peter Wadding to Luke Wadding, *IFD*, no. 83, 29.8.1638, Praha.
51 *IFD*, no. 19, 12.9.1631.

which would last for many years. He succeeded in writing a defence of the Prague college in which, against a broad historical perspective, he justified its existence, describing its foundation and enumerating all the authorities who had given their permission (the Emperor, the general of the order, the papal nuncio, the Archbishop of Prague and the commissary general), giving reasons why it should be separated from other houses and explaining why the other orders in Prague need not fear it for reasons of exceeding their jurisdiction or competition.[52]

Fleming himself, however, did not live to see further moves in the game. Soon after he had returned to Prague, he set out again for Vienna, accompanied by a deacon, Matthew Hore.[53] His mission in Vienna was to agree upon the conditions for the arrival of the remaining friars from the college, who had decided to leave Prague ahead of the advancing Saxon army. On 7 November 1631, Fleming and Hore were attacked by enraged villagers near Benešov by the village of Oleška. Fleming was killed on the spot by three blows to the head and his robbed body left lying on the royal highway, where it was later found.[54] The villagers dragged Hore off into the forest where they shot him three times in the chest, while at the same time stabbing him with a lance.[55] It is difficult to say whether the villagers were motivated by religious fanaticism, as Bruodin maintains,[56] or by the latent mob violence which had come to the surface in the difficult war years, or whether it was, perhaps, robbery. The truth, as usual, clearly lies somewhere in the middle. That the villagers were not acting solely for reasons of denominational intolerance is evidenced in part by the fact that the corpse was robbed, and in part by a comment made by Bruodin himself, referring to the bands of robbers wreaking havoc in the countryside using the Czech expression *"Petrovští,"*[57] while at the same time, for reasons of religious propaganda, adding the attribute *"Husitští pobudové,"* that is, "Hussite vagabonds."[58]

Fleming's body was found by Maria, Countess of Šternberk, and brought with that of his companion to Votice, where the earthly remains of the first guardian of the Irish Franciscan college were buried in the friary church of

---

52   Ibid., no. 32, *Apologeticus pro Collegii Pragensis Immaculatae Conceptionis ad S. Ambrosium.*

53   The spelling of the name varies from Hore to Hory or even Hoar, see Edward MacLysaght, *Irish Families, Their Names, Arms & Origins* (Blackrock: Irish Academic Press, 1991).

54   Bruodin contradicts himself when he immediately states that Fleming sustained five lethal blows.

55   For a description of the murders, see Bruodin, *Propugnaculum,* 751–753.

56   According to Bruodin, the Franciscans were attacked by the villagers who shouted: "Mactemus, mactemus monachos, patriae pestes, fideique nostrae hostes" [Let's kill the monks, the curse of our homeland and the enemies of our faith]. See Bruodin, *Propugnaculum,* 751.

57   Meaning "bandits," from "Petrovský," the name of the leader of a band of robbers in the seventeenth century.

58   "... ab Hussiticis grassatoribus (vulgo Petrowsky) ...," ibid. 752.

the Bohemian Franciscan province. The second Irishman, Matthew Hore, was laid to rest beside him on 12 November.[59]

No later than 18 November, the remainder of the college took refuge in Vienna. The Austrian Franciscans took a decidedly reserved attitude to their fellow Irish brothers, while at the same time the provincial gave them to understand who was in charge.[60] At the end of May 1632, however, the Imperial General Valdštejn drove the Saxons out of Prague and the Irish were immediately able to return.[61] Gerald Geraldin, who was, it seems, along with Patrick Taaffe, the only one still in correspondence with Rome and Louvain, in his letters to Luke Wadding refers to the military situation in Central Europe – the fear of another political and, consequently, religious upheaval was ever-present.

It seemed that the initial success of the Irish Franciscans in Prague was to be short-lived. They had never sought a place in the struggle between the Bohemian political parties and when the shadow of the Saxon invasion, during which their first guardian died, fell over them, all seemed lost. There was, too, the still unresolved question of whose authority the Prague college would come under. Louvain had an opinion entirely different from that of the general chapter. Until it was decided, as mentioned above, at the general chapter in Toledo in 1633, the College of the Immaculate Conception was placed under the control of the vicar general, who was not supposed to hinder or otherwise limit its activity.[62]

Anyone who supposed that the death of Patrick Fleming and the exile and then return to Prague of the members of the college had settled the dispute of the Irish Franciscans with the Capuchins would be greatly mistaken. Guided by their original intention to build a friary in close proximity to the Irish (as Gerald Geraldin writes in one of his letters: *"they have bought a place in our doore"*[63]) and expel them from the place, they initiated another instalment of the squabble. Following a complaint by the guardian of the Capuchins, Alexius Burgund, to Cardinal Harrach,[64] the Irish friars countered with two petitions

---

59 The iron grill which Sezima, Count of Vrtba, had made for their tomb was in the course of time removed and replaced by a board with a Czech inscription, which was attached to the pulpit. After the improvement of the interior in 1758, an inscription with similar wording was painted on the wall. When the church was being painted white in 1776, it was damaged and was again renovated by order of the provincial.

60 *IFD*, no. 35, 18.11.1631. Patrick Taaffe wrote from Vienna to Luke Wadding in St. Isidore's College in Rome that the local provincial was "quite contrarie" and that he was awaiting the decision of the general of the order to determine which province the Irish Franciscans of Prague would belong to, how they would live and what permissions they would have regarding the collecting of alms.

61 As early as 8 July, Gerald Geraldin wrote from Prague to Luke Wadding, see ibid., no. 41.

62 See ibid., no. 44, 29.7.1632, Praha. Patrick Taaffe to Luke Wadding in Rome.

63 Ibid., no. 58, 10.11.1632, Praha. Gerald Geraldin describes the whole story to Wadding and mentions that the guardian of the Capuchins bought "a place in our doore" for 9,000 florins in cash.

64 Ibid., no. 47, 2.11.1632.

to the papal nuncio in Vienna, Cyriaco Rocci,[65] but he froze the restoration of the college until the general chapter of the order was able to adjudicate.[66] Shocked by the strictest sanctions (excommunication) under which the prospective completion of the rebuilding was forbidden, in a series of petitionary letters the Irish turned to the influential Luke Wadding at St. Isidore's College in Rome. Wadding himself had for some time been inundating the Emperor, the Queen of Hungary[67] and wife of Ferdinand II, Eleonora of Mantua, Archbishop Harrach and the nuncio with letters of intercession.[68] The college was gripped by uncertainty because the chapter taking place in Toledo was too far away to be influenced by the Irish Franciscans or to obtain information adequate in quality and quantity. Gerald Geraldin wrote to Wadding: *"Our adversaries doe prepare themsealves against the Chapter General, and our fathers are a slipe; so that I cannot understand what they intend to doe; if I doe send them papers, I know wel that that wil not bee of such efficacie as if I had beene mesealf present, who knows the state of all the buisness ffrom beginnge, in this yor R. may admonish me what is to be don."*[69] On the other hand, support emerged in the guise of Archbishop Harrach, who demonstrated this by requesting the Irish Franciscans provide a lector in theology and a lector in philosophy for the archiepiscopal seminary, then under construction.[70] Not even the leadership of the Louvain college would accept that the College of the Immaculate Conception should meet an unpleasant fate, because reinforcements were soon to be sent from Louvain to the Prague college.[71]

---

65   Ibid., no. 48, 2.11.1632, and especially an extensive request with references to the foundation of other orders in Prague ibid., no. 49, sine dato. Jennings classified it as coming after 2 November. However, many newer documents follow so, according to the inner chronology, it must be a misprint.

66   Ibid., no. 51, 28.8.1632, Wien. Decree of the papal nuncio in Vienna. See also ibid., no. 55, 5.10.1632, Praha., where Geraldin communicated to Wadding that the previous day the Bohemian provincial had come with a mandate from the nuncio, which under the threat of excommunication prohibited any renovation until the general chapter gave its permission. The Capuchins were quiet. However, the most important parts of the college, i.e. the dormitory and chapel, had already been repaired.

67   Crowned also in 1627 in Prague as Queen of Bohemia.

68   *IFD*, no. 50, 21.8.1632, Praha. In a letter, Gerald Geraldin thanked Luke Wadding for the supplicatory letters which he had sent to the Emperor, the Queen of Hungary, Harrach and the nuncio; ibid. in no. 53, 1.9.1632, Praha, he thanked him again and mentioned a letter for the congregation *De propaganda fide*. See ibid. no. 56–58.

69   Ibid., no. 57, 4.11.1632, Praha.

70   Ibid., no. 62, 16.2.1632, Praha. Gerald Geraldin told Luke Wadding amongst other things, that Archbishop Harrach had requested from them two excellent lectors for the archiepiscopal seminary, one in theology and one in philosophy. This was the reason he asked for the four promised brothers.

71   Ibid., no. 63, 26.2.1633, Praha. Geraldin wrote to Luke Wadding that Robert (probably Chamberlain) had written him that in Advent they expected a provincial and a guardian who should determine which brothers would be sent to Prague.

Following the general chapter in Toledo, the minister general of the Franciscans of the Stricter Observance confirmed the foundation of the Prague college, whose construction had already begun, and in the text of the document expressly stated that it was to be completed. The minister general also took the college directly under his jurisdiction, at the same time appointing a special delegate to supervise, with the power and authority of a commissary general.[72]

With this, the situation quieted down somewhat, so that nothing prevented the Irish from entering their most famous period in Bohemia, that is, when they taught at the archiepiscopal seminary. As we know, of course, the Capuchins eventually built themselves the Friary of St. Joseph in the neighbourhood of the Irish Franciscans.

THE COLLEGE STATUTES: A VIEW OF THE HOUSEHOLD

What was life actually like inside the Prague college and according to what regulations was the community organised? Life in a religious house has always been considered as something very private, while at the same time a breach of the isolation within its walls by outside observers has aroused the promising, yet frequently unconfirmed, prospect of the revelation of scandal. Only rarely has the actual spiritual disposition of the conventuals and their personal attitudes been captured, and when they have been forced to publicly reveal their spiritual routines, it has usually been during a canonical visitation. Seeking answers to these questions is, in the case of the Irish college, all the more difficult in that we do not actually have at our disposal any original sources which would enable us to answer them adequately. Consequently, our look through the keyhole at the "household" in the early years of the college will have, in contrast to the later period, a rather official tone and will mainly be concerned with the structure of the community.

However, let us begin with the number of members of the college. Following the deaths of Patrick Fleming and Matthew Hore, Gerald Geraldin became guardian and, with several others, was the first to return to Prague. Delayed by illness, Patrick Taaffe followed him from Vienna a little later, accompanied by a confrère,[73] so that in the first half of November 1632, the

---

72   NA, ŘHyb Praha, nos. 9, 11, 12 and 15, 20.6.1633, Madrid, Lat. Juan de Campaña, general of the Franciscans of Stricter Observance, consented to the foundation of the College of the Immaculate Conception in Prague. The letter was also published by Jennings in *IFD*, no. 65, 270. In the text, it is mentioned that the previous general, Bernardino de Senis, had already equipped the Prague college with *all* necessary powers and freedoms.

73   *IFD*, no. 50, 21.8.1632, Praha. Gerald Geraldin informed Luke Wadding, among other things, that he was expecting the arrival of Patrick Taaffe and a companion from Vienna.

Prague college consisted of a mere half dozen people.[74] In the middle of the following year, Francis Farrell Fr. Aspol and a German lay brother arrived in Prague[75] and, from that time, the number of friars rose constantly, as we are informed, not only by the survey in Hammerschmid's *Prodromus*,[76] but also by the letter sent a year later, that is, in June 1634, by Francis Farrell to Luke Wadding. From 1632, the members of the college had tripled to eighteen.[77]

According to some descriptions, less than twenty-five years after its foundation the college already had seventy members, but it would be a mistake to ascribe this increase only to the growing persecution in Ireland.[78] In 1653, the Irish Franciscans had to leave the friary in Wieluń and some of them made their way to Prague. Registers from the years 1653 to 1654 show us that there were more than fifty friars in the Prague college at that time. Even so, this was quite a considerable number and the only reliable solution for the relief of the overcrowded college was to found a new one. This should have been Namslav in Silesia (now Namysłów, east of Wrocław in Poland). A Franciscan friary had been founded in Namslav in 1321. After the order was divided into the Friars Minor Conventuals (Minorites) and the Friars Minor of the Stricter Observance (Franciscans), it fell to the Franciscans of the Bohemian province. Shortly afterwards, however, in 1536, during the period of Reformation conflict, the friars had to leave Namslav and the empty friary became a hospital. It was restored to its former status in 1675.[79]

The Irish attempts were merely an episode which foundered on the opposition of the superiors of the Bohemian Franciscan province, who regarded the fact that the Irish would occupy one of their former friaries as a very unpleasant precedent with possible repercussions in the future. In addition, the Irish had avoided discussions with the Bohemian superiors over permission for a new foundation within the Bohemian province. In October 1653, the provincial, Konstantin Dubský, appealed to Luke Wadding to discourage his confrères from damaging the Bohemian province and, at the same time, turned to the Silesian provincial authorities (*suprema curia ducatus Silesiae*)

---

74   Ibid., no. 58, 10.11.1632, Praha. Gerald Geraldin wrote to Luke Wadding that the members of the college were "altogether ... six in number...".

75   Ibid., no. 66, 28.6.1633, Praha. Gerald Geraldin to Luke Wadding.

76   Hammerschmid, *Prodromus gloriae Pragenae*, 301–302, mentions as a newcomer in 1633 Fr. Francis Archepold (it is probably Fr. Aspol) who arrived with Farrell and a lay brother from Salzburg, "P. Ludovicus Machamius cum juniore novitio, fratre scilicet Patritio Colomano, quos mos secuti sunt P. Petrus Ô Moloy cum P. Paulo Frain, deinde P. Antonius Gavanus, item P. Laurentius Ô Bruin cum P. Jacobo Cavello in februario 1634. Quos eodem Anno P. Simon, P. Flemingus, frater Rochus, & frater Assius novitius secuti sunt" came from Flanders (i.e. from Louvain).

77   *IFD*, no. 74, 7.6.1634, Praha. Some other names, mostly in slightly distorted form, are stated again by Hammerschmid: Bonaventure Bermigham, Anthony Caron, Hugo Brinan, Kornelius Keoch, Evžen Chymanay, Patrik Warde and Bernard Lynsius.

78   Millett, *The Irish Franciscans*, 136; NA, AZK, carton no. 45, no. 60.

79   Vrbčanský, *Nucleus minoriticus*, 304–313.

in order to provoke a suitably negative attitude to the Irish. He wrote that the friars had not mastered the native tongue, so that they would not be able to preach or hear confessions, and also that *"the way that they conduct themselves is not in accord with this locality and, apart from their ineffectiveness, they would cause problems with non-Catholics."*

In the end, admittedly, the Irish received permission for a new foundation from the Emperor, but under the condition that in the college there would be several German priests or at least ones fluent in German, who would devote themselves to spiritual administration. Perhaps because of this condition (particularly when the Irish clearly intended to found another college to train missionaries and not a friary for pastoral work among the local inhabitants) and also because of further opposition in the Bohemian province, the Irish relinquished their plans to establish themselves in Namslav.[80]

Let us, however, return from the Silesian countryside to the Prague college. The basic norms for the Franciscan Order were represented by the general constitution and statutes, decreed by the general of the order and the general chapter.[81] From these, then, came the statutes of individual provinces, whose publication was under the supervision of the provincials.[82]

Friars were divided into priests (*patres*), clerics (*fratres*) and lay brothers (*laici*). Individual friars were then assigned to their roles; some acted as preachers (*concionatores, predicatores*), others as confessors (*confesores*). For the Prague college, teaching was especially important. Tuition was in the hands of lectors in philosophy and theology.

How the internal precepts of life in the college actually worked we can learn from the college statutes.[83] Unfortunately, only one authenticated specimen from 1744 has been preserved, but, nevertheless, we can determine at least approximately their original form because a note is appended, showing that it is in fact the wording from 1665 (Fig. 12).[84] All of the articles deleted in

---

80 Millett, *The Irish Franciscans*, 137–139. An undated petition by the Bohemian Franciscans to the Emperor, to which he refers in note no. 13, is stored in NA, ŘF, carton no. 22, together with other documents related to Namslav. The members of the Bohemian Franciscan province mainly used the argument that the Irish, due to their lack of language ability and ignorance of the situation, would not be able to impact on non-Catholics. At the same time, in Prague there were priests who could hear confessions in German as evidenced by the lists of persons suitable to send out on a mission which were sent to Cardinal Harrach in 1656–1657.

81 Quotes here from the order's regulations are from *Constitutiones et statuta generalia Cismontanae familiae ordinis sancti Francisci*, Romae 1663.

82 For the Bohemian province, we had at our disposal *Statuta et decreta fratrum minorum s. Patris Francisci reformatorum provinciae Bohemiae S. Wenceslai ducis et martyris*, (s.l.) 1673.

83 NA, ŘF, book no. 13. *Statuta domestica pro religio regimine fratrum minorum strictioris observantiae provinciae Hiberniae, collegii Immaculatae conceptionis B. V. Mariae Pragae.*

84 Ibid. In 1664, the regulations were reviewed, amended and confirmed by the general of the order, Michaelangelo de Sambuca. In the college, it was signed by the guardian Anthony Burke, *lector jubilatus* Daniel Bruoder, *lector jubilatus* Bernardine Clancy, *lector jubilatus sanctae theolo-*

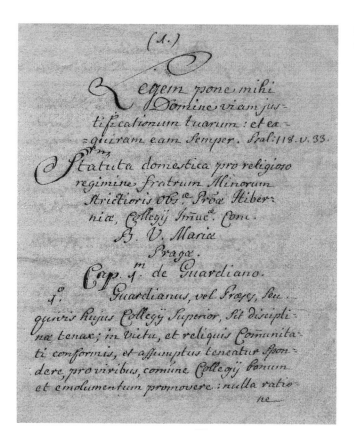

Fig. 12 The first page of the college statutes of 1655 (NA).

1774 were crosshatched on the original, which means that they were no longer valid. According to the postscript, it was a version from 1665 which had
been preserved in the college for many years before that. There is no doubt,
therefore, that this is the first code of conduct which had regulated life in the
college from the very beginning. The statutes contained fifteen articles. They
were to be read aloud at the beginning of January, April, July and October,
and then the general statutes in May and November.

The head of the college was the guardian (*guardianus*). He had to be of
indisputable morality and of appropriate age, experience and ability, that is,
he had to be at least thirty years old and to have been at the very least ten
years in the order. He was selected by the discreets who, every three years,
chose two or three suitable persons who came from the particular province
of Ireland[85] from which the new guardian was to be selected. Candidates
were then presented to the general of the order, who then appointed one of

---

giae Anthony Farrell, *lector jubilatus sanctae theologiae* and vicar Bernard O'Neill and, last but not
least, Anthony Donnelly, commissary visitator.
85   Ulster, Munster, Leinster or Connaught.

them guardian. It is noteworthy how much emphasis was laid on the rotation of guardians from the individual provinces of Ireland. It speaks eloquently of the jealousy which held sway inside the community and doubtless, too, of dissension, for only these could cause this article to have been incorporated into the text.

The three-year tenure of the guardian began the day the "literarum patentium" was published. When the office of guardian was vacant for various reasons (for instance, the guardian had not yet been elected, or had unexpectedly died, etc.), the praeses supplied a guardian. Unfortunately, the competences of the praeses were not clarified in the Prague copy of the statutes. If the new guardian came from the same province of Ireland as the praeses, his office began the day the praeses had begun to supply.[86] Otherwise, the three-year tenure began the day the praeses took office. In the exercise of his authority, at least in the most important respects, the guardian was monitored by the discreets. Without their written consent, he was not allowed to make a decision regarding the state of the college, accept or expel members, make unusual payments or demolish the building. If he overstepped his authority in these matters, he was suspended. He was also threatened with punishment if he did not promulgate in good time the edicts of his superiors, or even kept them secret.

The guardian enjoyed no special privileges. Like the praeses or any other friar, he could not, under any pretext, accept donations for himself, because, like everything else, these became the property of the community. This concerned books and other items, even if he had obtained them himself. He did not have separate meals; even if he was ill, he was not allowed to eat in his own cell, or even in the cell of another friar. If the guardian was seriously ill and had not recovered after three days, he was placed in the communal infirmary and treated there like any other friar. In short, he had to adhere to all aspects of communal life.

The discreets saw to it that the guardian properly managed the resources which served the collective life of the community and if he exhibited shortcomings, he was reprimanded and if he did not improve, he was relieved of his position. On the other hand, it was the guardian's responsibility to regularly determine whether the friars were obtaining superfluous items and if he found this to be the case, these were used for the community or given to those who needed them. If such a friar was thus found to have broken his vow of poverty, he was punished. On the other hand, the guardian had to ensure that the friar had whatever essential items he lacked.

---

86   According to information kindly provided by Joseph MacMahon OFM, this condition is not included in the copy of the 1665 statutes of the college in the library of St. Isidore's College in Rome.

The college was respected as an institution with its own way of life and its private problems, which is evidenced by the article which forbad a commissary who was temporarily managing the college from becoming involved with the affairs of the guardianate and the other offices of college administration. In the same way, a commissary was not allowed to interfere in the private affairs of the superiors; at most, he could support them. Neither could he make any changes in the important affairs of the college without consultation with the guardian.

The choice of candidates for commissary visitator (*commisarius visitator*) fell within the jurisdiction of the guardian and discreets, but the final decision lay in the hands of the general of the order.

In the guardian's absence, he was deputised by the vicar, who was appointed either by the chapter or the provincial.[87]

As mentioned above, the guardian had, also in order to correct his own decisions, an advisory council (*discretorium*) of which he himself was a member. The council consisted of discreets (*discretes*). The function of a discreet could only be taken by lectors in theology and that meant those who actually lectured as "*jubilati*" (see below). Besides the guardian, there were to be four older (*seniores*) lectors from the four provinces of Ireland; they were discreets *ipso facto*. They were joined by another four, again from the four provinces to maintain proportionality.

The discreets occupied a key position in the internal life of the college. This was because, in colleges lying outside their own province, the private judgement of a single person, however scrupulous, did not seem sufficiently safe. Individual discreets had both the right to advise and the right to make decisions. Anyone who did not seek their mandatory agreement and thus circumvented them thereby acted not only without permission but also without validity.

Discreets assisted the guardian with advice and supervision and informed him of the state of affairs of the college, not just once a year but more often in urgent cases. Without their written consent (or rather, majority consent), the guardian could not do anything of consequence related to the administration of the college. This consent was entered "*in libro conventus*," the book where everything connected with the administration of the college was recorded, from changes in it, through the decrees of the superiors, the names of the friars, to accounts of preaching missions and other activities.

The consent of the discreets was required for the appointment or removal of college officials, changes in food or dress, in the studies and ceremonies prescribed in the regulations of the order or province, also for building al-

---

87   Bruodin, *Corolla oecodomiae*, 295.

terations to the college, expenditure, debts, taxes, more serious and unusual punishment of the friars, all disrespect to the will of the superiors (when it was not possible to appeal to them) and cases requiring investigation. Once a month, in the presence of the discreets, there was an accounting of alms and expenditure, which was confirmed as correct by the discreets' signatures, but if a discrepancy was found, a protocol would be drawn up.

The college statutes also contained several articles concerning the discreets' approach to resolving problems. The most interesting of these is the one which exhorts them to reticence towards the other friars in matters of secrecy, and for these things to be resolved in the council chamber. If someone did betray a secret, they were, but with the support of two witnesses, to be reported to the guardian.

As is clear from very varied references, the teaching by the lectors was highly praised. The fact that the lectors were appointed by the general of the order confirms the importance attached to teaching. If possible, lectors were alumni of the college. Altogether, there were eight lectors: four taught scholastic theology and two always taught ethics and two philosophy. Even among lectors, the principle of proportionality was to be maintained with regard to the four provinces of Ireland, so each province had one teacher of scholastics and one teacher of either ethics or philosophy. In the system of scholarship, philosophy was traditionally subordinated to theology (*philosophia ancilla theologiae*), so that they began to gain experience by teaching philosophy initially and if they were to lecture in theology, they first had to pass a two-year course. Even so, they still had to wait until the position of lector became vacant. Lectors in theology who had taught for twelve years gained the "title" or position of *lector jubilatus*.[88]

The statutes enjoined the lectors to lecture without unnecessary aberrations; theology from the Scriptures, the Acts of the Apostles and Ecclesiastes, and more rarely they were allowed to introduce *"rationibus metaphysicis et Aristotelicis."* Twice a year, each lector had to participate in a public disputation with a published thesis. When teaching, they were to avoid exotic, singular and strange assumptions and the admixture of unorthodox opinions. Lectors could choose their own method, but when teaching they had to honour John Duns Scotus, called *doctor subtilis*; if they did not do so, they were relieved of their lectorate. All lectors, without exception, had to participate in each others' disputations, whether in public or in private. In terms of routine, lectors in theology lectured in morality and casuistry three times a week.[89] On Sundays and holy days, there were disputations *"de controversiis fidei,"* that is, polemics.

---

88 Ibid., 256.
89 These were the instructions for solving more complex cases which confessors might encounter.

In contrast to that, students had to comply with the timetable of study, not go out without permission and, in all other respects, behave according to the Rule, as it is for that matter to the present day.

Once a week, there was a two-hour disputation. The day before, students had to present their thesis to the guardian and the lectors, who were in this way invited to attend. The printed thesis were subject to the approval of the guardian and the discreets. Anyone who was to defend their thesis publicly was exempted from choir duty with the exception of first- and second-class holy days. A student who spoke without the invitation of a lector was subjected to a punishment which was, from today's viewpoint, rather humiliating; that is, during the next meal, he had to hold a stick in his mouth and apologise to the community on his knees.

Every three months, the guardian determined the progress and discipline of the students and, in the presence of the discreets, accordingly reprimanded or encouraged them. Students who did not have a twice yearly exhortation (the statutes do not explain in detail what this term covers, but it was clearly an address on a given theme), which it was the custom of the college for the guardian to prescribe, were deprived of all privileges and exemptions.

The statutes make it clearer to us how members of the college were accepted and discharged. Before teaching began on the philosophy course, the guardian, with the help of the discreets, reported in writing to the provincial on the state of the college and if there were no local aspirants, the provincial sent the required number of new students. The number of friars in the college was, however, set by the council and, if possible, at the beginning of a new guardian's three-year term of office.

When a friar arrived at the college, first his order, age, name, surname and the friary he came from were established. The guardian entered these data in the archive. Those arriving from Ireland were prepared for a year by the master of novices.

Those who were returning to Ireland as missionaries were trained for two months in casuistry, preaching and "fidei controversiis."

It is clear that teaching was the most important activity in the college. This is evidenced by the amount of space it is given in the statutes. This is understandable because from other comments it is clear that students were by no means only friars. The Prague college also served as an educational establishment for Irish Catholic youth, though the considerable remoteness of Prague from Ireland is perhaps why the number of secular students was not very high.

Besides lectors and students in the college, there were also other positions. There was the novice master (magister novitiorum), who was responsible for the preparation and guidance of novices, then the sacristan, who was responsible for the running of the church, including (pious and respectful) dealings with people and the management of the books in which Masses were recorded. One of the friars also acted as gatekeeper (*ostiarius*).

An important position was also occupied by the prefect of the infirmary or hospital. He had to have pharmaceutical training and to supervise the college pharmacy, which he stocked with preparations for mixing medicines according to a doctor's prescription. Patients were subjected to a rather strict regime. The statutes forbad them to ask for a change of food or clothing. This formulation suggests that illness was considered rather as a weakness. Apart from the *pater spiritualis* and the doctor, no secular person or stranger could enter the infirmary. The friars' access was also limited; they were allowed to visit a patient only in twos and at a certain time.

Besides articles relating to divine worship and contemplation, and, if need be, the observance of silence, with regard to individual friars the college statutes understandably also covered other aspects of daily life. These concerned domestic discipline; for example, the borrowing of books, meal times and the readings during them, spiritual exercises and also the friars' clothing. Here, we should mention the article that stipulated that no-one was permitted to have two habits or two tunics in his cell, and that winter clothing was returned in May and stored away, and issued again in October for the winter.

It is understandable that the norms also covered contact with the outside. This concerned not only visitors to the college but also in particular dealings with people from the outside world. Students (clearly those who were not friars) and the poor, who might be in the college to assist the friars, could attend to minor matters in the city, though too much *"familiaritas"* was forbidden. If someone was applying to join the order, he was not to live there long before being dressed in the habit of the order. There is also an interesting article which forbad any unfavourable talk about other nations, provinces or families.[90]

It was within the framework of the college statutes, then, that the members of the community of the College of the Immaculate Conception of the Virgin Mary in Prague's New Town lived in the early years of this house of the order and doubtless, in a modified form, in subsequent decades, too. It is clear that many members infringed the principles of communal life and that what has been preserved for us is only the form of the ideal. The confrontation of the ideal and the real is provided only by the record of the apostolic canonical visitation carried out after approximately one hundred years of the college's existence.

---

90 Here, the term "familia" means a family or group of provinces, for example, "familia Transmontana," the transalpine family.

3. THE IRISH FRANCISCANS IN THE SERVICE OF THE ARCHBISHOPS OF PRAGUE (1636–1692)

"Happy are you, Irishmen, whom Ireland bore as a mother and as a step-mother sundered: you, who suffer persecution for the sake of justice, are blessed by the voice of truth, and yours is the Kingdom of Heaven! Happy are you, who are banished by your own land and accepted by a foreign one: that land, overcome by a new plague inimical to your integrity, deserved not your presence! Happy are you, who through the imitation of St. Patrick and the example of Christ become righteous! Let us rather believe that it happened at the instigation of Providence itself, to lead you into these regions which will be fired with the innate ardour of your piety, and that it will bring a new benefit when that which was hidden, or at least enclosed, within Ireland, scholarship, endurance and virtue, will now win you, who are scattered around the world, eternal glory and good reputation."

With these words Hugo Teiser, a Premonstratensian from the Strahov monastery, addressed the Irish Franciscans assembled in the College of the Immaculate Conception on the Feast of St. Patrick, 17 March 1637. It was no accident that the Irish invited, as a renowned preacher, Teiser himself. In his time, Teiser became so famous for his eloquence that he became Professor of Rhetoric in the recently opened archiepiscopal seminary. Equally, Teiser's eulogising the Irish presence in Bohemia was no accident, even though his audience would have forgiven his polished address being somewhat exaggerated, they may indeed have expected it.[1]

For that matter, most of those present were, perhaps, aware of the situation. Not quite two years before, after all the delays caused by the Saxon invasion, regular tuition had finally begun in the seminary established by Archbishop Harrach. There were, however, very few experienced and, in particular, theologically knowledgeable men who could ensure the high quality education of priests, secular and regular. Admittedly, the Strahov Premonstratensians did try, but their strength was only sufficient to provide tuition in classes for minor seminarians. A single Premonstratensian, Alexius Perelcius, taught morality in the archiepiscopal seminary in the years 1637 to 1638. In 1630, he had himself attended lectures in philosophy by Charles Grobendonque at the Faculty of Arts in Prague, and then in the years 1633 to 1634 he had continued in his study of theology in Olomouc, where

---

1 Hugo Teiser, *Panegyricus factus aeternae memoriae … sanctissimi Patricii…*, Pragae 1637.

he defended his thesis in philosophy.[2] Hugo Teiser had also studied philosophy in Olomouc but only completed his theological education in 1637 at the
archiepiscopal seminary in Prague. When he preached to the Irish about
St. Patrick, he was not yet a priest.[3] Other colleagues of theirs, who later, in
the 1640s, taught in classes for minor seminarians, were in no better position. Bruno Lindtner and Bernard Sutor (Schuster) themselves continued in
their study of philosophy, or rather theology, at the archiepiscopal seminary.
Václav Želivský, who replaced Sutor, was only ordained priest in 1640 and
Kašpar Falco, entrusted in 1640 with the tuition of the youngest pupils, only
as late as 1643. In addition, the Premonstratensians in Prague's Old Town did
not have their own accommodation: the better informed among the listeners
to Teiser's sermon may have known that, less than a fortnight before, the Abbot of Strahov monastery, Kaspar Questenberg, had signed a contract with
the builder Melchior Meer for the construction of a college by the Chapel of
St. Benedict. The building site was not far from the archiepiscopal seminary
and for all that Questenberg valued the advantageous location of the future
institute of learning, he clearly did not enjoy recollecting the circumstances
in which a delapidated church and the area around it had been exchanged
for the Church of St. Nicholas and the adjacent parish in Prague's Old Town.[4]

The Cistercians, another of the orders on which the archbishop relied,
were in an even worse position. At the provincial chapter of 1616, they had
resolved to send a certain number of students to Prague, but until the 1630s
they could, understandably, only send them to Jesuit schools. Clearly, the
then Abbot of Zbraslav and vicar general, Johann Greifenfels of Pilsenburg,
was filled with enthusiasm by his friend, Abbot Questenberg, so that, as early
as 1635, Cistercian monks began to study at the seminary. With Questenberg's
support, in September 1637, Greifenfels finally bought a house not far from

---

2   Perelcius's lectures in moral theology have been preserved in SK, MS DA V 33. They were re-
     corded by the Strahov Premonstratensian Cyril Hofmann. Perelcius's notes from the lectures
     by Charles Grobendonque *Aristotelis Stagiritae philosophia rationalis* are under DD VI 33, and the
     Olomouc lectures by Martin Eismann under DA V 20 and DE VI 42. He defended his thesis in
     philosophy "pro doctoratu philosophico" in Olomouc 18 August 1634, under the chairmanship of
     Théodore Moret, see SK, CZ IV 40/b.

3   For the record of Moret's lectures *Tractatus in libros Aristotelis ... de generatione et corruptione*, see
     SK, MS DG VI 38, Bohumil Ryba, *Soupis rukopisů Strahovské knihovny. Díl III [An Inventory of the
     Manuscripts of the Strahov Library. Vol III]* (Praha: Památník národního písemnictví, 1979), no.
     1815. Theological lectures by Francis Farrell attended by Teiser as late as the first days of 1638
     have been preserved under shelf mark DD VI 19. Teiser was ordained priest in December 1637.

4   Hedvika Kuchařová, "Premonstrátská kolej Norbertinum v Praze 1637–1785" [The Norbertinum
     College of the Premonstratensians in Prague 1637–1785], BS 3 (1997): 15–57, there on pp. 21–23. The
     author recapitulated the topic in a broader context in her monograph *Premonstrátská kolej Nor-
     bertinum v Praze. Alternativy univerzitního vzdělání v 17. a 18. století [The Norbertinum College of the
     Premonstratensians in Prague. Alternative forms of university education in the 17th and 18th centuries]*
     (Praha: Casablanca, 2011) 78–90.

the archiepiscopal seminary, which was to serve as a Cistercian college. For the time being, however, there was no question of them being able to provide their own teachers.[5]

The situation was the same with the Benedictine monasteries. The day before the Feast of St. Patrick, the Břevnov provost, Šimon Chlodomasteus, appealed, not for the first time, to the Bohemian Chamber for a financial contribution for repairs to the monastery which had been plundered several times. The war had likewise damaged Broumov and in 1637 it was still feeling the aftereffects of famine and an epidemic of the plague, but at least things looked hopeful for the community there because of their numbers: in 1632, twenty-six monks had fled before the Saxon army. The economies of other Benedictine monasteries (Svatý Jan pod Skalou, Sázava, Kladruby and the Emmaus community which had recently moved to Prague's Old Town) were mostly in ruins and this was accurately reflected in the number of members. Any great activity in education seemed to be rather a luxury, necessary in the long term but at that time hardly achievable.[6]

It was clear, then, that if the archiepiscopal seminary was to become a worthy counterpart to the Jesuit schools, teachers would need to be found elsewhere. Within the mendicant orders, the Minorite college, Ferdinandeum, by the friary in Prague's Old Town, was of interest, but that served the internal needs of the order. We do not know whether the archbishop appealed to the Dominicans and Franciscans for assistance, but clearly this was hindered by the unconsolidated state of the Bohemian monasteries and the associated impossibility of providing qualified teachers from their own ranks.[7]

THE SEMINARY OF ARCHBISHOP HARRACH

The best solution in the mid-1630s was to fill, temporarily, the teaching posts with Irish Franciscans. This evidently also accorded with the archbishop's

---

5   Philibert Panhölzl ed., "Statuta capitulorum provincialium Ord. Cist. vicriatus Bohemiae-Moraviae-Lusatiae (1616–1784)," *Cistercienser Chronik* 22 (1906): 106; V. Bartůněk, "Jan Greifenfels z Pilsenburku, opat zbraslavský" [Johann Greifenfels of Pilsenburg, Abbot of Zbraslav], *ČKD* 84.4, 5 and 6 (1944): 217–229, 284–291 and mainly 321–354.

6   Milada Vilímková and Pavel Preiss, *Ve znamení břevna a růží* [In the Name of the Beam and the Roses] (Praha: Vyšehrad, 1989). On the state of the Břevnov monastery, see pp. 53–54, on Broumov p. 57, on other monasteries pp. 130–139.

7   For instance, in the Friary of Our Lady of the Snows, philosophy and theology was taught from 1617, though the lectors were from abroad. Studies were developed further in the 1640s and 1650s; at that time, the development was supported by the Irish from the College of the Immaculate Conception. See Klemens Minařík, "Provinciál P. Bernard Sannig, učenec, spisovatel a organisátor františkánské provincie. (1637–1704)" [The Provincial Fr. Bernard Sannig, Scholar, Writer and Organiser of the Franciscan Province. (1637–1704)], *ČKD* 61 (1920): 237.

other aims. The somewhat delayed opening of the seminary admittedly ful-filled the decree of the Council of Trent, but its foundation was connected with specific Prague conditions, in particular with Archbishop Harrach's dispute with the Jesuits over the university and his attempt to weaken their monopoly of higher education.[8] The teaching by Franciscans in the spirit of Duns Scotus was the corresponding intellectual counterpart to institutional independence. The Franciscans did not hesitate to send certain talented and promising members of the order (such as Patrick Fleming) who had gained an education in the order's colleges in Rome and Louvain to their own col-lege which was to exclusively serve the education of future missionaries The unfortunate events of 1631 did not weaken the college's calling for long.[9] We do not know the details of the discussions over the teaching posts, but they clearly took place even before the Saxon invasion. Among the first teachers to arrive at the archiepiscopal seminary in the mid-1630s were Malachy Fallon, Patrick Warde, Francis Fleming, Francis Farrell, Edward Tyrell and Ber-nardine Cavoc.[10] It was to these men in particular that the words of Teiser's sermon were addressed (Fig. 13).

Archbishop Harrach paid considerable attention to the college: in June and August of 1638, after ceremonial disputations in the seminary, he enjoyed a meal in the college[11] and he regularly joined in celebrations connected to the college such as St. Patrick's Day and the Feast of the Immaculate Conception

---

8   In 1622, Charles University in Prague, "guilty of heresy," was passed to the administration of the Jesuits who planned to reform it according to the custom of the order. They, however, met with the resistance of the Archbishop of Prague, the chancellor of the university, who in 1627 even enforced a ban on graduations; while Jesuits graduated their own students in accordance with the privileges of the order, the students of secular faculties left without graduating. The Emperor tried to solve the untenable situation in 1638 by again taking the Carolinum (the Facul-ties of Law and Medicine) away from the Jesuits and putting them under an appointed official called the Protector. The situation was resolved only by the decree of union in 1654. For the lat-est literature on the topic, see I. Čornejová ed., *Dějiny Univerzity Karlovy II, 1622–1802* [*The His-tory of Charles University II, 1622–1802*] (Praha: Univerzita Karlova, 1996) 23–57 or, in more detail, Ivana Čornejová, *Kapitoly z dějin pražské univerzity, 1622–1754* [*Chapters from the History of Prague University, 1622–1754*] (Praha: Karolinum, 1992). The figure of Cardinal Harrach was studied in detail by Alessandro Catalano in *Zápas o svědomí. Kardinál Arnošt Vojtěch z Harrachu (1598–1667) a protireformace v Čechách*, trans. Petr Maťa (Praha: Nakladatelství Lidové noviny, 2008). On the foundation of the seminary, see pp. 178–181.

9   In September 1633, the guardian of St. Anthony's College in Louvain sent four friars to Prague to study, namely Fr. Peter Molloy, Fr. Louis MacNamie, Fr. Peter Frame and Br. Donat Connolly. ŘHyb Praha, carton no. 45. On the literary activity of Patrick Fleming, see Benignus Millett, *The Irish Franciscans 1651–1665* (Rome: Gregorian University Press, 1964) 492–493. See also notes nos. 70 and 71 in Chapter 2.

10   See the list of friars at the end of this book.

11   Katrin Keller and Alessandro Catalano eds., *Die Diarien und Tagzettel des Kardinals Ernst Adalbert von Harrach (1598–1667)* (Wien: Böhlau, 2011), Band 4, 467 and 484. Theological disputations took place at examinations and sometimes also on special occasions such as visits to the seminary; the latter were referred to as ceremonial disputations.

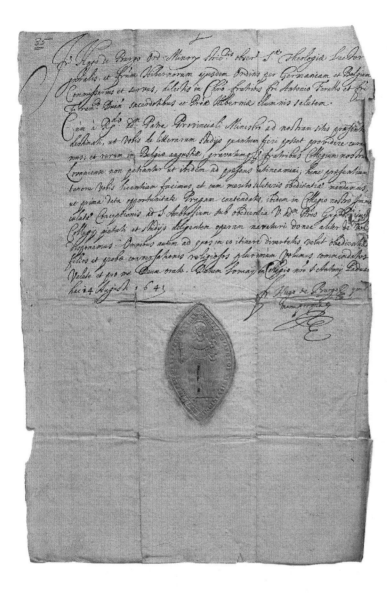

Fig. 13 Hugh Burke, lector general in theology, sends Anthony Farrell and Francis Duin to the Irish Franciscan college in Prague, 14 August 1641 (NA).

of the Virgin Mary. On St. Patrick's Day in 1654, Jan Caramuel of Lobkovice preached in the church,[12] on the Feast of the Immaculate Conception in 1657, Leopold I, King of Bohemia, joined the Mass and a banquet afterwards.[13] During one of his visits to Rome in 1637, Cardinal Harrach also visited St. Isidore's College and devoted considerable space to it in his diary (Fig. 14).[14]

12   Ibid., Band 3, 791.
13   Ibid., Band 6, 397 and Band 4, 278.
14   Ibid., Band 2, 200–1.

Fig. 14 Ernest Adalbert,
Cardinal Harrach, Archbishop
of Prague. Engraving, Prague
1646 (SK).

Fig. 14 Ernest Adalbert,
Cardinal Harrach, Archbishop
of Prague. Engraving, Prague
1646 (SK).

Malachy Fallon, was, as mentioned above, one of the founders of the Prague college. He gained teaching experience partly in Rouen (possibly at the Franciscan *studium*) where he was Professor of Philosophy, then later as Professor of Theology at St. Anthony's College in Louvain. By virtue of these qualifications, he was appointed *professor primarius* in theology at the archiepiscopal seminary and finally, on 28 August 1637, he was named *lector jubilatus* by the general of the order, Juan de Campaña.[15] The zeal in his relations with the newly founded seminary brought him two appointments as superior of the seminary, which were not, however, free of bitterness and disputes.[16] In 1641, his lectures at the seminary became the focus of attention of the noted Jesuit philosopher and theologian, Roderigo Arriaga, who perceived them to be inspired by the opinions of Cornelius Jansen, whose works at that time were causing considerable controversy. The Jesuits in

---

15   NA, ŘHyb Praha, carton no. 45.

16   However, in the petition written together with the rector of the archiepiscopal seminary, Jiří Peischel, around 1638 (definitely before 1641), Fallon is listed as guardian. NA, APA, carton no. 2014.

Louvain, who were among the first to oppose Jansen and who obtained Arriaga's opinion, concluded that measures should be taken against Fallon, but that this should be done by someone from an order other than the Jesuits. In the Bohemian Crown Lands, however, there was no suitably qualified theologian.[17] The accusation of preaching the "Jansenist error" against the then deceased Fallon (he had died on 9 January 1651) was also contained in the anonymous pro-Jesuit tract *Idea gubernationis ecclesiasticae*, which most probably originated in 1653 and blamed the Capuchins, Basilius d'Aire and Valeriano Magni for the fact that the Departments of Theology and Philosophy at the archiepiscopal seminary (regarded by the author of the tract as a very dubious institution, whose foundation and functioning was not guided by the precepts of the Council of Trent) *"had been entrusted to some foreign friars from Ireland and the former* [the Department of Theology] *at one time to a certain Brother Malachy, infected by heresy and by Jansenist errors, which is clear from his public lectures."*[18]

Another of the notable friars who passed through both the college and the seminary was Francis Farrell. Born in Ireland in the diocese of Ardagh in 1597, after entering the order he studied theology at the Louvain college and in 1625 was ordained priest in Brussels. In 1632, he stayed for a while in Salzburg, where he taught at the Franciscan *studium*. At the beginning of June 1633, he arrived at the Prague college as a lector in theology and later taught both theology and philosophy at the seminary. He was appointed *lector jubilatus*. In 1644 to 1645, he returned to Ireland where he was appointed guardian in various friaries in turn (Enniscorthy, Multyfarnham and Ballinasaggart), and in 1655 he became provincial. He died in 1663.[19]

We have a great deal less information on the others. According to the register of 1697, John Barnawall, teacher of philosophy and theology in the archiepiscopal seminary and *lector jubilatus*, became provincial. Francis Harold also attained the higher offices of the order.[20] In the 1697 register,

17   Stanislav Sousedík, *Filosofie v českých zemích mezi středověkem a osvícenstvím* [*Philosophy in the Bohemian Crown Lands between the Middle Ages and the Enlightenment*] (Praha: Vyšehrad, 1997) 104–107. The topic was also dealt with by Lucian Ceyssens, "Florence Conry, Hugh de Burgo, Luke Wadding, and Jansenism," *Father Luke Wadding* (Dublin: Clonmore & Reynolds, 1957) 295–404.

18   Antonín Rezek, *Tak zvaná "Idea gubernationis ecclesiasticae" z časů kardinála Harracha* [*The so-called "Idea gubernationis ecclesiasticae" from the Time of Cardinal Harrach*] (Praha: Královská česká společnost nauk, 1893).

19   Millett, *The Irish Franciscans*, 43–45.

20   The question is whether he was identical with the lay brother, John Barnavall, who was sent to Prague in July 1635. NA, ŘHyb Praha, carton no. 45, no. 19. Francis Harold became the order's annalist. The stock of the former library of the Franciscan friary in Hájek includes the preserved *De oculo morali aureus libellus Ioannis Gualensis*, published by Luke Wadding in Viterbo 1656, which Harold (Haraldus) donated to an unknown recipient in St. Isidore's College in Rome in the same year. However, how the book appeared in Hájek is not clear. The books from the stock are now stored in the Strahov library.

Patrick Warde the Elder is shown as a long-serving teacher of philosophy and theology and *lector jubilatus*. It can be inferred that he spent many years in Prague.[21] Francis Fleming is mentioned only as *philosophiae & theologiae lector emeritus*, as is Bernardine Cavoc. Anthony Gavan became an apostolic missionary in Ireland. Francis Warde arrived in Prague from Louvain in the autumn of 1640 and that same year began to teach philosophy. In the registers of the first half of the 1650s, which were published by Millett, Warde's name, like the three other above-mentioned names, is missing.[22] *Lector jubilatus* Louis Cooney (Connaeus) twice taught the philosophy course at the archiepiscopal seminary and also taught theology at the Franciscan Friary of Our Lady of the Snows, where he was assigned as lector in philosophy as early as 1644. He died on 14 April 1652, and was buried at the College of the Immaculate Conception.[23] Edward Tyrell, also *lector jubilatus*, reportedly taught theology in the seminary for four years, although he had previously served as guardian of the college.[24] At the beginning of the second half of the seventeenth century, Maurice Conry, author of the work on persecution in Ireland *Threnodia hiberno-catholica* and of an Irish dictionary, also taught in Prague.[25]

At this point, it should be mentioned that the seventeenth century was a period of intellectual rise for the Irish Franciscans when many respectable historiographical and theological works were created in the continental colleges. A special role was played by the Louvain college which became a centre of Irish historiography and hagiology shortly after its foundation. The Annals of the Four Masters, a fundamental work on Irish history, originated there in 1626 to 1636 with the support of the Irish Franciscans. The main purpose of compiling the Annals was to record and preserve legends about Irish saints.[26]

---

21   This name is included in the list of confessors from around 1656 whom the guardian of the college was able to supply to the consistory for missionary purposes. However, it is more probable that this Patrick Warde, who spoke German, was the second of the friars of this name, listed as "the Younger" make a distinction, appearing in the lists published by Millett in 1650/1651 as a student of theology and later as a lector in philosophy. NA, APA, carton no. 2100. See Benignus Millett, "Some lists of Irish Franciscans in Prague, 1656–1791," *Collectanea hibernica* 36–37 (1994–5): 61–62.

22   For an accompanying letter for Francis Warde and Br. Francis Ravell dated 28.9.1649, see NA, AZK, carton no. 45. Millett, *The Irish Franciscans*, 135–137, notes nos. 6 and 8.

23   See the list from 1697. There he is described as "a zealous restorer of the local studies." Permanent theological studies were established at Our Lady of the Snows in 1647 based on the initiative of the provincial, Ludwig Gesner. See Minařík, "Provinciál P. Bernard Sannig," 237. Also Bruodin, *Armamentarium theologicum*, see note no. 63.

24   In sources available to us, his activities in the archiepiscopal seminary are evidenced for 1646 and 1648, as guardian for 1641 and 1642 (NA, ŘHyb Praha, carton no. 45, no. 36).

25   Millett, *The Irish Franciscans*, 493.

26   Bernadette Cunningham, "The Louvain achievement I: the Annals of the Four Masters," *The Irish Franciscans 1534–1990*, eds. E. Bhreathnach, H. MacMahon, OFM and J. McCafferty (Dublin: Four Courts Press, 2009) 177–188.

At the centre of the Franciscans' plans to process Irish hagiography were Hugh Ward and Patrick Fleming, whose violent death in Bohemia was described above. After Ward's death in 1635, responsibility for the project was taken over by John Colgan and Mícheál Ó Cléirigh (died 1643). Unfortunately, even Colgan did not manage to complete the original idea and only the first of four planned volumes of *Acta sanctorum Hiberniae* was printed. Colgan's next work, *Triadis Thaumaturgae* is dedicated to the trinity of great Irish saints: Patrick, Brigitta, and Colum Cille.[27]

The renowned historian Luke Wadding was also an Irish Franciscan theologian. It was precisely this aspect of scholarly activity of the Irish Franciscans that was most important from Cardinal Harrach's point of view. As well as Wadding, who was also the editor of John Duns Scotus's works, the most significant names in Irish Franciscan theology of the first three quarters of the seventeenth century were Florence Conry, Hugh Cavell, Anthony Hickey, John Punch and Bonaventure Baron. The activities of these men connected colleges in Salamanca, Louvain, Rome and Prague.[28] The role of Prague college members in preserving and studying the Irish language and literature has been underestimated by Czech researchers to date.[29]

War affected the running of the archiepiscopal seminary, as it doubtless also affected life in numerous expanding colleges.[30] Moreover, the Emperor intervened in the dispute of 1641 to 1642 with the archbishop, which had begun with a dispute over the university, by decreeing that the seminary, despite all written papal privileges, could serve only as a private school.[31] This dispute also affected the Irish Franciscans. That is, at the end of November 1641, the seminary, together with Norbertinum, was occupied by the military and the supreme burgrave, Jaroslav Bořita, Count of Martinice forbad the Irish professors to teach at the seminary. As with the dispute with the Capu-

---

27   Pádraig Ó Riain, "The Louvain achievement II: hagiography," *The Irish Franciscans 1534-1990*, 189–200.

28   M.W.F. Stone, "The theological and philosophical accomplishments of the Irish Franciscans: from Flaithrí Ó Maoil Chonaire to Bonaventure Baron," *The Irish Franciscans 1534-1990*, 201–220.

29   Mícheál MacCraith and David Worthington, "Aspects of the literary activity of the Irish Franciscans in Prague, 1620-1786," *Irish Migrants in Europe after Kinsale, 1602-1820*, eds. T. Connor and M.A. Lyons (Dublin: Four Courts Press, 2003) 118–134.

30   In 1642, it had thirty members, at the turn of 1650/1651, forty-four, and three years later, fifty-one. See Millett, *The Irish Franciscans*, 135–136. The note, probably from 1653, that there were sixty brothers in the college and that more were expected seems slightly exaggerated, see NA, ŘHyb Praha, carton no. 45, no. 60.

31   The teaching in the archiepiscopal seminary was interrupted in spring 1639 due to concerns about the invasion of Bohemia by Banér's troops, and because a hospital was later established in the building, the interruption lasted till the following year. In November 1641, a dispute between Archbishop Harrach and the Emperor about the character of the seminary culminated. In 1638, the archbishop obtained a papal bull for the seminary, which gave it powers corresponding to the university type of study. The last interruption was the war intermezzo during 1648 and 1649.

chins during the building of the college, the Irish found themselves caught between two sides and it was not advisable to become enemies of either. The archbishop was not happy that they had retired into seclusion and stopped teaching, and tried by repeated appeals to persuade them to resume teaching as quickly as possible. For fear of angering the Emperor, the Irish Franciscans discussed Harrach's appeals with the burgrave, who understandably rejected them. The Irish even submitted a memorandum to the Emperor, but instead of a clear answer they received a recommendation to wait until the matter had been investigated. Increasing pressure from the burgrave persuaded the Irish to adopt an openly "pro-Harrach" position in 1642, and when the situation had quietened down somewhat, they returned to the seminary.[32]

Not until the beginning of the 1650s was there the promise of longer term uninterrupted development, but this was when the first more serious dispute with the archbishop occurred. Its roots lay deep in the not entirely clarified institutional relations between the college and the Irish province.

In September 1647, Patrick Taaffe was elected guardian of the college at the provincial chapter in Rosserilly. This was clearly contrary to the statutes of the college. It was customary, as evidenced by the wording of these, that before the expiry of the term of office of the current guardian, the discreets would choose several suitable candidates and the general of the order would choose the new guardian from among them.[33] When the news reached Prague, it caused considerable astonishment in the college because the guardian of the college had, from the same year, been Bernardine Clancy, appointed according to custom by the general of the order. Clancy was from Munster, so he was supported by his fellow countrymen from Munster and, in particular, by two priests, Daniel Bruoder and Francis Harold; Taaffe was supported by his fellow countrymen from Ulster, among whom were the vicar, Magennis, and a number of lectors in philosophy. The two opposing factions were distinguished by their differing opinions as to whether the college should be subordinate to a commissary general (as Clancy wanted) or to a special commissary for the colleges. This confused situation lasted two years. Only at the beginning of 1650 did the general of the order, Daniel a Dongo, place the college under his direct authority and, at the same time, permit the new guardian to be chosen at the following provincial chapter in Ireland. In view of the fact that Clancy's term of office had just expired, this decision helped to calm the situation.[34]

---

32   ÖSW, FA Harrach, carton nos. 177 and 179 (further).
33   Millett, *The Irish Franciscans*, 117–118.
34   The commissary general of the order proposed in October 1648 that Clancy remain in office as guardian until the chapter of the Irish province decided otherwise. For a copy of Daniel a Dongo's decision dated 25.2.1650, see ÖSW, FA Harrach, carton no. 177. For the year 1648, see *Die Diarien und Tagzettel*, Band 1, 124–125, 128.

This did not last long, however, because in the summer of 1650 the discretorium of the college set the members of the college and the wider community against each other with a request sent to the superiors of the Irish province that, out of the eight lectors, Ulster, Munster, Leinster and Connaught should each have one lector in philosophy and one lector in theology. It is probable that this measure was to be a means of personnel changes among the teachers at the archiepiscopal seminary (including both of Clancy's supporters and, from 1650, Clancy himself) and we can then guess how it was connected with Clancy and his adherents. These plans met with the displeasure both of the Irish Franciscans and Archbishop Harrach and resulted in a special visitation of the college being ordered in September 1650. The visitation took place in November and the visitator, Paul de Tauris, former provincial of the Hungarian province, who was charged with negotiating with Archbishop Harrach over the filling of professorial posts in the seminary and, at the same time, settling the disputes in the community, managed to bring matters to a successful conclusion. Clancy was named a discreet and continued to teach as a lector in both the college and the seminary; Malachy Fallon, as praeses, became temporary head of the college until the arrival of a new guardian.[35] Harrach's displeasure was most likely caused by the fact that the composition of the teaching staff had been influenced by a decision by the superiors of the College of the Immaculate Conception. It is possible to interpret the appointment of three teachers from the Minorite Friary of St. James in Prague's Old Town, namely Bonaventura a Leodio to teach philosophy and Laurentius Fabri and Martius Coriolanus to teach theology, at the beginning of the 1650/1651 school year, as a possible reaction to the situation among the Irish Franciscans.[36]

The peace which was established during the visitation of Paul de Tauris was, however, very short-lived. At the end of December, the news reached Prague that an Ulsterman, Philip O'Reilly, had become the new guardian and not someone from Connaught as had been requested and which would have been in accord with the rotation of offices and functions within the college among the natives of the individual Irish provinces. Also, an Ulsterman, John Colgan, who was incidentally the translator of St. Francis de Sales into Irish,[37] was named commissary for the colleges in Prague, Wieluń and Louvain. Fallon, in particular, received the news with distaste. He immediately complained to the general of the order and Paul de Tauris, but before it came to a dispute between him and the new guardian, Fallon died.[38]

---

35   Millett, *The Irish Franciscans*, 156–157.
36   SK, MS DJ IV 1, *Anály Norbertina I. [The Annals of Norbertinum I]*, f. 78.
37   Mícheál MacCraith, "Gaelic language links with Prague," a lecture delivered at the conference entitled "The Irish in Europe 1580–1850," Maynooth 2000.
38   For the appointment of John Colgan, the commissary for the colleges in Prague, Louvain and Wieluń, see the section "The Irish province of Franciscans." Colgan was forced to resign in 1652.

Another measure should have affected the teachers of theology at the archiepiscopal seminary, Bernardine Clancy and Anthony Donnelly. According to the agreement between the commissary, Colgan, and the discreets of the college, they should have been replaced by Bernardine Higgins and Anthony Farrell at the beginning of 1652. Bernardine Clancy, who clearly had reason to be sensitive to changes affecting himself, left Prague at the end of September 1651 with Colgan's permission to undertake a pilgrimage to Loreto, stopping in Vienna where Archbishop Harrach also happened to be. Harrach insisted on Clancy remaining at the seminary because he did not want teachers who had admittedly proved themselves in the teaching of philosophy but had as yet no experience with theology. The new guardian, O'Reilly, however, regarded this demand as impossible. If implemented, it would, in his opinion, have led to unrest in the college. The archbishop, however, was not particularly interested in internal disputes in the college and was determined not to lower academic standards at the seminary, which could, in his opinion, have happened if he had given up Clancy and Donnelly.

The archbishop evidently objected to the arrogance with which the superiors of the college manipulated the composition of the teaching staff at his institution. In his letters to Harrach, O'Reilly made clear his self-importance as the leading representative of the college; the question is, however, whether such behaviour in relation to his dealings with a person of the archbishop's standing and connections was sufficiently prudent. Millett details Harrach's attempts to find teachers among Irish Franciscan circles independent of the Prague college: he wanted Bernard Fallon from Louvain, but because this was not possible, he turned to Anthony Bruodin (then a member of the Bohemian Franciscan province). More significantly, however, was that in November, Hilger Burghof, a Cistercian from the Austrian monastery in Lilienfeld and superior of the Cistercian college, Bernardinum, began to teach philosophy.[39] His arrival meant not only more interference with the Franciscan teaching staff but also a dogmatic divergence from the previous teaching in the spirit of Scotism, the extent of which it is possible to understand from the comment by the Premonstratensians that when, following his election as Abbot of Sedlec in 1654, Burghof resigned from his teaching post and was replaced by Bonaventure Bruodin, who changed the conception of his predecessor according to Scotism, *"it was to the detriment and confusion of the pupils' thoughts."*[40] Indeed, the view of secular observers was that Burghof's arrival at the seminary was the cause of the split between the archbishop and the

---

In as much as the function of the commissary ceased to exist, his powers over the colleges were transferred from 1662 to the order's commissary for Upper Germany.

39 Millett, *The Irish Franciscans*, 159–161. SK, MS DJ IV 1, f. 80.
40 Kuchařová, "Premonstrátská kolej Norbertinum v Praze," 29.

Irish Franciscans, most certainly not its likely result, which is evidenced by the annals of the Premonstratensian college, Norbertinum. The true cause was the too great claims the Irish Franciscans made on the teaching posts, or on how they were managed; in this version, however, their behaviour was unequivocally provoked by Burghof's arrival. When the archbishop recognised Clancy's innocence in the matter, he did not prevent him or his colleague, Bonaventure Bruodin, from teaching at the seminary. However, to protect them against the insinuations of their confrères, he allowed them to live away from the Irish college, first with the Emmaus Benedictines and later, when the weather worsened and attendance at the seminary became difficult, with the Franciscans at Our Lady of the Snows.[41]

Reality, of course, was more complex. When Clancy returned from his pilgrimage, O'Reilly confined him to the college. Harrach gave Clancy his full support and made his decision known in letters sent to the leading representatives of the order and the Irish province – to the general, Pedro Manero, Wadding and Colgan. In the middle of December, the general of the order sent the archbishop the necessary obediences for Clancy and Donnelly so that they could remain at the seminary, but the guardian, supported by a majority of the discreets, maintained his position. At the beginning of 1652, Bernardine Clancy had to leave the Irish college and live at Our Lady of the Snows (it is difficult to say when he lived with the Benedictines) and with him went Bonaventure Bruodin, another teacher at the archiepiscopal seminary. Anthony Donnelly remained in the college and discontinued his lectures at the seminary.[42]

Unfortunately, it was likely that while O'Reilly remained guardian, prospects of a peaceful resolution were poor. This was also the opinion of Clancy and Bruodin. The dispute, however, helped the Bohemian and Moravian monastic communities whose members were studying at the archiepiscopal seminary, especially the Cistercians and Premontratensians, with whom Harrach made an agreement in the autumn of 1652 confirming and clarifying their part in tuition at the seminary. The teaching staff was also increased by Benedictines and Franciscans of the Bohemian province.[43] Even a change of

---

41   SK, MS DJ IV 1, ff. 81–82. Due to gaps in her knowledge of the broader context, this interpretation was also adopted by H. Kuchařová in her work on the Norbertinum college.

42   Millett, *The Irish Franciscans*, see note 39. In January 1652, the guardian and discreets of the college said that it was not possible for two lectors to continue to teach in the archiepiscopal seminary without the permission of the superiors of their order without this being detrimental to the order. However, if the archbishop wished them to teach in the seminary, the college would not stand in their way. ÖSW, FA Harrach carton no. 177. Catalano, *Zápas o svědomí*, 259–277.

43   From the academic year 1652–1653, philosophy was taught (however, in the Scotist spirit) by the Strahov Premonstratensian Vít Rössler, then in the following year by the Benedictine, Jan Manner, and in 1655 for the first time by Franciscans from Our Lady of the Snows. If it was an emergency solution, then it was in favour of those orders which were interested in the running of the seminary and wanted to fill the teaching posts with their own members.

guardian made no marked difference. In October 1656, when the college, led by the guardian, Anthony Connor (Conorus), and the commissary, Anthony Daly, appealed for the return of the Irish Franciscans to the archiepiscopal seminary, Harrach replied politely but firmly that all the teaching posts were taken and that it would be nonsensical to duplicate them.[44] From the record of student lectures, it is nevertheless clear that the seminary did not go without lectures by the Irish Franciscans and, apart from the two "deserters", others also taught in that tense period, possibly even in the school year just before the submission of the appeal.[45] From the viewpoint of the Irish Franciscans, a complete return to the teaching posts was impossible so long as Fathers Clancy and Bruodin remained outside the college and thus demonstrated continued disunity and division. The burden of finding a solution rested with the commissary, Anthony Daly, who achieved partial success in the autumn of 1657. Bernardine Clancy expressed his willingness to return to the College of the Immaculate Conception, provided that the archbishop raised no objection to this and that he would not be accused of disobedience by his superiors. Bonaventure Bruodin clearly had no great wish to return. Later, his transfer to the Bohemian province was discussed, with the involvement of Anthony Bruodin. The extension of both Franciscans' stay outside the college was most likely the result of a lack of trust; namely Bruodin's and Clancy's misgivings as to whether their return to the college would happen without measures being taken against the "malefactors" and Harrach's demand for a guarantee that the situation of 1650 to 1651 would not be repeated. The distrust of the "apostates" was finally exorcised by the pronouncement by the commissary, Bernardine Barry, in August 1659, in which their departure was judged to be just and legitimate, they were absolved of all accusations of apostasy from their own college and also expressed their gratitude to the Franciscans who had protected them. Not long afterwards, Clancy did return to the college.[46] His exoneration before his confrères culminated the follow-

---

44 NA, APA, carton no. 2100. A record in the Archbishop's diary from 4 October 1659 reflects the situation. On that day, he participated in a celebration of St. Francis of Assisi's Day in the Irish Franciscan college, while in other years he had regularly attended the Capuchines' celebration. He perhaps wanted to demonstrate that he was not angered by some "differences" with the Irish Franciscans.

45 This may only have become possible after the end of O'Reilly's guardianship; in 1655–1656, lectures in philosophy were delivered by Francis Fenell and then repeatedly in 1659–1660 together with Francis O'Beirne, see SK, MSS DG VI 36 and DG VI 8, and see Hedvika Kuchařová and Jan Pařez, "On the trail of Irish émigrés in the collections of the Strahov Abbey Library in Prague," *The Ulster Earls and Baroque Europe. Refashioning Irish Identities, 1600–1800*, eds. Thomas O'Connor and Mary Ann Lyons (Dublin: Four Courts Press, 2010) 202.

46 In his letter of 3 November, the rector of the seminary, Jiří Meckenburger, informed Archbishop Harrach of this. Anthony Bruodin's letter of 22 October 1659 to Archbishop Harrach is in ÖSW, FA Harrach, carton no. 177.

ing year, when he became guardian of the college.[47] Bonaventure Bruodin, who was not in the best of health, received permission to return to Ireland.[48]

During the same period, through his intermediary, Father Basilius d'Aire, Harrach also negotiated his own conditions.[49] The declaration by the general of the order, Michaelangelo de Sambuca, on 10 January 1660, to some extent sidelined both parties because the right to appoint or dismiss Irish professors at the archiepiscopal seminary would henceforth appertain only to the general of the order and his successor. Teachers at the seminary should enjoy all the privileges which were customary among Franciscans in the Irish province, but, at the same time, all scholastic lectures (*lectiones scholasticae*) which were provided at the archiepiscopal seminary were forbidden in the college, with the exception of tuition in morality and pastoral theology. In this way, study was centralised. In the summer of the same year, Anthony Farrell (Fig. 15) was appointed to replace Clancy and he was guardian of the college for the next three years.[50] In June 1661 in Valladolid, the general chapter also revised the appointment of the guardian, who would be selected by the general of the order from the candidates nominated by the discreets.

The ruling that lectors be appointed by the general of the order was also inserted into the statutes of the college, which were approved there in 1665, having been previously approved by the general.[51] There is no mention in the statutes of tuition at the archiepiscopal seminary, but if the ruling that students must take the greater part of their study programme at the seminary and that further studies at the college were unnecessary was observed, then the article in the statutes devoted to lectors related entirely to teachers at the archiepiscopal seminary and so it was pointless making any distinction between them. Lectors were obliged to participate twice a year in a public disputation with printed thesis, to adhere faithfully to the teachings of John

---

47   NA, APA, carton no. 2100.

48   Millett, *The Irish Franciscans*, 164. See AZK, carton no. 45, no. 86, where the appointment of Clancy as guardian by the provincial, Bernard Egan, is dated 1 April 1660. In his letter dated by Harrach to 1661, Bonaventure Bruodin requested at least a year's sick leave, which would enable him to travel home. ÖSW, FA Harrach, carton no. 177. For Cardinal Harrach's role as a mediator, see Catalano, *Zápas o svědomí*, 315–317.

49   NA, APA, carton no. 2100. According to the proposal by Basilius d'Aire dated 7 August 1659, the teachers should swear an oath to the archbishop that they would remain in the seminary for the requested period. According to Millett, Harrach was not overly excited by the return of the teachers, but the circumstances would, in any case, have forced him to replace Clancy and Bruodin.

50   Ibid., carton no. 2100. Millett, *The Irish Franciscans*, 164–165.

51   NA, ŘHyb Praha, carton no. 45, no. 91. The general of the Franciscan Order, Michaelangelo de Sambuca, confirmed the text of the statutes of the Prague college to Fr. Laurence Molloy on 7 October 1662. According to the notes in the manuscript of the statutes, they were (again) reviewed, confirmed and corrected by the general of the order in 1664, then authorised in the college on 4 September 1665.

Fig. 15 The title page of the recorded lectures of Anthony Farrell. Engraved cartouche by Cornelis Galle, written inscription by the learner, 1662–1664 (SK).

Duns Scotus, to take a two-year course in philosophy before receiving a credit in the field of teaching and, so as to prevent friction between the natives of the four Irish provinces, to maintain the principle of proportionality within the teaching staff.[52] The whole dispute, which reveals the fragile balance within the college, however, was a boon to the Cistercians and the Premonstratensians, the two main supporters of the archiepiscopal seminary, on whose young people and their education the Irish had a great influence. Although there were few teachers from these two orders in the seminary in the 1650s, they first began to appear more regularly during the 1660s, and they would clearly have found it more difficult to establish themselves if the Irish Franciscans had displayed reliability and unity.[53] At the same time, members of other religious orders had the opportunity to assert themselves as teachers of future secular and regular clergy.

The Irish Franciscan teachers whose work was in some way stigmatised by the division belonged, in comparison with Fallon, Cooney or Francis Farrell, to another generation. As individuals, they met with very different fates. In the end, Bernardine Clancy taught for twenty-seven years at the archiepiscopal seminary and became guardian of the college for the second time in August 1673. He died on 5 May 1684, apparently at the age of seventy-two.[54] Bonaventure Bruodin, cousin of the well-known Anthony Bruodin who will be mentioned again later, returned to Ireland precisely when the province was divided by the efforts of Peter Walsh. In the wake of the Cromwellian terror, James Butler, Duke of Ormonde, was attempting to moderate the government's approach to Catholics. In return, of course, Catholics were to recognise the supremacy of the state and renounce the papal right to depose the head of state.[55] Peter Walsh fully supported these attempts while Bruodin, who had returned from exile, used all his influence to prevent them

---

52   NA, ŘF, book no. 13. That these articles applied to the teaching at the archiepiscopal seminary is supported by the finding that in the 1740s, when the statutes were reviewed, they were deleted as irrelevant. Millett is partially right that the general of the order did not want to exacerbate the situation with further regulations, especially when Harrach showed a certain concern about the upcoming confirmation.

53   Thanks to their activities in the archiepiscopal seminary, the intellectual influence of the Prague Irish Franciscans reached beyond the Bohemian Crown Lands because the Cistercian and Premonstratensian colleges were attended by students from various monasteries of central Europe. Direct evidence can be found, for instance, in the library of the Premonstratensian monastery in Geras in Austria where a manuscript of the lectures by Anthony Bruodin from 1656 (together with the bound thesis of Nicolaus Jacob Imann, catalogue no. 27) and the manuscript of the lectures by Louis O'Neill from 1689 to 1692 (catalogue no. 38) are stored. Gottfried Gröniger from Geras began studying in Prague in 1654. Joseph Natzer is listed in the Norbertinum, Premonstratensian college in Prague, in 1690. See Josef Pfiffig, "Handschriftenkatalog der Stiftsbibliothek Geras," *Geraser Hefte* 33 (1994): 5–23.

54   See *Quartum quod incedit.*

55   Theodore W. Moody and Francis X. Martin eds., *Dějiny Irska* [*The Course of Irish History*] (Praha: Nakladatelství Lidové noviny, 1996) 155.

and to restore peace in the volatile conditions of the province. Consequently, Bruodin was imprisoned in Dublin and, as a result of his imprisonment, died there in 1671. His name was also entered into the necrology of the Bohemian province.[56] Among the other long-serving teachers at the archiepiscopal seminary were *lector jubilatus* Anthony Donnelly (died 20 May 1682) and Anthony Farrell, also *lector jubilatus* (died 12 January 1681), both of whom served as guardian.[57] In about 1664, another teacher at the seminary, Bonaventure O'Connor Kerry, published his work *Iubilaeum iubilum, portiunculae seraphicae* in Prague.[58]

It is clear from the above that the Irish Franciscans studied mainly at the archiepiscopal seminary. The above-mentioned printed register shows more than forty students, but it is probably not complete because when the register was being compiled, relations between the seminary and the college were much looser. Higher positions were gained by James Taaffe, who became the papal nuncio for Ireland, Anthony MacGeoghegan, who became the Bishop of Clonmacnoise (1647–1657) and the Bishop of Meath (1657–1664),[59] Anthony O'Neill, who served in various offices of the order (*inter alia*, he was guardian in Armagh several times), Bonaventure Burke, who was active in the Holy Land,[60] Francis Connor, who was shown as *guardianus Romanus* (at St. Isidore's College), James Coghlan, later guardian at the Prague college and teacher at the Benedictine monastery in Kladruby, Louis MacNamara, who was also guardian in Prague and, from the younger generation, Francis O'Devlin, who served at the Cistercian monastery in Waldsassen (Fig. 16).

---

56 Bonaventure Bruodin also taught at Our Lady of the Snows. See Kevin MacGrath, "The Bruodins in Bohemia," *The Irish Ecclesiastical Record*, 5ᵗʰ series, 77 (1952): 341–343. 28 May is considered to be the anniversary of his death, see *Martyrologium Franciscanum* (Rome: Librarium Collegii S. Antonii, 1938) 197.

57 Anthony Farrell was sent to Prague in 1641, see NA, ŘHyb Praha, carton no. 45. Of the other Franciscans listed as teachers in *Quartum quod incedit*, the following can be mentioned in connection with this period: Daniel Bruoder, *lector jubilatus* and commissary visitator of the college, died 30.9.1687; Anthony Burke, *lector jubilatus*, guardian of the college and later provincial of the Irish province; Patrick Warde the Younger, *lector jubilatus*, died in 1678; Philip O'Reilly, *lector jubilatus*, guardian, died 26.5.1680 (not to be confused with his namesake, also a guardian; he is said to have been born around 1640); John Clancy, *lector jubilatus*, recorded in the seminary at the beginning of the 1670s, died 19.10.1680.

58 Millett, *The Irish Franciscans*, 485. Because there were several men with the name of Bonaventure O'Connor, Millett successfully attempted to determine the author of this work.

59 Millett, *The Irish Franciscans*, Appendix 1.

60 He became lector in theology in the friary in Bethlehem. For period illustrations and descriptions, see, for example, Franciscus Caccia, *Jerusalem, seu Palestina nova...*, Wien 1706.

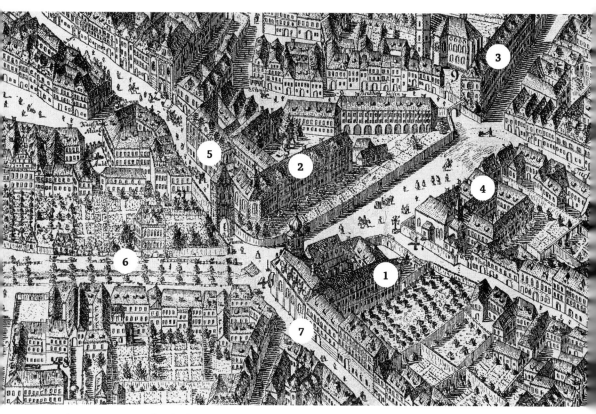

Fig. 16 A section of Huber's plan of Prague, which depicts the Irish Franciscan college and its vicinity in the year 1769 (Facsimile copy, *Obraz barokní Prahy*, ed. by J. Hofman, Prague 1944). 1. Irish Franciscan college; 2. Archiepiscopal seminary; 3. Premonstratensian college of Norbertinum; 4. Capuchin friary; 5. Powder Gate; 6. Na Příkopě street; 7. Hybernská street

ANTHONY BRUODIN:
THE DOUBLE EXILE OF THE SCOTIST SCHOLAR

The most significant figure, however, among the Irish Franciscans in the third quarter of the seventeenth century was unquestionably Anthony Bruodin, despite the fact that he is connected with the Bohemian rather than the Irish province. By his own account, he arrived in Prague on 25 May 1650,[61] accompanied by John Brady, to fulfil the teaching duties of Louis Cooney, whose strength was declining while the number of young students was increasing. He clearly had a somewhat antagonistic nature; according to McGrath, *"he was known for his lack of tact and blunt expression,"* but he was definitely very

---

61   For more information about his origins, see below in the text.

Fig. 17 The title page of *Corolla oecodomiae* by Anthony Bruodin. Prague, 1664 (SK).

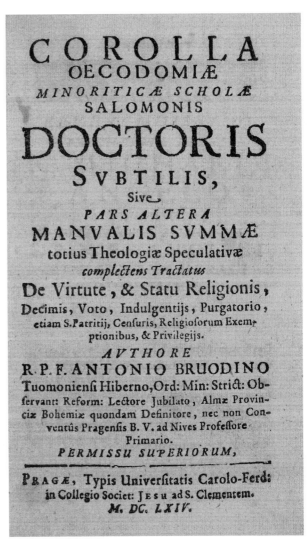

COROLLA
OECODOMIÆ
MINORITICÆ SCHOLÆ
SALOMONIS
DOCTORIS
SVBTILIS,
Sive
PARS ALTERA
MANVALIS SVMMÆ
totius Theologiæ Speculativæ
complectens Tractatus
De Virtute, & Statu Religionis,
Decimis, Voto, Indulgentijs, Purgatorio,
etiam S.Patritij, Censuris, Religioforum Exem-
ptionibus, & Privilegijs.
AVTHORE
R. P. F. ANTONIO BRUODINO
Tuomonienfi Hiberno, Ord: Min: Strict: Ob-
fervant: Reform: Lectore Jubilato, Almæ Provin-
ciæ Bohemiæ quondam Definitore, nec non Con-
ventûs Pragenfis B. V. ad Nives Profeffore
Primario.
PERMISSU SUPERIORUM,

PRAGÆ, Typis Univerfitatis Carolo-Ferd:
in Collegio Societ: JESu ad S. Clementem.
M. DC. LXIV.

able. The reasons for his transfer to the Bohemian province are not at all clear. Together with another Irishman, Peter Lorcan, he was incorporated into the Bohemian province in November 1651.[62] Soon afterwards, he was sent to Olomouc to teach philosophy and then, for the same reason, to the friary in Jindřichův Hradec. In 1654, he returned to Prague to teach in place of his colleagues from the Irish province, Bernardine Clancy and Bonaventure Bruodin. Later, he also began to teach at the archiepiscopal seminary, where, by his own account, he worked for six years. At the provincial chapter

---

62   MacGrath considers the claim that he was excluded from the province to be unreliable, nor was a more or less private dispute with Luke Wadding the reason.

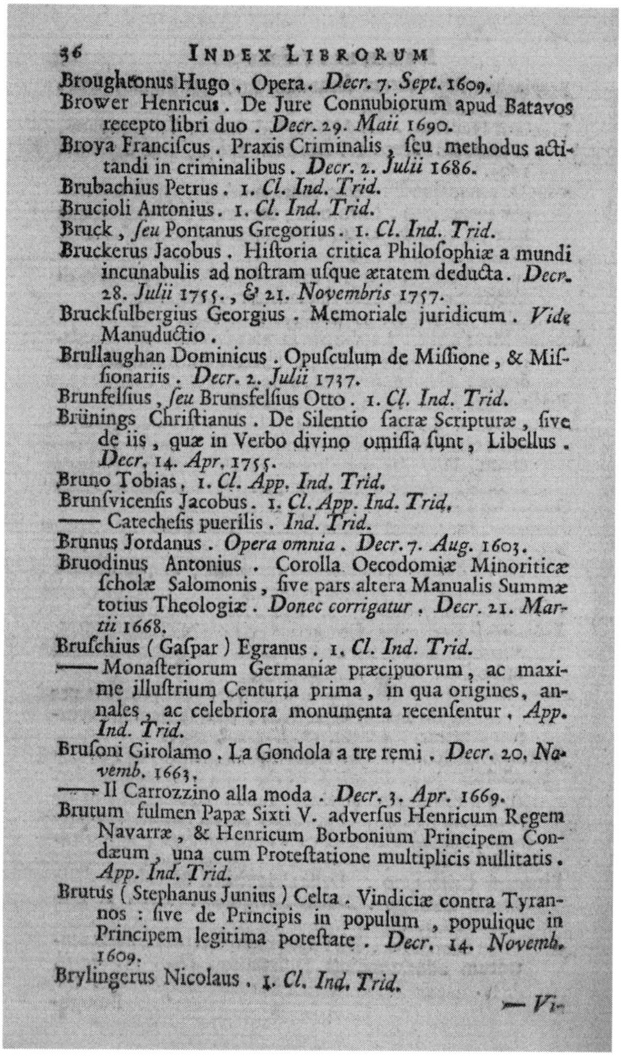

36   INDEX LIBRORUM

Broughtonus Hugo . Opera . *Decr.* 7. *Sept.* 1609.
Brower Henricus . De Jure Connubiorum apud Batavos
    recepto libri duo . *Decr.* 29. *Maii* 1690.
Broya Francifcus . Praxis Criminalis , feu methodus acti-
    tandi in criminalibus . *Decr.* 2. *Julii* 1686.
Brubachius Petrus . 1. *Cl. Ind. Trid.*
Brucioli Antonius . 1. *Cl. Ind. Trid.*
Bruck , feu Pontanus Gregorius . 1. *Cl. Ind. Trid.*
Bruckerus Jacobus . Hiftoria critica Philofophiæ a mundi
    incunabulis ad noftram ufque ætatem deducta . *Decr.*
    28. *Julii* 1755., & 21. *Novembris* 1757.
Bruckfulbergius Georgius . Memoriale juridicum . *Vide*
    Manuductio .
Brullaughan Dominicus . Opufculum de Miffione , & Mif-
    fionariis . *Decr.* 2. *Julii* 1737.
Brunfelfius , feu Brunsfelfius Otto . 1. *Cl. Ind. Trid.*
Brünings Chriftianus . De Silentio facræ Scripturæ , five
    de iis , quæ in Verbo divino omiffa funt , Libellus .
    Decr. 14. *Apr.* 1755.
Bruno Tobias . 1. *Cl. App. Ind. Trid.*
Brunfvicenfis Jacobus . 1. *Cl. App. Ind. Trid.*
—— Catechefis puerilis . *Ind. Trid.*
Brunus Jordanus . *Opera omnia* . *Decr.* 7. *Aug.* 1603.
Bruodinus Antonius . Corolla Oecodomiæ Minoriticæ
    fcholæ Salomonis , five pars altera Manualis Summæ
    totius Theologiæ . *Donec corrigatur* . *Decr.* 21. *Mar-
    tii* 1668.
Brufchius (Gafpar) Egranus . 1. *Cl. Ind. Trid.*
—— Monafteriorum Germaniæ præcipuorum , ac maxi-
    me illuftrium Centuria prima , in qua origines , an-
    nales , ac celebriora monumenta recenfentur . *App.*
    Ind. Trid.
Brufoni Girolamo . La Gondola a tre remi . *Decr.* 20. *No-
    vemb.* 1663.
—— Il Carrozzino alla moda . *Decr.* 3. *Apr.* 1669.
Brutum fulmen Papæ Sixti V. adverfus Henricum Regem
    Navarræ , & Henricum Borbonium Principem Con-
    dæum , una cum Proteftatione multiplicis nullitatis .
    App. Ind. Trid.
Brutus (Stephanus Junius) Celta . Vindiciæ contra Tyran-
    nos : five de Principis in populum , populique in
    Principem legitima poteftate . *Decr.* 14. *Novemb.*
    1609.
Brylingerus Nicolaus . 1. *Cl. Ind. Trid.*

                    — Vi-

Fig. 18 Anthony Bruodin's *Corolla oecodomiae* in the Index librorum prohibitorum, 1758 (SK).

in Jindřichův Hradec in 1659 he was elected definitor, and then from 1663 he was guardian at the Friary of the Immaculate Conception of the Virgin Mary in Olomouc (Fig. 17; Fig. 18). As guardian, he attended the general chapter in Rome, and, in the Ara Coeli Friary, he presided over the disputation at which Vilém Antonín Brouček, later provincial, defended his thesis. When he was in Rome for the second time in 1667 for a disputation, he met Bernard Sannig. After his term of office in Olomouc ended, he devoted himself to teaching until April 1668, when he became guardian at Our Lady of the Snows in Prague. During his term of office, he had some improvements made (the construction of a larger dormitory and a pharmacy), he had the cloister decorated with pictures, supplied the library with books and the sacristy with vestments. In 1671, he was sent to Hostinné, where a friary had been established in 1666. Because of the difficulties caused by a poorly selected site, he decided to start building on another, more suitable one. He spent fifteen months there, before being elected guardian at Jindřichův Hradec, where, again by his own account, he improved the friary in every way until 1674. In addition, he made visitations to friaries in Poland and, in late 1674 and early 1675, he attended to the business of the order in Vienna. At that time, Bruodin was at the height of his powers and his career. His functions enabled him to interfere in the life and administration of the province and also became the cause of his downfall.

In the seventeenth century, German-speaking friars predominated in the Bohemian Franciscan province in terms of numbers and culture and, understandably, they also occupied the leading positions. This caused dissatisfaction among the Czech-speaking friars and, occasionally, they made attempts to gain greater influence, the first of which was in 1675 when they tried to push through a Czech candidate for the post of provincial. The leading representative of the Czechs, Engelbert Putomský, came under consideration, but he died in 1673. His place was taken by Anthony Bruodin; the question remains whether, as a member of a small and at that time oppressed nation, sympathy for the Czech friars on the defensive or his own ambition played a greater role. His rival for the post of provincial was also of high calibre, that is, it was Bernard Sannig, who made a great impression on the visitator, the Bavarian Franciscan, Fortunatus Huber (whose task was to check the state of the province and arrange the election of the provincial). Considering that Huber made no secret of his sympathies in the friaries he visited, Bruodin sent a written message to the Turnov friary, asking the guardian not to support Sannig's candidature during the visitation and to be as vague as the Prague guardian in expressing his opinion. By mistake, however, the message ended up in the visitator's hands. Huber took this as an illicit electoral machination, which in addition led to the suspicion that similar messages had also been received in other friaries, and relieved Bruodin of all functions, excluded him from all elections at the prepared provincial chapter and imposed a penance on him. Bruodin could not bear such humiliation; he preferred to request a discharge from the province. When he obtained it, at the end of May 1675, he withdrew to the Irish college, where he died during a plague in 1680.[63]

---

63   For Anthony Bruodin's biographical data, apart from MacGrath, see also Stanislav Sousedík, *Jan Duns Scotus. Doctor subtilis a jeho čeští žáci* [John Duns Scotus. Doctor Subtilis and His Bohemian Pupils] (Praha: Vyšehrad, 1989) 167; the biographical data related to his candidature for the post of provincial is in Bruodin's introduction to his own work *Armamentarium theologicum*, Pragae 1767, also translated and published by Stanislav Sousedík in the cited work p. 325ff. The national circumstances in the province, the plans for its division and Bruodin's intervention against Sannig are discussed in detail in Minařík, "Provinciál P. Bernard Sannig," 144–150 and 197–201.

Bruodin's writings are outstanding. His first work was a two-volume textbook on Scotist theology, intended to be a continuation of the philosophical handbooks published by Bruodin's pupils, Vilém Antonín Brouček and Arnošt Schaff in 1663.[64] The first part of Bruodin's work was published towards the end of 1663, the second part in March 1664. Sousedík's evaluation was that it was a relatively modest textbook; in the preface, the author himself mentions that it was begun for practical reasons, so that his pupils would have a comprehensible printed handbook available. It was, however, the first work of Scotist theology printed in the Bohemian Crown Lands. The second volume was described as objectionable by the official Catholic censorship and changes were demanded.[65] From the viewpoint of cultural history, it is interesting, in part for the register of Bruodin's students from the Bohemian Franciscan province, printed in the preface to the second volume, and in part for the minor digressions in the text; for example, in the section on purgatory, he refers to the pilgrimages to St. Patrick's Purgatory in Ireland and, in the section on privileges, he refers to various functions within the Franciscan Order.[66]

In the years 1667 to 1668, Bruodin worked on his extensive *Propugnaculum catholicae veritatis*, which was published a year later (Fig. 19).[67] Of the planned ten books in two volumes, only half appeared, with the subtitle *pars historica*. Even so, this partially realised plan became "first-class propaganda" for the oppressed Catholic Church in Ireland. The work is dedicated to Václav, Jan, and Ignác, Counts of Šternberk, who, as Bruodin recounts in the preface, covered the cost of printing, and it is conceived with truly Baroque efficiency. The first book is on the concept of heresy and all heresies, not just from the beginning of Christianity, but right from the beginning of the world up to the end of the fifteenth century. It is noteworthy that Bruodin allotted

---

64 Vilém Antonín Brouček and Arnošt Schaff, *Domus sapientiae ... ad mentem Joannis Duns Scoti complectens philosophiam*, Pragae 1663. From Bruodin's teaching activity in this period are the well-known theological thesis *Conclusiones theologicae ex primo sententiarum ad mentem ... Joannis Duns Scotti*, copy in NK, MS 31 J 58, defended by Antonio de Venetiis in the friary in Jindřichův Hradec under Bruodin's chairmanship.

65 For example, it can be found in *Index librorum prohibitorum*, Romae 1758, 36, with reference to a decree of 21.3.1668. According to the note *donec corrigatur* [until a correction is made], these were probably less serious faults; no "amended" version, however, was published. It was not the only book by the Baroque theologian from the Bohemian environment that appeared in this somewhat demonised list: on page 126 of the same edition, there are two works by the Strahov abbot Hieronymus Hirnhaim.

66 Anthony Bruodin, *Oecodomia ... Doctoris subtilis ... hoc est: Universae theologiae scholasticae manualis summa...*, Pragae 1663; the same author, *Corolla oecodomiae ... sive pars altera manualis summae totius theologiae speculativae*, Pragae 1664. For an evaluation of the work, see Sousedík, *Jan Duns Scotus*, 167–168.

67 Anthony Bruodin, *Propugnaculum catholicae veritatis... Pars prima historica...*, Pragae 1669. SK, BCh VIII 35.

Fig. 19 The title page of
*Propugnaculum catholicae
veritatis* by Anthony
Bruodin. Prague, 1669 (SK).

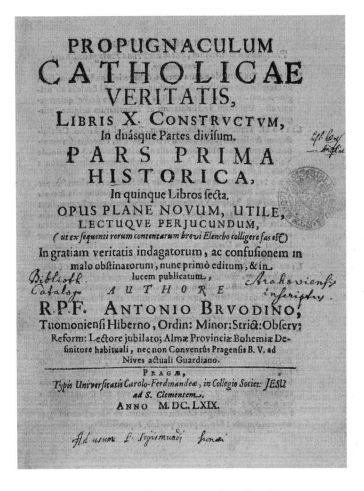

four chapters to Hussitism. He was particularly concerned with John Huss
and his adherents, and only dealt marginally with the subsequent movement.[68] Although he does not acknowledge his sources at all systematically,

---

68   According to Bruodin, Wycliffe's teaching was brought to Bohemia by the nobleman Peter
Faulfisch, who was in Oxford (here, there is a clear confusion with Nicholas Faulfisch to whom
primacy is not attributed in this respect). Huss's fondness for Wycliffe caused his disagreement
with the German teachers and eventually (understandably for ethnic reasons) he convinced
King Wenceslas to expel the German teachers and students from Prague (according to Bruodin
24,000!). Of the more important clergy, Jan, a renegade from Strahov monastery (a clear
confusion with Jan Želivský) and Jerome of Prague adhered to Huss's teaching. It is followed by
a list of Huss's mistakes according to the Articles of the Council of Constance and the progress of
heresy in Bohemia (in accordance with Aeneas Silvius, from whom he probably drew, Bruodin
considers Peter of Dresden to be the ideological originator of the lay chalice, thus making a
double error, and Jakoubek of Stříbro is systematically called Jakoubek of Dresden), up until
Huss's and Jerome's death. For Peter of Dresden, see František Šmahel, *Husitská revoluce II. Kořeny
české reformace* [*The Hussite Revolution II. The Roots of the Czech Reformation*] (Praha: Univerzita
Karlova, 1993) 58.

it is clear that he knew Pavel Stránský of Zhoř, with whom he argued over the etymological origin of the name Tábor.[69] The second section is dedicated to the Reformation of the fifteenth century on the European mainland, with a chapter on missions in India and America. Only in the third section does Bruodin reach England, Scotland and Ireland, firstly describing the advance of the Reformation beginning with the reign of Henry VIII. The closing comprehensive twentieth chapter is devoted to martyrs for the faith who suffered from 1535 until the beginning of the reign of Charles I in the lands under the sceptre of the King of England. Charles's reign, followed by revolution and the Cromwellian period, is described by Bruodin in the fourth section, ending with chapters on the Irish martyrs after the death of Charles I (literally "killed by rebels and regicides") and on the death of Patrick Fleming in Bohemia, as quoted above. The end of the chapter on the Irish, however, is also connected to Bohemia, if not to the Franciscans. The Jesuit John Meagh who had studied in Italy, was sent to the college in Kutná Hora in 1638 to prepare himself for missionary work in Ireland. The following year, he and two confrères were ordered to go to the college in Jindřichův Hradec by the Kutná Hora rector, through fear of the Swedish forces under Johan Banér, but on the way they were killed by enraged villagers on 31 May 1639. Their bodies were buried in Kutná Hora.[70] The fifth and final section concerns historical and contemporary Ireland; Bruodin appends to it a geneological survey of the O'Brien family, a list of the Irish kings and a list of the families of the Irish nobility.

Bruodin was criticised for a number of errors, even by his contemporaries. In 1670, a work by Thomas Carve was published entitled *Enchiridion apologeticum contra sordidorum mendaciorum faraginem R. P. Antonii Bruodini* (*An Apologetical Handbook against the Farrago of Sordid Mendacities of the Reverend Father Anthony Bruodin*). It was not, however, simply a reaction to the factual inaccuracies, which could be explained by the fact that Bruodin had left Ireland in about his twenties and that his information on his contemporaries was inadequate, or at best second-hand. There was more to it than that. Behind it lay the antipathy of the old Irish (including Bruodin) towards the Anglo-Irish, the differing opinion of these groups on Irish history and the nuances in their conception of it, and with what kind of treatment and with

---

69   According to Bruodin, Stránský is lying if he claims that the name was not taken over from the name of the Palestinian biblical mountain and that it developed from the word "tábořiště" [camp] (in the original *castrum*). According to Bruodin, "castrum" is translated into Czech as "ležení" [camp] and those who belong to it are called "vojenští" [soldiers] (in the original *castrenses*); "tábor" [camp] is not even a Czech word. It would be better to use the expression "a sacred place" (in the original *fanum*), for which Bruodin gives the word "zbor" [corps]. Taborites would be then called "zborníci" [corpsmen]. See *Propugnaculum*, 110.

70   See Mathias Tanner, *Societas Jesu usque ad sanguinis et vitae profusionem militans...*, Pragae 1675, 112–114. According to Tanner, Meagh's guides were called Martin Ignatius and Václav Trnoška.

what legitimacy this history was presented. It also related to their view of the Irish bards, their fabulation and their way of portraying important events, a natural component of national culture, although difficult to translate into Central European terms.

In *Propugnaculum*, in the chapter entitled *De Carve, seu Carrani erroribus et imposturis* (*On Carve's or Carran's Errors and Impostures*), Bruodin replied to Carve's *Itinerarium*, published in three volumes in the years 1639 to 1646, and to his work *Lyra hibernica*, first published in 1666. He questions not only Carve's distorted conception of Irish history (the assertion in *Itinerarium* that the Irish became civilised through contact and trade with the English must have seemed particularly abhorrent), but also the author's character and the reasons for his departure from Ireland. A response might have been expected, but no preserved copy of the above-mentioned *Enchiridion* has yet been found (its title is known from *Anatomicum examen*). In 1671, Cornelius O'Mollony replied to *Enchiridion* in his *Anatomy examination* (*Anatomicum examen, inchiridii apologetici … quo Carrani imposturae, et calumniae religiose re-futantur*), published by the Jesuit printing house in Prague. Millett justifiably considers the otherwise unknown O'Mollony to be Bruodin's pseudonym. For that matter, the writer was exposed by Carve himself, for whom his opponent's choice of pseudonym was clear, Bruodin's mother being named O'Mollony. O'Mollony-Bruodin reproached Carve for his poor Latin and the surreptitiousness of what he had done (according to the introduction to *Examen*, Carve's work had been published without it being stated where and by whom it had been printed). Of course, Bruodin also strived to refute, step by step, each of his opponent's assertions and defended himself, which gives today's reader the chance to reconstruct the contents of *Enchiridion*; at the same time, Bruodin appended a list of Irish martyrs, which he had not included in *Propugnaculum*. Carve had the last word in the dispute in 1672, when he published in Sulzbach his *Responsio veridica ad illotum libellum cui nomen anatomicum examen* (*The True Answer to the Foul Volume Entitled Ana-tomicum Examen*).[71]

The core of the dispute was the false picture of Ireland as outlined by Carve. This, however, was quickly lost in the writers' accusations and coun-ter-accusations. Carve himself, despite his prejudices and his lack of critical feeling in relation to ancient Irish history, wrote well and objectively about events in contemporary Europe. *Itinerarium* originated, so to speak, in the

---

71 Millett, *The Irish Franciscans*, 245–246. Apart from this, Carve wrote a short work with the title of *Epitome rerum Germanicarum … ab Anno MDCXVII ad XLIII. gestarum...*, a critical new edition of which was published as late as 1760 in Leipzig. Unlike Bruodin's critique of Carve's Latin style, the editor praised *Epitome* as "graviter eleganterque scripta...". On Carve (Carew), see M. MacCraith and D. Worthington, "Aspects of the literary activity of the Irish Franciscans in Prague," 125–128, 130–131.

Fig. 20 *Armamentarium theologicum* by Anthony Bruodin, the title page. Prague, 1676 (SK).

midst of battles and the author was clearly not too concerned with remote academic questions; in his later disputes with Bruodin he did not even try so much to defend his conception as to inveigh against his opponent. He had quite enough opportunities to do this, beginning with his family. Not only did he ridicule the possessions and seat of the Bruodins (described in *Anatomicum examen*), but he also ridiculed the head of the family, the bard

Thaddeus Bruodin (Tadhg MacDaire MacBrody), whose sad end he had seen with his own eyes. The inspiration of the family, the imagination and fabulation of the bards were very clear to Carve from *Propugnaculum*; he found them in the passages on Irish saints and martyrs, many of whom had been "canonised" by Bruodin, and he generally wrote very ironically about the bards. His criticism of Bruodin's superficiality was not without foundation; it is possible to observe the boldness with which Bruodin launches into Czech etymology. This rift, at least in the form it took, would clearly not have happened in the first half of the seventeenth century when figures such as Luke Wadding managed to keep the innate outspokenness and vehemence of his fellow-countrymen in check.[72]

In the same year as *Propugnaculum*, Bruodin published his minor work on the Spanish Franciscan Pedro de Alcántara who was proclaimed a saint in 1669.[73] Anthony Bruodin was then silent for several years. Apart from the dispute with the critic of *Propugnaculum*, his functions clearly occupied his time and clearly a temporary lack of access to the necessary literature was also a reason (most probably in Hostinné and on visitation journeys). His final work, *Armamentarium theologicum*, which perhaps in part arose because he was forced into seclusion, remained unfinished (Fig. 20).[74] In a remarkable preface to this work, undoubtedly in an attempt to defend himself against his opponents, he describes his work in the Bohemian province and his introduction of Scotist philosophy and theology to the Bohemian Crown Lands. In losing Bruodin, the Irish Franciscan community and at the same time the Bohemian province lost a significant figure. Although his theological works were never more than school compendiums, their publication was pioneering. What is indisputable is Bruodin's importance in acquainting the educated public with the history of Ireland and events in that country.

THE CHURCH BY THE POWDER GATE

One of the reasons for the attempt to found a friary in Namslav was the inadequate capacity of the college in Prague, a problem which the friars suffered from in later years as well. It was not, however, always caused by

---

72   See a detailed analysis of the literary dispute between Bruodin and Carve written by Thomas Wall, "Bards and Bruodins," *Father Luke Wadding*, 438–462. According to Wall, Carve's *Enchiridion* was published in Nuremberg.

73   Anthony Bruodin, *Synopsis vitae, virtutum, et miraculorum S. Petri de Alcantara*, Pragae 1669. Humprecht Jan, Count Černín of Chudenice, to whom the book is dedicated, participated at that time in the decoration of the Church of Our Lady of the Snows – according to Bruodin's data, he donated a lamp worth 300 imperial florins.

74   Anthony Bruodin, *Armamentarium theologicum*, Pragae 1675–1676.

a flood of young newcomers. The repression in Ireland in the early 1650s certainly forced a greater number of the religious into emigration, while at the same time deterring the young from entering friaries there, which as a result meant a reduction in the number of students coming to the colleges in mainland Europe to be prepared for missionary work. The inadequacy was only felt some years later. In May 1658, at the request of the guardians of the colleges in Prague, Louvain and Paris, it was submitted to the Congregation of Bishops and Regulars that they be permitted to accept novices after a period of one year. Only in 1667 did the general of the order, Ildefonso Salizanes, grant the Prague college in perpetuity the right to accept novices, together with the right for the guardian to issue friars with the permission necessary to receive ordination.[75] Also, only Irishmen could be accepted into the novitiate.[76]

The beginning of the 1650s saw the continued development of the Prague college. On 15 August 1652, in the presence of Ferdinand III, the foundation stone of the new Church of the Immaculate Conception of the Virgin Mary was laid. The ceremony performed in the presence of Archbishop Harrach and the relic of St. Patrick was embedded in the church's substructure.[77] As late as 1949, the plaque commemorating this event was photographed in the former church (Fig. 21).[78] The building was apparently designed by Carlo Lu-

---

75 NA, ŘHyb Praha, carton no. 45, nos. 99 and 100. The privileges are dated 20.7.1667 in Madrid.
76 It was emphasised by the decree of the general of the order, Pietro Marini Sormani, of 24 March 1683 in which he forbad the Prague Irish Franciscans under penalty to accept Czechs or Germans as he had heard that the Irish Franciscans were accepting into the novitiate youngsters of Czech origin, which understandably harmed the Franciscans of the Bohemian province, see NA, ŘF, carton no. 22.
77 *Die Diarien und Tagzettel*, Band 6, 623.
78 Today it bears a Latin inscription:
ANNO 1652 DIE XV MENSIS AVGVSTI INNOCENTII X, /
SVMMI PONTIFICIS A[NN]O VIII. FERDINANDI III. IMPERATO/
RIS A[NN]O 16. FERDINANDI IV. HVNGARIAE ET BOHEMI/
AE REGIS A[NN]O 7. PROVINCIAM HIBERNIAE FRAT/
RVM MIN[ORUM] STRICT[IORIS] OBSER[VANTIAE] REGENTE R[EVERENDO] A[DMODUM] P[ATRE] FRANCI/
SCO Ô SVILLEVAN ET IN HOC COLLEGIO IMMACV/
LATAE CONCEPTIONIS NEO PRAGAE GVARDIANO/
EXISTENTE P[ATRE] PHILIPPO Ô REILLI POSITVS EST/
PERIPSVM AVGVSTISSIMVM IMPERATOREM/
LAPIS PRIMVS CONSECRATVS AB EM[INENTISSI]MO CAR/
DINALI AB HARRACH IN FVNDAMENTO/
ECCLESIAE DICTI COLLEGI [!] SVB TITVLO/
IMACVLATAE [!] CONCEPTIONIS.
"On the fifteenth day of the month of August, the year of 1652, in the eighth year of [the pontificate of] the noble sovereign pontiff Innocent X, in the sixteenth year of the reign of Emperor Ferdinand III and in the seventh year of King Ferdinand IV of Hungary and Bohemia, during the tenure in office of the honourable Father Francis O'Sullivan [Provincial] of the Irish Province of the Franciscan Order of the Stricter Observance and Father Philipp O'Reilly, the

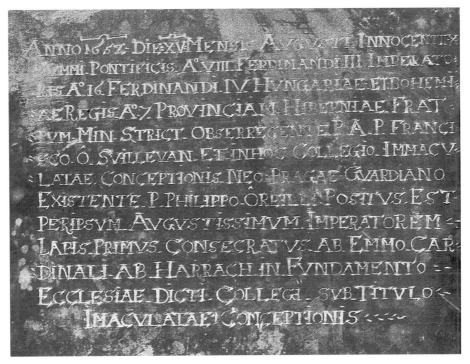

Fig. 21 A panel with a memorial inscription about laying the foundation stone of the Irish Franciscan church (NPÚ).

rago. The community was so poor that work on the costly construction had to be stopped just the following spring, so the Irish Franciscans turned to the Emperor with a request for financial assistance, and were granted 2,000 florins. After a year, however, further problems occurred: after the foundations had been laid and the pillars erected, it turned out that the width of the church was slightly greater than its length. The Irish Franciscans tried to obtain permission from the city council to move the façade of the church onto ground belonging to the city, but without success.[79] It is possible that

current guardian of the College of the Immaculate Conception in the New Town of Prague, the cornerstone was laid by the said noble emperor in the foundations of the church of the said college which bears the name of the Immaculate Conception, and was blessed by the noble Cardinal Harrach."

The photography is stored in Národní ústav památkové péče in Prague [The National Institute for the Preservation of Monuments], inv. no. 155.300. The unusual abbreviation R.A.P. in front of the name of Francis O'Sullivan could possibly be only an erroneously carved A.R.P.

79 On the construction of the church, see Millett, *The Irish Franciscans*, 139–141, also Růžena Baťková ed., *Umělecké památky Prahy. Nové Město, Vyšehrad, Vinohrady* [*The Artistic Monuments of Prague: New Town, Vyšehrad and Vinohrady*] (Praha: Academia, 1998) 189–191; ibid. on building development after the dissolution of the college. Jan Florian Hammerschmid, *Prodromus gloriae Pragenae*, Vetero-Pragae 1717, 302–303 lists in detail the patrons of the church. The consecration of the Immaculate Conception was based on the fact that the Franciscans (as well as the Jesuits)

the opposition they met with persuaded them to appeal to Ferdinand III for Imperial protection against all opponents of their foundation. The document in which the sovereign took the Irish under his protection was promulgated on 4 November 1654.[80] From then on, they counted on the support of the ruling house in carrying out the construction, as is apparent from their requests for wood from the Třeboň estate in late 1656 and early 1657. It is, however, understandable that money for the construction of the church must also have come from sources other than the Emperor's charity and almsgiving. It may not, perhaps, have been so much, but over the years they succeeded in having several restrictions regarding this removed from the foundation charter. In January 1652, with the support of influential patrons, Ferdinand III confirmed all their privileges and, in addition, extended them somewhat. That is, the clause was removed from the foundation charter which stated that friars were not to be accepted into the college unless they were provided with sufficient means of support (this measure benefitted friars forced to flee Ireland as a result of oppression) and permission to collect alms anywhere in the Kingdom of Bohemia, with the exception of Prague, was reconfirmed.[81] This limiting clause in the foundation charter of Ferdinand II, intended to protect the local mendicant orders, was only abolished on 5 April 1659, by Leopold I in a decree which permitted the Irish Franciscans to collect alms in Prague as well.[82] By the end of 1661, construction of the church was more or less completed. According to Archbishop Harrach's diaries, Mass was read in the new church for the first time on the Feast of the Immaculate Conception that year.[83]

Private individuals continued to be important patrons. The first who should be mentioned is Walter Buttler, whose bequest, like those of the other soldiers involved in the Valdštejn murder, was discussed in Chapter 2. Likewise, through the bequest of Gerhard, Baronet of Wachtendung, the Irish Franciscans received, in addition to 2,000 florins for the funeral, 13,000

---

honoured this teaching even before its proclamation as dogma in the nineteenth century (unlike, for example, the Dominicans). For the Feast of the Immaculate Conception as well as for the Feast of St Patrick, ceremonial speakers were invited to the church. They included not only church dignitaries but also educated laymen. See Antonín Podlaha, "Učení o neposkvrněném početí Panny Marie v Čechách před prohlášením učení toho za dogma" [The Doctrine of the Immaculate Conception of the Virgin Mary in Bohemia before the Declaration of Teaching as Dogma], ČKD 45.7–8, 9 (1904): 480–494 and 554–569. There is also a list of the sermons related to this topic delivered in Prague (mainly in Týn and at the Irish Franciscan college).

80   NA, L 2, ŘH sA, document no. 1224.
81   Millett, The Irish Franciscans, 143–144. The original of the document is in NA, L 2, ŘH sA, document no. 1223. In the early 1650s, the number of supporters and patrons of the college had decreased because the generation of Irish soldiers in the Imperial service who had been among their main supporters in the first decades of its existence was steadily dying off.
82   NA, L 2, ŘH sA, document no. 1226.
83   *Die Diarien und Tagzettel*, Band 7, 143.

florins after the sale of real estate and the subsequent settling of the deceased's debts. There was also Ferdinand Leopold Benno, Count of Martinice, at whose expense the high altar in the church was created. The connection between this Bohemian nobleman and the college can be found most probably in the person of his chaplain, Molloy, also mentioned above. Count of Martinice, provost of the Vyšehrad Chapter house, inherited from his father, Jaroslav Bořita of Martinice, outstanding debts which he passed on to the Irish Franciscans. The Royal Chamber, however, decided that the greater part of the capital should remain within the donor's family and thereby prevented the creation of a damaging precedent, which would have made it possible to give such gifts to the Irish Franciscans. In March 1658, in connection with the Count of Martinice's donation, Emperor Leopold I permitted the lesser part of the capital to be passed on to the Franciscans and for them to be paid a commission from the Royal estates to this account. The Franciscans used the donations not only for the construction of the church but also for securing the community's means of living. In 1659, for example, they appealed for iron to make the windows of the church, and in 1661, on the intervention of the Emperor, they were paid 300 florins. In the period 1658 to 1666, they received gifts amounting to 4,147 florins 20 kreutzer from the Count of Martinice.[84] He also showed goodwill towards individuals of Irish nationality; in 1659, he provided for the meals of a "high-born Irishman" in Žitenice (this was probably a member of the clergy), but he considered his liberality towards the Irish college to have been finished in his lifetime and it was not remembered in his will, despite substantial bequests to other monastic institutions.

Other bequests were smaller and more often concerned the furnishings of the church. It was often the case that the deceased wished to be buried in the college. Jan of Talmberk left 1,100 florins for the building of the church, but it was, as in other instances, apparently a long time before the bequest was released.[85] Another bequest was made by Anna Marie Golčová. Although Don Martin de Hoff-Huerta left the college as much as 7,000 florins, the bequest was in practice unclaimable, as became evident during a hearing at the archbishop's consistory in April 1641. De Hoff-Huerta's wife, the executor of the will, fulfilled her husband's last wishes only in small part, by having a lamp made for the church. The Irish Franciscans were not the only ones to suffer; the Discalced Carmelites were also adversely affected in this way. They turned to the Emperor for help over the settlement of the will, but he referred them to the support of the relevant officials.[86] Hammerschmid pres-

---

84 Millett, *The Irish Franciscans*, 144–147. Here, on another bequest by Countess Dvořecká.
85 See NA, L 2, ŘH sA, document no. 1227. In 1662, Vilém of Talmberk handed over a promissory note of 1,000 florins to the Franciscans.
86 NA, APA, carton no. 2100. More than the unwillingness or greed of the heirs, the troubles they experienced after the death of Hoff-Huerta played a role. In 1638, his adoptive daughter and

ents interesting details on how construction progressed: a certain Šimon Bohuslav Morávek bequeathed the Irish Franciscans 100 florins for the construction of the tower which was added to the church later; in 1672, the friars raised another contribution towards its construction at the Royal Chamber. Building surveys show that it was mainly made of wood, because its siting is not reflected in the ground plan of the construction.[87]

Johann Anton, Count Losy of Losinthal, contributed to the costs of refurbishing the high altar, as well as ordering the picture *The Immaculate Conception of the Virgin Mary* from Karel Škréta. In connection with this, Hammerschmid mentions that the count donated 100 florins, while the remainder was raised by collecting special alms around Prague.[88] He also had the Chapel of St. Anthony built and apparently decorated it with a picture by Škréta. If we step outside the time frame of this chapter, we can present a picture of the entire internal arrangement of the church as it was described in the second decade of the eighteenth century. On the gospel side of the high altar was a side altar (Franz Anton, Count Sporck had this built) and on the same side was the Altar of the Virgin Mary of Neukirchen, "of the Holy Blood," paid for by Vilém Václav, Baronet Michna of Vacínov.[89] By the entrance to the sacristy were the Altar and Chapel of St. Francis with more pictures by Karel Škréta (*The Baptism of Christ* and *The Conversion of St. Paul*) which had been donated by Jan Norbert, Count of Šternberk, and his brothers, Ignác

---

also heiress was forced to give up Písek and the Písek estate when she was threatened with the withdrawal of almost all her heritage, on the basis of proven dishonest machinations on the part of her adoptive father, see *Ottův slovník naučný. Díl 11 [Otto's Encyclopedic Dictionary. Vol. 11]* (Praha: J. Otto, 1897) 840–841. On the August negotiations with the Emperor, see NA, SM, H 99/6. There is probably some truth in the claim made by Hammerschmid in *Prodromus gloriae Pragenae* that 7,000 florins were bequeathed to the college by Don Martinus Paradis, Hispanus.

87 See Baťková ed., *Umělecké památky Prahy*, see note no. 79. On the requests to the Bohemian Royal Chamber, see NA, NM, K2 H1.

88 Jaromír Neumann et al., *Karel Škréta 1610–1674. Katalog výstavy NG v Praze [Karel Škréta 1610–1674. Catalogue of the Exhibition in the National Gallery in Prague]* (Praha: Národní galerie, 1974) 200–221. According to the data given in František Ekert's *Posvátná místa král. hl. města Prahy. Svazek II [Sacred Places of the Royal Capital City of Prague. Vol. II]* (Praha: Dědictví sv. Jana Nepomuckého, 1884) 453, and mainly in Jan Bohumír Dlabač ed., *Allgemeines historisches Künstler-Lexikon für Böhmen und zum Theil auch für Mähren und Schlesien*. Vol. III (Prag: Stände Böhmens, 1815) columns 64–66, in the church there was later a fresco by Johann Ferdinand Schor (1686–1767), which was destroyed, according to Dlabač's testimony, in 1809.

89 There are two links with this Bavarian place of pilgrimage, also popular with pilgrims from the Bohemian Crown Lands: in Neukirchen, there was a Franciscan friary from 1657, from which the place of pilgrimage was managed, and the Michna of Vacínov family were clearly amongst the local pilgrims and patrons. The unidentified Baronet Michna (possibly identical with Vilém Václav) had the organ in Neukirchen repaired in 1681. Walter Hartinger, "Neukirchen bei Heiligen Blut. Von der geflüchteten adonna zur Flüchtlingsmadonna," *Wallfahrt kennt keine Grenzen. Themen zu einer Ausstellung des Bayerischen Nationalmuseum und des Adalbert Stifter Vereins, München*, eds. Lenz Kriss-Rettenbeck and Gerda Möhler (München: Schnell & Steiner, 1984) 411.

Karel and Václav Vojtěch. Then there was the Altar and Chapel of St. John of Capistrano with stucco decoration (paid for by General de la Crone) and the Chapel of the Virgin Mary of Svatá Hora, financed by Maria Mechtilde de Dieten, née de Bois.[90] Finally, on the gospel side, there was the Chapel of St. Patrick, to which the stuccoist, Cometa,[91] contributed, while its completion was funded by the provisor of the archiepiscopal seminary, Jiří Kryštof Hájek, who was buried here. The cult of St. Patrick, who was rather exotic for Bohemia, did not spread at all in Prague in the seventeenth and eighteenth centuries. Nevertheless, every year on his saint's day, the Irish Franciscans would invite a famous preacher, whose sermon was presumably limited to those who knew Latin. Apparently, the Fraternity of St. Patrick, which gained papal confirmation in March 1656, gathered at this very altar, or was supposed to have gathered there. That is, however, the only proof yet found of its existence and, because its promulgation need not necessarily mean that the sodality actually existed, it is possible that either the fraternity was not established at all, or that it came to an end after a short time without leaving any identifiable traces.[92] When the college was dissolved, there was a picture of St. Patrick by František Xaver Palko[93] on the altar.

On the opposite side, the epistle side, was an altar dedicated to the Assumption of the Virgin Mary (paid for by Jobst of Schwartzenwolf), the above-mentioned Chapel of St. Anthony, the Chapel of St. Isidore which was contributed to by one of the Lurago family of builders, then the Chapel of St. Thomas of Villanova, paid for by Count Černín of Chudenice, and lastly the Chapel of St. Wenceslas, financed by Ferdinand Christoph of Scheidlern. To the right of the entrance to the church was the Chapel of All the Faithful Departed, but because no patron for this was found, it remained untended and unfinished. At the beginning of the eighteenth century, the development of the church's interior was clearly complete in its main features. The inventory of the church's valuables, which originated after its dissolution, specifically mentions some of the altars: the Altar of the Virgin Mary of "the Holy Blood," the Altar of St. Francis, the Altar of the Virgin Mary of Svatá Hora on which

---

90   We deal with her last will in the section *The Irish Franciscans and the nobility*. Zimprecht's picture was probably placed here.

91   Probably Giovanni Bartolomeo who died in 1687 and was buried in the church, as had been his son Innocenzo before him (died 1681). Prokop Toman, *Nový slovník československých výtvarných umělců. Díl I [The New Dictionary of Czechoslovakian Artists. Vol. I]* (Ostrava: Výtvarné centrum Chagall, 1993) 131.

92   Archivio segreto Vaticano, Sec. brev., Indulg. perpet., book 3, f. 57v. St. Patrick's Day was supposed to be the main feast day of the fraternity, then also St. Columba's Day, the day commemorating the stigmatisation of St. Francis, St. Didacus's Day and St. Brigid's Day. The document was issued on 3.3.1656. Generally on Baroque fraternities, see Jiří Mikulec, *Barokní náboženská bratrstva v Čechách [Religious Fraternities Baroque in Bohemia]* (Praha: Nakladatelství Lidové noviny, 2000).

93   Jaroslav Schaller, *Beschreibung der … Residentzstadt Prag … Vierter … Band*, Prag 1797, 169 and Toman, *Nový slovník československých výtvarných umělců. Díl II.*, 239.

was a little crown and children's clothing on a copy of a graceful statue, the Altar of St. Thomas of Villanova with an unspecified picture of Mary, and the Altar of St. Patrick. The only new addition was the Altar of St. Joseph.[94]

Nevertheless, a description of the church interior from the period of abolition of the college varies in details. The main altar apparently had no altar picture but, instead of this, a fresco was painted on the wall, with two large gilt statuaries of saints on either side. On the gospel side, the above-mentioned sequence of altars continued; after St. Patrick's altar, that of St. John of Nepomuk was added with a statue of the saint (probably installed after his canonisation, i.e. after 1729), a small Marian picture and one of Salvator, as well as an altar of the Crucifixion with miniature Marian pictures. In the eighteenth century, the altar of the Most Sacred Heart of Jesus was placed on the epistle side between the chapels of St. Anthony and St. Isidore. St. Walpurga's altar with a sculpture of the saint and St. Joseph's altar were placed after St. Wenceslas's altar and before the chapel of All Faithful Departed. The aforementioned description also lists other pictures and their locations in the church. Apart from several non-specific Marian paintings, the church was decorated with the following pictures: *Ecce homo* at St. Francis's altar, the Holy Trinity at St. Patrick's altar, Mary Magdalene at St. Isidore's altar, St. Peter of Alcantara at St. Wenceslas's altar, St. Thecla at St. Walpurga's altar, and Judas Thaddaeus at St. Joseph's altar. The décor of the church documented the influence of old and new cults, Franciscan spirituality and patron saints of both nations together with the veneration of Marian pictures popular in Baroque Bohemia.[95]

Thanks to the art historical research in recent years and to the inventory discovered in the Prague City Archives by Radka Tibitanzlová, we can partially reconstruct what happened with the church furnishings. Two paintings by Karel Škréta have been preserved. His *Baptism of Christ* is owned by the Knights of the Cross with the Red Star, *St. Paul's Conversion* is in the Archdiocesan Museum in Olomouc.[96] *The Crucifixion* was probably first installed in the chapel of All Faithful Departed and then moved with other altars to the Church of Levín near Litoměřice. This church was later damaged by several fires and the catalogues available do not provide any information about other items from the Irish Franciscan college. A picture which was recently discovered in the Church of Nativity of St. John the Baptist in Čížkov near Plzeň was identified as St. Anthony of Padua.[97] Karel Škréta Jr., was commissioned

94   NA, ČG Publ, carton no. 2730.
95   NA, CSÚ, carton no. 293. The inventory was completed in August 1787.
96   For the most recent information about both paintings, see texts by Štěpán Vácha in *Karel Škréta 1610-1674. Doba a dílo* [*Karel Škréta 1610-1674. His Work and His Era*], eds. Lenka Stolárová and Vít Vlnas (Praha: Národní galerie, 2010) 136-139.
97   Radka Tibitanzlová and Štěpán Vácha, "Nově nalezené dílo Karla Škréty. Sv. Antonín Paduánský

to paint an altar picture for the St. Francis Chapel, but only a drawing, per-haps a draft by Karel Škréta Sr., (now in the National Gallery in Prague), has been preserved. Another of Karel Škréta Jr.'s planned works was the *Stigma-tisation of St. Francis* and a picture with a Trinity motive, the *Descent of the Holy Spirit*. On the basis of a fragment which has been preserved to this day, wall paintings in the St. Francis Chapel can be ascribed to Giacomo Tencalla.[98] A contemporary of Karel Škréta Sr., was Matěj Zimprecht. Today we know about his picture of the *Holy Family with St. Anne* (now in the possession of the Knights of the Cross with the Red Star). His painting of the visitation disappeared before the middle of the nineteenth century but a drawing of this from 1814 has been preserved.

Part of the church interior was taken to the depositary in the former Barnabite college, St. Benedict Church in Hradčany, that was handed over to Carmelite nuns in 1791. Despite being formally abolished, their community survived reforms by Emperor Joseph II and after his death and suspension of some of his decrees, it was allowed to continue to exist. According to their chronicle, the Carmelite nuns kept the following items from the former Irish Franciscan furnishings in their church: the tabernacle, altar stone and three oak steps from the main altar, a marble balustrade, before which commu-nicants used to kneel, kneelers, two confessionals, a marble lavabo for the refectory, fourteen pictures of Stations of the Cross to be hung in the lower corridor, a picture of St. Joseph, now sometimes ascribed to Jan Petr Moli-tor (1702–1757),[99] sacristy furnishing, high-quality chasubles and an altar cloth.[100] This list is almost identical to one found in the Archives of Prague archbishopric.[101] The organ from the Irish Franciscan church still remains in St. Benedict Church to this day.

Apart from the above-mentioned churches in Levín and Čížkov, the rest of the mobiliary from the former Church of the Immaculate Conception was disseminated to the churches in Pyšely (south of Prague), Hostivař (now a part of Prague), Lobendava (near Děčín) and Nezabudice (near Rakovník). In

s Ježíškem a obrazová výzdoba kostela hybernů na Novém Městě pražském" [A Newly Discovered Painting by Karel Škréta: St Anthony of Padua with the Infant Jesus and the Painting Decorations in the Church of the Irish Franciscans in the New Town of Prague], *Umění* 62 (2014): 118–140.

98 Martin Mádl, "Kresba Stigmatizace sv. Františka z Assisi a Šternberská kaple v kostele pražských hybernů" [Drawing Stigmatisation of St Francis of Assisi and Šternberk chapel in the Irish Franciscan church in Prague], *Ars linearis II. Grafika a kresba českých zemí v evropských souvislostech*, ed. Alena Volrábová (Praha: Národní galerie, 2010) 58–65.

99 Pavel Vlček ed., *Umělecké památky Prahy. Pražský Hrad a Hradčany* [*Artistic monuments of Prague. Prague Castle and Hradčany*] (Praha: Academia, 2000) 131.

100 SK, MS without a shelf mark, *Chronic oder Geschichts-Verfassung Anderter Theil des Closters deren … baarfüssigen Carmeliterinen … in Prag*, 119.

101 NA, APA, C 141/2, *Inventáře předmětů ze zrušených klášterů a kostelů* [*Inventories of items from abolished religious institutes*], 18th century, document no. 3744, carton no. 2218. The authors would like to thank Radka Tibitanzlová for the transcription of the inventory.

the last location, two items from the Irish Franciscans are to be found in St. Lawrence Church: a Rococo pulpit and Altar of the Most Sacred Heart of Jesus. The provenance of the latter is not known.[102] We expect further searches of churches and research in archival documents to lead to the discovery and accurate identification of other items of the mobiliary.

---

102 The altar is dated 1758. See *Umělecké památky Čech. Díl II.* [*Artistic Monuments of Bohemia. Vol. II*], ed. Emanuel Poche (Praha: Academia, 1978) 473.

4. THE INVOLUNTARY PATH TO SECLUSION (1692–1730)

At the end of the 1680s, disputes broke out in the college. No more detailed information can be provided because the sources from this period have been only partially preserved at best. We only have more detailed information about the preceding period from the rebuke the Irish Franciscans received from the general of the order in 1683. They had allegedly taken youngsters of Czech nationality into the novitiate, to the detriment of the Bohemian province. Bernard Sannig even had the general's decree confirmed by the Emperor. In 1685, however, Pope Innocent XI ratified a different decree by the general of the order from the previous year, in which Pietro Marini Sormani had confirmed the right of the guardian of the Prague college to accept lay brothers from the Bohemian province and adjacent regions, against which the representatives of the Bohemian province had made no objections.[1]

PROLONGED TENSION IN THE COLLEGE

Obviously, the instability also showed itself in disagreements between teachers at the seminary, as a result of which the quality of teaching suffered: in this respect, the rebuke from the Archbishop of Prague, Jan Bedřich of Valdštejn, was ineffective. It is possible that, among other things, the teachers gave precedence to alms gathering rather than to teaching, although their teaching responsibilities were also honoured. In any case, in the later period this abuse increased. The archbishop realised that if the dissatisfied members of other orders, who were in the majority at the seminary, decided to boycott teaching in some way, it would mean, at the very least, lengthy and unpleasant negotiations. The Cistercians and Premonstratensians had definite reasons for resentment: their chances of breaking the monopoly of the Franciscan Order in the teaching of theology were minimal and the Department of Canon Law could only have been small consolation to them. It had been established in the autumn of 1674 at the instigation of the Strahov

---

1   See note no. 76 in Chapter 3. The confirmation of Leopold I dated 8.8.1684 (orig.) and a copy of the confirmation of Innocent XI dated 7.4.1685 in which the decree of the general of the order of 13.11.1684 is inserted, in NA, NM, K2/H1/1/8.

abbott, Hieronymus Hirnhaim, and the Cistercians and Premonstratensians lectured there alternately. In the meantime, their grievances fell on deaf ears. In 1673, the Premonstratensians were passed over for the right to fill the position of supply teacher at the Department of Theology. In December 1675, some students (understandably through their superiors) complained of the unclear, muddled and practically useless exposition of the Franciscan teachers. It ended with the Franciscans being reprimanded and threatened with expulsion from the seminary (Fig. 22).[2]

In the second half of the 1680s, Bonaventure Burke taught theology at the seminary. According to the testimony of Adolf Vratislav, Count of Šternberk, he was a highly educated and honourable priest, who later attained a distinguished position in the order (he was a lector in theology at St. Isidore's College in Rome and was appointed *lector jubilatus* and *scriptor ordinis*).[3] One of his colleagues, Peter Marian Murry, first lectured in speculative theology in Bologna, then later taught in Prague and, for two years, in the Cistercian monastery in Waldsassen, eventually becoming guardian of the Prague college. Philosophy was taught by Anthony Murphy (the Elder), John Scot and Bonaventure O'Flynn.[4] A printed list from 1697 includes further names: Francis O'Neill, guardian in Prague and commissary visitator to the Louvain college (died in Prague 31 January 1696); Peter Farrell, teacher of philosophy; Francis MacKenna, whose work at the archiepiscopal seminary ended with his death in October 1684; Francis Philip Burke,[5] teacher of philosophy; Michael Deane, later guardian in Louvain (died 4 April 1697); Bernardine Gavan, general visitator of the Irish province, who was also guardian in Louvain around 1697; and Louis O'Neill, who taught first at the Louvain college and then taught theology for two years at the archiepiscopal seminary.[6]

---

2   Augustin Neumann, "Výpisy z menších řádových archivů římských" [Extracts from Smaller Archives of Roman Catholic Religious Orders], ČKD 73.1 (1932): 97. These are the letters in which the Archbishop explained to the patrons of the Irish Franciscans why he had decided to remove them from the archiepiscopal seminary. About the complaint, see SK, MS DJ IV 1, f. 156v.

3   Neumann, "Výpisy z menších řádových archivů římských," 97, also *Quartum quod incedit*. Regarding Burke's paedagogical activity, both the records of his lectures and a printed thesis have been preserved, see Hedvika Kuchařová and Jan Pařez, "On the trail of Irish émigrés in the collections of the Strahov Abbey Library in Prague," *The Ulster Earls and Baroque Europe. Refashioning Irish Identities, 1600–1800*, eds. Thomas O'Connor and Mary Ann Lyons (Dublin: Four Courts Press, 2010) 198–199.

4   Murphy and Scot were appointed to the teaching posts in autumn 1688. Before this, John Scot taught philosophy for three years in Louvain; Murphy had taught in the archiepiscopal seminary earlier and he taught theology at the college. Their names are also included in the list of students in the academic year 1689–1690 produced by the lecture recorder in the Strahov manuscript DD VI 6.

5   His presentation for the professorship of theology from 12 January 1678 has been preserved, NA, APA, carton no. 2100.

6   *Quartum quod incedit.*

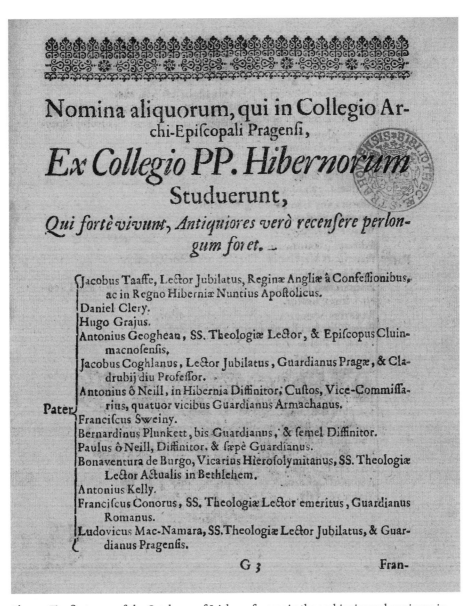

Nomina aliquorum, qui in Collegio Ar-
chi-Epifcopali Pragenfi,

Ex Collegio PP. Hibernorum
Studuerunt,
Qui fortè vivunt, Antiquiores verò recenfere perlon-
gum foret.

Pater

{Jacobus Taaffe, Lector Jubilatus, Reginæ Angliæ à Confeffionibus, ac in Regno Hiberniæ Nuntius Apoftolicus.

Daniel Clery.

Hugo Grajus.

Antonius Geoghean, SS. Theologiæ Lector, & Epifcopus Cluin-macnofenfis,

Jacobus Coghlanus, Lector Jubilatus, Guardianus Pragæ, & Cla-drubij diu Profeffor.

Antonius ô Neill, in Hibernia Diffinitor; Cuftos, Vice-Commiffa-rius, quatuor vicibus Guardianus Armachanus.

Francifcus Sweiny.

Bernardinus Plunkett, bis Guardianus, & femel Diffinitor.

Paulus ô Neill, Diffinitor. & fæpè Guardianus.

Bonaventura de Burgo, Vicarius Hierofolymitanus, SS. Theologiæ Lector Actualis in Bethlehem.

Antonius Kelly.

Francifcus Conorus, SS. Theologiæ Lector emeritus, Guardianus Romanus.

Ludovicus Mac-Namara, SS. Theologiæ Lector Jubilatus, & Guar-dianus Pragenfis.

G 3   Fran-

Fig. 22 The first page of the Catalogue of Irish professors in the archiepiscopal seminary in Prague. Prague, 1697 (SK).

The visitation of the college in 1670 promised improvement. The guardian at the time was Francis Burke and the visitator the above-mentioned Louis O'Neill. The college, led by the guardian, had reservations about the visitator, but, as had happened in previous cases, the friars were divided into supporters and opponents of one side or the other. Personal relations between the guardian and O'Neill were extremely tense; in correspondence with the archbishop dated August 1690, each made accusations against the other. The protest against O'Neill occupying this position, signed by twenty-seven friars and the guardian on 11 August 1690, presented the archbishop with these objections: O'Neill is biased against Burke, so, by appointing him, the guardian's rights are impaired and he is, in effect, removed from office. The visitator should himself be subjected to a visitation.[7] O'Neill, however, had plenipotentiary powers from Rome and, moreover, Valdštejn, like his predecessors, may have had very little desire to be judge and jury between antagonistic factions in the college. To ensure that the Franciscans submitted and that the visitation was entirely impartial, a second visitator was appointed, Christian Pfaltz of Ostritz, canon and archdeacon of the Cathedral of St. Vitus.[8]

Christian Pfaltz, a man of strict morality, was appalled at relations within the college. In his reports of 20 and 24 August, he wrote emotionally: "*Vulgo dicitur die Christen stehen in der Welt und in den Christen sey auch Welt, id verificatur in conventu hybernorum!*"[9] He found that the visitation was absolutely necessary. There was neither love nor concord in the college; on the contrary, disobedience predominated. Violence by one brother against another went unpunished, on the contrary, it was praised. Discipline had entirely lapsed, there was an active night life, choral worship was neglected and alms were squandered. It was clear that, if the college was not to become a scandalous example (if it was not already) of how monastic life could also be, reform had to be implemented. Pfaltz suggested the following solutions: disturbers of the peace and of peaceful coexistence should be transferred; if this dismal state of affairs is caused by the great distance from their superiors, let them be made subordinate to the Bohemian provincial; alms gathering should be done only in pairs; visitations must be carried out more often; and entry to those parts of the college intended only for the use of the friars must be strictly forbidden to lay persons.[10] It was not possible, however, to implement reform overnight, and, in the meantime, the friars were still able to completely ruin their reputation at the archiepiscopal seminary.

---

7   NA, APA, book no. B 65/13, f. 427. Neumann, "Výpisy z menších řádových archivů římských," 92. On the edition of the complaint, see Benignus Millett, "Some lists of Irish Franciscans in Prague, 1656-1791," *Collectanea hibernica* 36-37 (1994-5): 65-66.

8   On Christian Pfaltz of Ostritz (died 1702), see Antonín Podlaha, *Series praepositorum, decanorum, archidiaconorum aliorumque praelatorum et canonicum, S. Metropolitanae Ecclesiae Pragensis a primordiis usque ad praesentia tempora* (Praha: Metropolitní kapitula sv. Víta v Praze, 1912) 189-191.

9   "Simply put, Christians live in the world and the world is supposed to live in them – this is the rule in the Irish convent!" NA, APA, book no. B 65/13. This visitation and the one in 1773 are also mentioned by Eduard Winter, *Josefinismus a jeho dějiny. Příspěvky k duchovním dějinám Čech a Moravy 1740-1848* [Josephinism and its History. Contributions to the Religious History of Bohemia and Moravia 1740-1848] (Praha: Jelínek, 1945) 116.

10   NA, APA, book no. B 65/13.

In a short report dated 13 March 1691, the chronicler of Norbertinum described the reason for the departure of the Irish Franciscans from the seminary: "*In place of Father Bonaventure de Burgo a Hibernian, Professor of Theology at the archiepiscopal seminary, Father Louis O'Nelly, also a Hibernian and currently commissary of the Hibernians, was appointed at the same department, in a certain contention and dispute which broke out at that time between the above-mentioned Father Bonaventure and Father Marian, the second Professor of Theology, and as a result of which the Hibernian Fathers were later withdrawn from the Department of Theology.*"[11] The heart of the matter is made clear in a letter from Juan Pérez López, general of the Franciscans, to the Archbishop of Prague, dated by Neumann to 1692. López wrote that when, due to various excesses, one of the priests of the college was designated visitator, some of the lectors, including Father Burke, were dismissed. The unnamed visitator was O'Neill, which can be deduced from the protests which his nomination provoked, and also from the dismissal of Bonaventure Burke, the first name on the signed "anti-O'Neill" letter. Other victims may well have been his colleagues and fellow signatories, Anthony Murphy and Bonaventure O'Flynn. Father Scot (the above-mentioned John Scot, whose subsequent peripatetic life accurately corresponds with the very short curriculum vitae given in the 1697 register), who was living at the time in St. Isidore's College in Rome, took such pity on the talents of Father Bonaventure that he made sure that Burke came to Rome and took his place in the college while he went to Prague. He travelled there with Father Warde, who had accompanied Father Burke on his journey to Rome, with the necessary documents from Juan Pérez López, the general of the order. When they arrived in Prague, the guardian kept their documents to himself, however, and the lectors, Fathers Peter Marian Murry and Louis MacNamara remained in post. The two lectors insisted that Scot's position was already filled by Father Bernard Lorcan, who had been appointed the previous year despite the fact that the general had no intention of allowing this. That is to say, Murry and MacNamara had the audacity, firstly, to disobey binding patents from both the general and the archbishop, secondly, to appoint a student (Father Lorcan) as lector in theology against all the regulations and practice of the order, thirdly, to act thus against a right which appertained to the general of the order alone, and fourthly, to appropriate the supreme power of the general to appoint and remove from office. Scot accordingly appealed to the archbishop to correct these excesses and punish the guilty parties.[12]

It is unlikely that the superiors of the order and the Irish province imagined that the archbishop would punish the wrongdoers by depriving the Irish

11   SK, MS DJ IV 1, f. 211v.
12   Neumann, "Výpisy z menších řádových archivů římských," 93.

Franciscans of all teaching posts. Later, the college did not lack advocates, but the archbishop was indisputably tired of Irish squabbles and indifferent discipline at the college, which was bound, sooner or later through the teachers, to reflect badly on the seminary. At the same time, he was aware of the ambitions of the orders whose members studied at the seminary, especially the Cistercians and Premonstratensians, who were, to say the least, decidedly exasperated by the disharmony of the Irish Franciscans.[13]

There were, nevertheless, attempts at reform. At the end of January 1692, López, the general of the order, sent the Irish Franciscans in Prague a list of sixty-two articles intended to improve discipline in the college. Besides these, the following regulations were to be introduced; everyone, apart from the gatekeeper, the cook, those who were sick and those who were actually performing a duty in the college, must, under threat of severe punishment, attend the chapter and the choir, every priest must celebrate Mass daily, and the clerics and lay brothers take communion. Everyone must have the same food and eat in the refectory, with the exception of the sick, convalescents and aged friars. Schooling which is also attended by the laity must not be held in the refectory but in a special room, study must be solely before meals, and students must not wander about the town but walk to and from the seminary together. We must suppose that daily liturgical responsibilities were generally considered to be a non-compulsory recommendation, to talk of meals being communal is pointless, apart from the fact that the refectory fulfilled the function of a communal area and friars were prone to succumb to the temptation to have a look around the town as a distraction (this was not, of course, only a problem of Irish youth). The sixty-two articles covered ecclesiastical music, studies (Articles 4–26 were on the organisation and timetabling of study, disputations and examinations and the preparation of lectures) and the novice master and discipline. The final section was patently aimed at shortcomings revealed during the visitation. At the same time, it is clear from the regulation on studies that the 1660 ruling by the general of the order was no longer valid in practice, and lectures on philosophy and theology were being held in the college itself and other students were attending these lectures. The degeneration of the college is shown by the list of what was forbidden: sitting about and drinking in the cells at night; the access of lay persons to the college (benefactors and persons of high position were exempt from this); returning after hours; drinking with laymen in the town; the dishonest drawing of travel money for the journey to Ireland (this

---

13   It is possible that some of them pointed out the decline of the college in Rome; this would be evidenced by the note written by Neumann that the letters of many aristocrats and prelates to the procurator general of the order forced the superiors of the order to consider rectifying the situation.

was in such disorder that a reliable member of the college had to guarantee that those who requested travel money would actually go to Ireland); and the retention of sums of money. On the other hand, it was directed that the sick be properly treated (Bonaventure O'Flynn, suffering from the expectoration of blood [haemoptysis], had to accept the hospitality of the Benedictines).[14]

It begs the question of how this situation arose: the great distance from the centres and superiors of the order, the relative isolation in the Bohemian environment, dwindling missionary fervour and thus the decline of the main role of the college, and the contentiousness of Franciscans from various parts of Ireland all contributed. Considering that most of these factors were, at the very least, difficult to alter, not even remedial measures could have too great a hope of success. A temporary improvement at least could be brought by a strong and respected figure appointed to lead the college, but there was no such individual among the Irish at that time. The general of the order decided to appoint Amandus Hermann as head of the college. However, as the general had written in the introduction to the above-mentioned articles of correction, some members of the college, for personal reasons, preferred a less able, younger and immature superior. Hermann was a member of the Bohemian Franciscan province and one of their leading representatives.[15] The Irish may have felt affronted by such interference, but López, in writing at least, appointed Hermann as commissary in order to implement the articles of correction in the college. Whether this actually happened and how successful it was, we do not know, and we do not even know whether he served as guardian of the college; in 1696, both Gerald Geraldin and Thomas Dolan were mentioned as guardian.[16]

On 10 November 1692, Archbishop Valdštejn signed an agreement with representatives of the Cistercians (it was signed by the Abbot of Plasy and vicar general, Andreas Troyer, as well as the Abbots of Sedlec, Osek, Zbraslav, Zlatá Koruna and Vyšší Brod) and the Premonstratensians (represented by the Abbots of Strahov, Teplá and Želiv), to whom he had already granted the Departments of Theology and Philosophy. In line with the agreement of 1670, the Benedictines participated in teaching.[17] Opinion was unequivocal about

---

14   Neumann, "Výpisy z menších řádových archivů římských," 93-97.
15   In the period 1687 to 1690, he was provincial of the Bohemian Province, in which he held an important position after his term of office ended. In Rome in 1700, he was elected definitor general of the order. He was also active in terms of literature. See Klemens Minařík, "Provinciálové františkánské české provincie v letech 1600-1750" [The Provincials of the Franciscan Bohemian Province 1600-1750], SHK 18 (1917): 88-90 and Stanislav Sousedík, Jan Duns Scotus. Doctor subtilis a jeho čeští žáci [John Duns Scotus. Doctor Subtilis and His Bohemian Pupils] (Praha: Vyšehrad, 1989) 175-176.
16   NA, APA, carton no. 2100 and ibid., carton no. 2101. In 1696, a new guardian was elected; if the usual regulations were complied with, the previous election must have taken place in 1693.
17   In this contract, they formally confirmed their commitment to provide a suitable teacher (for

the departure of the Irish Franciscans, who were called to the seminary by Harrach only when there were not enough Cistercian or Premonstratensian lectors and *ex pura gratia*; experience had long shown that the students were adversely affected by the sudden and often unexpected changes of Irish Franciscan teachers, whose appointment should no doubt have been at the discretion of the archbishop, but whose continued work at the seminary or withdrawal lay, because of their membership of a religious order, in the hands of their superiors. Accordingly, from that time onwards, the only ones who would teach were those who did so at the discretion of the archbishop and directly of their abbots. In order to prevent possible disputes, there were clearly defined conditions in the contract which laid out how the members of the individual orders were to take turns. The proposal proved effective because, as far as we know, no disputes arose on this point.[18]

The members of the local orders proved themselves capable of quickly resolving an issue that had been the subject of dispute among the Irish Franciscans for more than fifty years. It may be supposed that this development of events did not arouse enthusiasm in the Irish college and that the explanatory letters, from the first half of November 1692 and sent by Valdštejn to some cardinals, were perhaps intended to prevent a new reversal of the situation in favour of the Irish Franciscans, which might have been enforced from above. The Irish teachers, however, had to leave the seminary. Shortly afterwards, Peter Marian Murry was teaching at the Cistercian monastery in Waldsassen.[19] As early as 1696 under Archbishop Breuner, the existing state of affairs was confirmed by the papal bull of Innocent XII; there is a brief mention in the text of the teaching of the Irish Franciscans and of their replacement brought about by the new flourishing of the orders teaching at the seminary.[20] The Irish Franciscans were hardly able to do anything about this, but nevertheless they refused to admit defeat. In July 1698, Archbishop Breuner wrote to the Cistercian vicar general and visitator, saying that the Irish were not only attempting, step by step, to regain the departments at

---

the Department of Philosophy) or to pay an established amount to ensure cover. At the same time, for personal reasons, they requested to be allowed to appoint a teacher of their own after the Premonstratensians and Cistercians had alternated twice.

18 Hedvika Kuchařová, "Premonstrátská kolej Norbertinum v Praze 1637-1785" [The Norbertinum College of the Premonstratensians in Prague 1637-1785], *BS* 3 (1997): 32-33.

19 Francis O'Devlin was there at the same time. Preserved in the National Library in Prague is Murry's *Disputationes theologicae de gratia et sanctificatione, de justificatione et meritis*, which Nivardus Götzl defended in Waldsassen in 1695 (MS 46 D 115) and O'Devlin's *Theses theologicae de fide, spe et charitate* from the same year (MS 46 E 141). Two years later, O'Devlin was back in Prague.

20 The bull was issued on 6 July. A version of the bull was printed by the Premonstratensian historian Charles Louis Hugo in *Sacri et canonici ordinis Praemonstratensis annales ... pars prima*, Nanceii 1734.

the seminary but also securing the most powerful support (*potentissima patrocinia*) of the Emperor, of his chief ministers, especially the Supreme Chancellor (at that time, František Oldřich, Count Kinský of Vchynice), as well as of the Spanish Ambassador, although the archbishop was assured that nothing could be reinstated or changed in contravention to the papal bull by whose authority the Department of Theology had been entrusted to the other orders. It seemed to Breuner that it would be better if Troyer and the other interested parties drafted a memorandum of the aforesaid compelling arguments for the retention of the department in the hands of the Cistercians and Premonstratensians and sent this to him as archbishop. In this respect, he promised them the greatest possible help on his part. If it was not possible to deter the Irish Franciscans without conflict or greater difficulties with the court, it was decided to leave them with only the Department of Canon Law. The required memorandum, signed by the Abbot of Strahov, Vít Seipl, as well as Troyer, was not ready even a fortnight later. The Irish Franciscans would like to return to the seminary, wrote both prelates, but by what right? In Rome, Louvain and Prague, they had their own colleges where they spread their teachings. The Cistercians and Premonstratensians did not want to be removed from the seminary, where the Irish would teach their monks to no avail, sometimes for up to a year, until the students could understand their foreign pronunciation of Latin well enough to be able to follow their lectures without difficulty. If the Irish Franciscans taught canon law, the prelates said, it would be sure to cause laughter at the university.[21]

Understandably, good relations were maintained outwardly, or at least the Irish attempted to do so.[22] This is not too surprising: with personal contact, the Irish were obviously able to gain powerful supporters, which, especially in view of the interconnections of individual families and their contacts, reaching up to the court, cannot have been too problematic. However, they mostly undermined their own status, at one time so high, in Church circles in Prague precisely at a time when their work at the seminary would not have been observed by the Premonstratensians and Cistercians, who found it hard to bear that the teaching of theology was not entrusted to them, with any great enthusiasm even if it had been accompanied by an irreproachable morality.

Besides the teachers, all of the Irish youths also left the seminary, it being contrary to the regulations of the order and statutes of the college for them to be educated in any theological teaching other than Scotism. The young

---

21   Státní oblastní archiv v Litoměřicích [State Regional Archives in Litoměřice], Cisterciáci Osek, carton no. 70. Breuner's letter is from 16 July, the memorial from 27 July.

22   In the same year, Louis Ryan from the College of the Immaculate Conception published a poetic composition *Eucharisticon*, SK, AB VIII 44/36, in Troyer's honour.

Irish novices, who could have been granted permission to be ordained by the guardian of the college in accordance with the privilege of 1667, were, however, ordained by the Archbishops of Prague or by auxiliary bishops. Six were ordained in the years 1695 to 1699, four in 1700, five in 1702, as many as nine in 1704, three in 1703 to 1707, and five in 1709. Up until 1700, it was usually Archbishop Breuner who conducted ordinations, and then from 1702, they were solely conducted by auxiliary bishop Vít Seipl, already known to us as the Abbot of Strahov.[23]

From then on, the Irish Franciscans concentrated on their literary and scholarly activities solely within their own college. The most significant (or, in terms of literature, most active) figure in the late seventeenth century and early eighteenth century was Francis O'Devlin, who was also renowned for his work in Irish. In about 1695, he was at Waldsassen, the Cistercian monastery (his *Theses theologicae de fide, spe et charitate* was published); two years later, he was lector in theology and philosophy at the Prague college, where he presided at Anthony Tuite's defence of his thesis.[24] In 1698, he is referred there as teacher of Holy Theology and the Word of God (*SS. Theologiae ac Verbi Dei Lector*); on the occasion of Louis Ryan's defence of his thesis in the same year, his theological work *Gladius spiritus* was published, dedicated to his former ward, Franz Anton, Count Sporck, and decorated with a notable engraving which referred to the military successes and Church patronage of members of this family.[25] The title page of the thesis which Patrick Babe defended in 1704 under O'Devlin's chairmanship also bore a dedication

---

23 Antonín Podlaha, *Dějiny arcidiecése pražské. Díl II. Doba arcibiskupa Jana Josefa hraběte Breunera* [*The History of the Diocese of Prague. Volume II. The Period of Archbishop Johann Joseph, Count of Breuner*] (Praha: Dědictví sv. Prokopa, 1917) 221–232. Sometimes various investigations were involved, for instance, when Thaddeus O'Crowley lost his birth certificate and was unable to obtain a new one due to the poor circumstances in Ireland (233). The numbers of those ordained during Archbishop Breuner's time are available in the cited monograph, but it would also be possible to complete them for other periods from the ordination registers. This was done by Matthäus Hösler, who included excerpts from these books in his work "Irishmen ordained at Prague, 1629–1786," *Collectanea hibernica* 33 (1991): 7–53. The additions were provided by Benignus Millett in his article "Irishmen ordained at Prague, 1628–1700: additions and corrections to Matthäus Hösler's lists," *Collectanea hibernica* 39–40 (1997–8): 23–31. The lists also contain the names of secular priests and members of orders other than Franciscans. From Podlaha's work we also learn about two other two Irishmen in Prague, namely Bernard Farrell and Michael Bell who were altar servers at St Vitus's in 1703, although it is not clear what their relation to the Irish Franciscan college was. In the college archives, however, there is a decree of the consistory about the inheritance after Farrell's death, issued on 10 September 1705 (NA, ŘHyb Praha, carton no. 45, no. 148). Farrell is said to have mastered seven languages, including Czech.

24 It is possible to attribute to O'Devlin the work *Compendium universae philosophiae ad mentem Doctoris subtilis*, which was published for the occasion, although in January 1698 the praeses Anthony MacNamara used the same text during the defence of Laurence Dalton. The text related to Tuite's defence is dedicated to the Strahov Abbot Vít Seipl.

25 See the section *The Irish Franciscans and the nobility*.

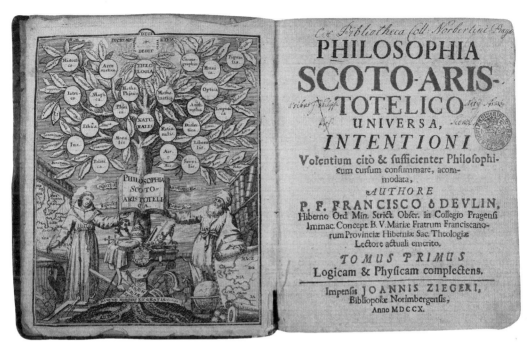

Fig. 23 The title doublepage of *Philosophia Scoto-Aristotelico-universa* by Francis O'Devlin. Engraving, Nuremberg, 1710 (SK).

to Sporck and, besides a depiction of the Virgin Mary, contained the same Sporck motifs as the *Gladius* engraving.²⁶ The frame of the scene is formed by medallions with portraits of Franciscan saints, popes and high dignitaries of the Church, scholars and martyrs. The youngest of those portrayed died in 1702, for among the martyrs are Patrick Fleming and his companion, as well as a representative of the Franciscans of Our Lady of the Snows who had been killed in 1611. The author of the design was O'Devlin himself. John Toland met him when visiting the Prague college in 1708.²⁷ Toland's edition of works by English republican James Harrington is included in the catalogue of the Irish Franciscan library. Harrington's *magnum opus* is listed there as *Oceana*. Perhaps this was a reminder of Toland's stay in the Prague college. In 1710, paid for by the bookseller Johann Zeiger, the first part of O'Devlin's textbook, *Philosophia scoto-aristotelica*, was published. It was clearly intended as a teaching aid for young noblemen (Fig. 23) (which is evident from phrases in the approval by Francis Donoghue from the Prague college: *"I found that the work was ... written for the use of the young in their studies, verified several times*

---

26 Heinrich Benedikt, *Franz Anton Graf von Sporck (1662–1738). Zur Kultur der Barockzeit in Böhmen.* (Wien: Manz, 1923) 412–413. The engraving is now stored in NA, SbR, inv. no. 236.

27 Joseph MacMahon OFM, "The silent century, 1698–1829," *The Irish Franciscans 1534–1990*, 100.

recently by the outstanding progress of the young counts and noblemen who are pupils of this priest..."). The manuscript was certainly ready in 1706, because it was in that year that O'Devlin was permitted to print it by the general procurator of the Franciscan Order and the imprimatur shows that there was also to be a second work (although no copy of this has been found). The work was dedicated to the nephews of Franz Anton, Count Sporck.[28] The youngest one, Johann Rudolph, a future Auxiliary Bishop of Prague, defended his philosophical thesis the following year under the chairmanship of O'Devlin. The printed work was entitled *Nucleus fundamentalis ac theses ex universa philosophia.* We meet this work again in 1712, when it was published on the occasion of the defence by Count Octavius Piccolomini.[29] It shows that, as in other Prague monasteries, young noblemen were taught at the Irish college; although it is clear from López's regulations that there was some form of teaching of the laity even earlier. The departure of the Franciscans from the archiepiscopal seminary may have been an incentive to extend such activities. It is difficult to say to what extent this tuition was carried out, but it is known from elsewhere that when they continued these activities up to a certain point and became a sort of "aristocratic academy," naturally the Jesuits from Prague University responded. In comparison with the university, the very best tuition at the college remained incomplete in the sense that the students could not gain an academic degree. One of O'Devlin's colleagues whose name we know was John Malone is documented as lector in theology at the college in 1703.[30] In 1714, O'Devlin returned to Ireland and joined a circle of scholars and writers in Dublin who focused on the Irish language.[31]

"THE HIBERNIANS, FOR MONEY"

The financing of the general running of the college caused certain problems. In the 1660s, the friars were, besides alms, already primarily dependent on sums paid by the Bohemian Chamber from the liberal settlements of previous years. Appeals for disbursement usually have the laconic Czech comment *"Hyberni, o peníze"* ("The Hibernians, for money") written on the back. As a rule, in the introduction to such an appeal, the college pleaded intolerable necessity and then requested the payment of, most commonly, 100 florins or,

---

28   Kuchařová and Pařez, "On the trail of Irish émigrés," 218–219.
29   Richard J. Kelly, "The Irish Franciscans in Prague (1629–1786): Their literary labours," *Journal of the Royal Society of Antiquaries of Ireland* 52 (1922): 172–173.
30   Kuchařová and Pařez, "On the trail of Irish émigrés," 177.
31   Mícheál MacCraith and David Worthington, "Aspects of the literary activity of the Irish Franciscans in Prague, 1620–1786," *Irish Migrants in Europe after Kinsale, 1602–1820*, eds. T. Connor and M.A. Lyons (Dublin: Four Courts Press, 2003) 131–133.

from the Chamber estates, such provisions as fish, meat or wheat – and all this once or twice a year.

Resources were not, understandably, unlimited. At the end of 1666, the Royal Revenue Office presented the Bohemian Chamber with a statement of the balance of the amount granted to the college from the Martinic donation and the balance of the bequest of Kateřina Ludmila Dvořecká, née Countess Šliková. Altogether, there remained 591 florins 40 kreutzer; the rest had dwindled away in the previous eight years. In the years 1667 to 1669, the Irish Franciscans requested the payment of an additional 400 florins, and, besides this, in July 1668, Emperor Leopold I ordered the Revenue Office to pay the Irish Franciscans another 200 florins for the construction of a college infirmary. However, in the early 1670s, in terms of a secure income, the Irish were impoverished.

The Emperor subsidised them again with the decree of 27 July 1671, on the basis of which they were to be supplied with provisions from the Chamber estates to a total value of 600 to 700 florins and the Royal Chamber was to pay them 500 florins as a contribution to the construction of a bell tower, a contribution which the Irish applied for again in 1672. They requested in advance rams and beef cattle to the value of 400 florins from the dominion of Zbiroh, fish (mostly carp and pike) to the value of 200 florins from the dominion of Poděbrady, and butter and wheat to the value of 100 florins from elsewhere. In November 1673, in the request for four hundredweight of carp and two hundredweight of pike, they estimated the balance of the Emperor's allowance to be more than 100 florins. By 9 September 1675, the merciless Revenue Office had calculated the balance to be 25 florins 15 kreutzer: there was nothing for it but more humble petitions.

In subsequent years, the custom was established that, when their request was made, the President of the Court Chamber Council (*President Hofkammerräthe*) would charge the Bohemian Royal Chamber with supplying them with, "in place of alms," a certain quantity of provisions from the Chamber dominions. In 1682, for example, they were to receive a hundred strychs (strych or korec = 93.587 litres) of corn, six hundredweight (centnýř = 61.728 kg) of carp, two hundredweight of pike, four oxen and fourteen rams. In 1687, however, the allowances for the Irish Franciscans were to be put on par with those of the Capuchins of Hradčany, which meant only twenty strychs of corn, four hundredweight of pike, six hundredweight of carp and seven hogsheads of wine.

However, over the years, the Royal Chamber showed further inclination to save money and, in October 1702, only allowed the Irish Franciscans half of the provisions they had received the year before, that is, two oxen and seven rams from the dominion of Pardubice, three and a half hogsheads of wine from Brandýs, three hundredweight of carp and two hundredweight of pike

Fig. 24 The Irish Franciscan church and its vicinity according to a veduta by Folpert van Ouden-Allen of 1685 (SK).

from Poděbrady, and ten rafts of firewood from the building office (*Bauamt*), everything *"ohne einzige Consequenz,"* that is, without the right to receive the same allowance the following year. Fortunately, they did, but it was only a reprieve before the final refusal. In March 1705, the Accounting Department of the Royal Bohemian Chamber (*Cammer-Buchhalterey*) announced that "all Chamber estates have been leased, and, therefore, they can no longer supply provisions, but during the current complete exhaustion of the Revenue Office, it is hardly possible to buy provisions from the lessees." This is also the last document on this matter it has been possible to find.[32]

Before the end of the seventeenth century, they were helped by the last will of their former benefactress, Maria Mechtilde de Dieten. Besides the mentioned bequest to the Irish Franciscans, she left half of her fortune to her grandson, Franz Anton of Billau; however, if he should die before he came of

---

32   NA, NM, K2/H1.

age, the money would go to the Irish Franciscans. The child died of the plague in 1680, but the Franciscans only asked for the bequest in 1692, evidently after the death of his mother, Anna Franziska. In May of that year, Ondřej Frischmann, a sworn provincial barrister, whom Anna Franziska of Billau had named as her heir, declared that he knew of the conditions attached to the will and that he was not demanding any of the property originally intended for Franz Anton. The Revenue Office then calculated the amount for the Irish Franciscans at 6,001 florins 52 kreutzer; the annual allowance was supposed to be 600 florins, but it was often not even as much as this. By the end of 1699, a total of 4,410 florins had been paid. The final request for a withdrawal from the bequest was in May 1702 (Fig. 24).[33]

Decidedly more bizarre was the request made in 1699. Václav Vojtěch, Count of Šternberk, was probably behind this affair. That is, the Irish Franciscans were requesting an unpaid debt which the builder Jean Baptiste Mathey owed the Bohemian Chamber for the construction of the Imperial Riding School and which had been estimated at 400 florins. Because Mathey left for France without the sovereign's permission, after his death his estate went by default to the Treasury and was later given by the sovereign to Václav Vojtěch, Count of Šternberk, who agreed with his heir, Prudentius Renaut de Bisón, that the outstanding debt would be transferred to the Irish Franciscans. In the end, the result of the pile of handwritten papers was evidently the recommendation that the Irish Franciscans appeal to the heir. In the absence of any confirmation that they drew on the money, it is unlikely that they succeeded in obtaining any of it.[34]

It is no surprise that the Irish Franciscans resorted to such measures. Admittedly, we cannot forget the income the college had from alms gathering, from Mass offerings, payments for funerals and so on, but the time of generous single gifts, which had for a number of years represented the assurance of the college's existence or the opportunity to undertake extensive construction, clearly came to an end for the Irish Franciscans towards the end of the seventeenth century and it might have been difficult to find a benefactor who did not want his money used for a specific purpose, as the Count of Šternberk had in the building of the library. The unfinished Chapel of All the Faithful Departed, as Hammerschmid informs us, was also evidence of a definite waning of interest. The astounding sums of the foundation period and the one immediately afterwards, it must be admitted, sometimes existed only on paper, as we have seen, or they were swallowed up by the construction of the college and the church, but fifty years later, the friars no longer found fellow countrymen and patrons in Central Europe who might be willing in

---

33   Ibid., K2/H1/1/10.
34   Ibid., K2/H1/1/7.

this way to ease their consciences a little. The generosity of the Emperors, too, had its limits. And at the beginning of the seventeenth century, when the Irish Franciscan province had to face escalating persecution in Ireland and the continental friaries were overcrowded after the exodus of many friars from their home country, it was no small wonder that the Prague college asked the Chancellery at Court to confirm its old privileges, including being able to seek alms during Advent and on festivals. State authorities exempted the Prague friary from paying fees for the confirmation that was issued on 1 September 1718.[35]

SAPIENTIA AEDIFICAVIT SIBI DOMUM[36]

Even in this period, however, the Irish college still, to a certain degree, retained the goodwill of its patrons. If we start with demonstrable expressions of such goodwill, besides Count Sporck, the Šternberk family remained faithful to the Irish. As mentioned above, they contributed to the decoration of the church and Anthony Bruodin dedicated his *Propugnaculum* as a New Year gift for 1699 to the brothers Václav Vojtěch, Jan Norbert and Ignác Karel. From the Irish side, the Šternberk family gained the attention not only of friars; in 1697, William MacNeven O'Kelly, Baron of Aughrim, dedicated his eulogy *Templum gloriae in monte stellari extructum* to this family.[37]

Jan Norbert died as early as 1679, and Ignác Karel in 1700. Among other things, Ignác Karel left a large and famous library, probably kept originally at the Šternberk chateau, Zelená Hora (Fig. 25). Because he had no descendants, the inheritance was divided equally between his older brother, Václav Vojtěch, and his nephew, Jan Josef, but the latter did not long outlive his uncle, dying tragically the same year. His part of the library was intended for Prague University, but the bequest was not realised and the library remained the property of Václav Vojtěch[38] who attained high provincial office and was, at the same time, an influential "spiritual father" or officially apostolic syndic

35   Jan Kahuda, "Panovnické konfirmace priviliegií českých klášterů v 18. století" [Royal Confirmations of Privileges of Bohemian Religious Institutes in the Eighteenth Century], *Paginae historiae* 9 (2001): 55.

36   "Wisdom has built her house."

37   *Templum gloriae in monte stellari extructum et ... familiae Sternbergicae consecratum...*, Neo-Pragae 1697.

38   Petr Mašek, "Příspěvky k dějinám zámeckých knihoven západních Čech (Chodová Planá, Lázeň, Merklín, Poběžovice, Zelená Hora)" [Contributions to the History of the Manorial Libraries of Western Bohemia (Chodová Planá, Lázeň, Merklín, Poběžovice, Zelená Hora)], *Sborník archivních prací* 41.2 (1991): 511–536, on the Šternberk library mainly pp. 530–532. Zdeněk Tobolka, *Národní a universitní knihovna v Praze, její vznik a vývoj I* [*The National and University Library in Prague, its Foundation and Development I*], (Praha: SPN, 1959) 108–112 (ibid., also a list of the shelf marks of the Šternberk books in the National Library).

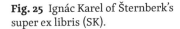

Fig. 25 Ignác Karel of Šternberk's super ex libris (SK).

of the College of the Immaculate Conception of the Virgin Mary. He decided that the inherited books would be used for the benefit of the friars.

The plan was rather generous and, as early as March 1701, the first stone was laid for the construction of a new library. Over the next few years, the count paid the bills for the building work; in 1706, Baltazar Fischer from Prague received 200 florins for joinery in the library, another 78 florins for unspecified expenditure was paid to the guardian, Francis More, and 125 florins to Antonio Lurago for building alterations.[39]

In his will of 1708, Václav Vojtěch stipulated that the entire library of the deceased Ignác Karel should be deposited in the Irish Franciscan college and that it should be accessible to the public (*ad usum publicum*). From his inheritance, 150 florins were spent each year to pay two librarians and on essential expenditure and a further 150 florins from Maria Theresia, the then nine-year-old daughter of Jan Josef, to whom he was guardian. The execution of the will, however, gradually ran into difficulties on both sides. Maria Theresia, whose married name was Countess Paar, refused to pay the sum of 150 florins which Václav Vojtěch had left for her to pay *"sine jure"* in his last

---

39 Alžběta Birnbaumová, "Příspěvky k dějinám umění XVII. stol. z archivu Šternbersko-Man-derscheidského" [Contributions to the History of the Art of the Seventeenth Century from the Šternberk-Manderscheid Archive], PA 34 (1925): 492–497; on the library of the Irish Franciscans mainly pp. 496–497.

will. His heir, František Leopold, Count of Šternberk, referred to the poor
state of the inheritance, from which, once all outstanding debts had been
settled, it was not actually possible to pay the Irish Franciscans the promised
sum. The friars evidently began to use the space intended for the library for
other purposes, so they found it difficult to clear out "the best part of the
college" and, moreover, under conditions of reclusion. Besides this, the university remembered its rights. In 1724, therefore, František Leopold came to
an arrangement with the Irish Franciscans in which they stated the aforesaid
impediments and the fact that Václav Vojtěch could not freely dispose of half
of the library, and they decided on the following: half of the library would
be transferred to the Carolinum so that it could be used by the Faculties of
Law and Medicine and the other half would remain with the library of the
Irish Franciscans, but no longer with the condition that it be accessible to
the public. If the library could not be divided in half, the deficiency would
be compensated for in cash. The Count of Šternberk permitted the friars to
freely use the building which had been constructed at his expense for their
needs, but with the express condition that the Šternberk coat-of-arms should
be placed in commemoration on the outside, which indeed happened.[40] With
this agreement, all responsibilities imposed by Václav Vojtěch on Countess
Paar were rescinded.[41] It seems probable that in reality the library remained
with the Count of Šternberk until 1724. Two years later, selected books were
officially handed over to the university, and it is clear that it was not until
representatives of the university had indicated which books they wished to
take that the Irish Franciscans could be given the remainder.

The Irish Franciscans' own library, however, came into being together
with the college; its foundation was one of the first concerns of the friars
after they arrived in Prague.[42] This is what Patrick Fleming told Robert Rochford, lector in philosophy at the Louvain college, in April 1631.[43] Despite this, it
was possible to find some interesting works in Prague itself, as evidenced by
two volumes gained from the property of the Mělník dean, Jan Václav Tlappa
of Wainberg – an edition of the medical writings of Constantinus Africanus

---

40 This coat-of-arms on the façade facing the current square, náměstí Republiky, is clearly visible
    on the engraving of the coronation procession of Leopold II. See Johann Debrois, *Urkunde über
    die vollzogene Krönung seiner Majestät des Königs von Böhmen Leopold des Zweiten und ihrer Majestät
    der Gemahlin des Königs Maria Louise, gebornen Infantinn von Spanien* (Prag: n.p., 1818) picture
    no. 44. At that time, the college had been dissolved but the building had not yet undergone
    structural alterations.

41 The text of the agreement is printed in Raphael Ungar ed., *Bohuslai Balbini E S. I. Bohemia docta,
    opus posthumum editum, Pars III.* (Praha: Kolej sv. Benedikta, 1780) 73–78.

42 The informative article was devoted to the library of the college of Irish Franciscans by Kevin
    McGrath, Kevin MacGrath, "The Irish Franciscan Library at Prague," *Franciscan College Annual
    1951,* (Multyfarnham 1951): 29–33.

43 See the section *Patrick Fleming and his death,* note no. 28 in Chapter 2.

from 1536, which were registered in the college library in 1643; and somewhat later, with Anthony Farrell as intermediary, the Lyon edition of the writings of St. Jerome from 1518 was added.[44] This second acquisition also includes the Scotist theological writings of the Franciscan Stephan Brulefer published in Basel in 1501, which, with James Cavell as intermediary, were given by the Kutná Hora archdean, Matouš Černovský, together with a volume of Pietro Tartareto's commentaries on Aristotle and Petrus Hispanus (later Pope John XXI) in the Paris edition of 1514.[45] These works can also be found in a 1503 Lyon edition of Tartareto, which is provenanced by a college note from 1632.[46] More detailed information about the Strahov library book collection which has become available since the publication of the present volume in Czech allows us to formulate a hypothesis that the Irish Franciscans obtained basic theological works, editions of Church Fathers as well as other authors, as donations only in Prague, often from priests. Many of these donated books were incunabula or post-incunabula. It is possible to presume that the donors recorded these books as valuable because of their antiquity but, at the same time, they did not use them since they had modern editions at hand. It is evident from the Flemish translation of the work by St. Bonaventure, *Speculum disciplinae ad novitios*, published in Antwerp in 1605 by the Plantin printing house,[47] that some of the books were brought by the friars.

The question of the extent and content of the library before the Šternberk acquisition is now in fact unanswerable. A single catalogue has been preserved, which records the contents only after the settlement with the Šternberk family in the 1720s. The entire stock of the library, however, has not been preserved, having been scattered after the dissolution of the college. It is impossible to untangle, even in part, the contents of the Šternberk and Franciscan libraries from other sources. According to the information in the literature, the Šternberk library contained 2,500 books and more than ten manuscripts.[48] In the Strahov library, there is preserved a catalogue

---

44 *Summi in omni philosophia ... Constantini Africani medici operum reliqua ... Basileae 1536*, now SK, CR I 20. *Epistole sancti Hieronymi ... Lugduni 1518*, SK, BH III 28; in this volume, there is a Czech note by the imprint about his age, dated 1646. It is doubtful that anybody in the college would have used Czech here. The Irish Franciscans had another Lyon edition of St. Jerome, *Epistole sancti Hieronymi ... Lugduni 1513*, now in SK, BE V 31.

45 *Excellentissimi ... Stephani Brulefer ... reportata ... Basileae 1501*, SK, BE VI 120. *Commentarii Petri tatareti in libros philosophie naturalis et metaphysice Aristotelis ... Expositio magistri Petri Tatareti super textu logices Aristotelis ... Parrhisiis 1514. Expositio magistri Petri Tatareti in summulas Petri Hispani ...* Today SK, ED III 59.

46 *Clarissima singularisque totius philosophie necnon methaphisice Aristotelis magistri Petri Tatareti expositio*, [Lyon] 1503, SK, JB III 36. The work was obtained thanks to James Buttler. See the section *The Irish Franciscans and soldiers*.

47 *Spieghel der goeder manieren...*, Antwerpen 1605, SK, BD II 61.

48 Tobolka, *Národní a universitní knihovna v Praze*, 110. The estimate is based on the works in the National Library identified as originating from Šternberk.

of works of mathematics, astronomy, geography, military science and the occult sciences in the library of Ignác Karel, Count Šternberk, which was compiled at the beginning of the 1680s. The catalogue containing 218 works is composed in part of books filed under location number *D* and in part from an alphabetical inventory of these books. The question is whether there were any more catalogues based on subject or location in the library.[49]

We have no intention of attempting a reconstruction of the Franciscans' library here, although it would be an interesting task, only to summarise what is possible to determine with relatively superficial research. Anyone who embarks on this painstaking operation, whose results are, as a rule, not too appealing to the reader, is obliged, if not in possession of encyclopaedic knowledge, to combine the statistical viewpoint, aiming at the identification of as many represented authors as possible, with research aimed at known fields of literary creation. This, with the best will in the world, may lead to unique (even by their representation in the library) works from fields the researcher is not familiar with being overlooked. The work is also made more difficult by the way it is recorded in the catalogue, being limited to the name of the author and, expressed euphemistically, the Latinised term. We therefore concentrated primarily on the basic specification of the theological works in the library, especially those by Scotist authors and by friars working in the college. Secondly, we attempted to complete the cataloguing of the works connected with Ireland, England and Scotland, which was an unmistakably unique collection in Prague, and, thirdly, we noted the occurrence of works in Czech – that is, to what extent the library was open to Czech literary production. With the first two groups, we can legitimately presume that the books were directly acquired by members of the community, while with the third group it is possible that they were partly accessions from the Šternberk library. In the first group, we deliberately almost entirely omit older authors and concentrate on theology from the sixteenth century onwards. It is thus possible to verify how contemporary schools and tendencies were represented in the library.

The catalogue of the college library is now in the National Library in Prague.[50] It was begun by Patrick Hackett in August 1752.[51] The books are

---

49   Bohumil Ryba, *Soupis rukopisů Strahovské knihovny. Díl IV* [*An Inventory of the Manuscripts of the Strahov Library. Vol. IV*] (Praha: Památník národního písemnictví, 1970) no. 2011, MS DH V 27. It is not possible to agree entirely with the explanation which Ryba gives to confirm his statement that entries were made in the catalogue after von Šternberk's death. He based it on the ephemera from 1684 to 1712, but ephemera for a certain period were usually published in advance so their year of completion might not automatically also mean the year of publication.

50   NK, MS IX I 2. See Josef Truhlář, *Catalogus codicum manu scriptorum latinorum qui in c.r. Bibliotheca publica atque universitatis Pragensis asservantur.* Vol. 2 (Praha: Regia societas scientiarum Bohemica, 1906) 30.

51   Truhlář read the name incorrectly as Hackell.

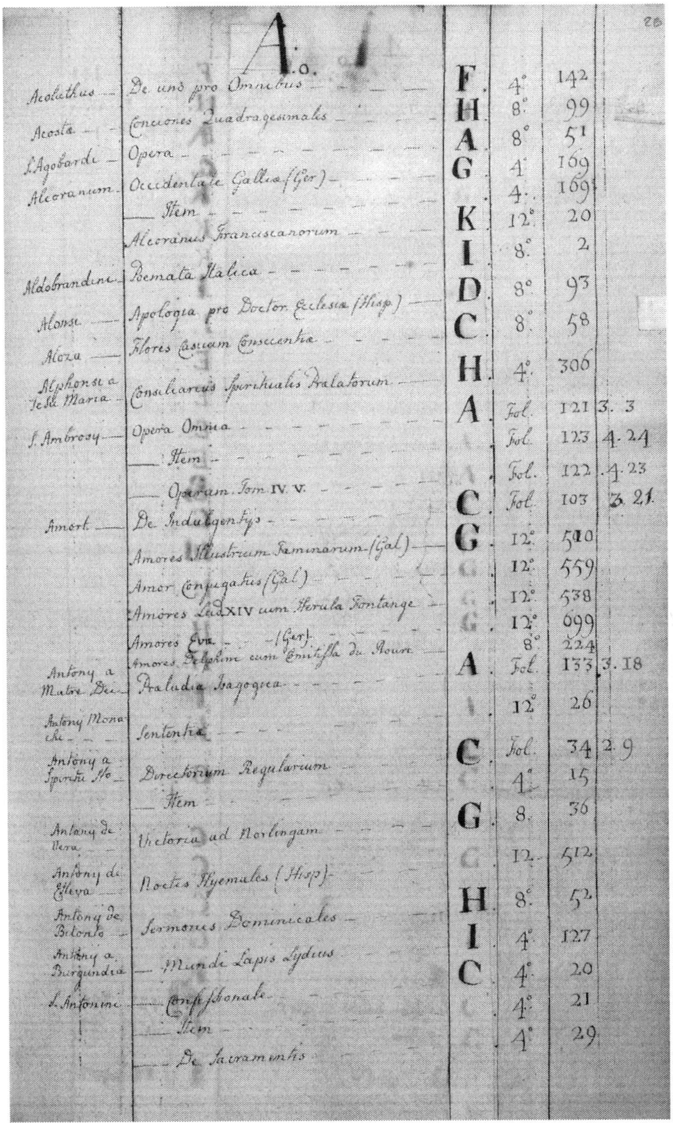
A.o.
Acoluthus — De uno pro Omnibus — F. 4° 142
Acosta — Conciones Quadragesimales — H. 8° 99
S. Agobardi — Opera — A. 8° 51
Alcoranum — Occidentale Galliae (Ger) — G. 4° 169
— Item — 4. 169
Alcoranus Franciscanorum — K. 12° 20
I. 8° 2
Aldobrandini — Poemata Italica — D. 8° 93
Alonsi — Apologia pro Doctor. Ecclesiae (Hisp.) — C. 8° 58
Aloza — Flores Casuum Conscientiae — H. 4° 306
Alphonsi a Jesu Maria — Consiliarius Spiritualis Praelatorum — A. Fol. 121 3. 3
S. Ambrosy — Opera Omnia — Fol. 123 4. 24
— Item — Fol. 122 4. 23
— Operum Tom IV. V. — C. Fol. 103 3. 21
Amort — De Indulgentiis — G. 12° 510
Amores Illustrium Faeminarum (Gal) — 12° 559
Amor Conjugatus (Gal) — 12° 538
Amores Lud. XIV cum Herula Fontange — 12° 699
Amores Eva — (Ger) — 8° 224
Amores Delphini cum Comitissa du Roure — A. Fol. 133 3. 18
Antony a Matre Dei — Praeludia Isagogica — 12° 26
Antony Monachi — Sententia — C. Fol. 34 2. 9
Antony a Spiritu S.to — Directorium Regularium — 4° 15
— Item — G. 8. 36
Antony de Vera — Victoria ad Norlingam — 12. 512
Antony de Esleva — Noctes Hyemales (Hisp) — H. 8° 52
Antony de Bitonto — Sermones Dominicales — I. 4° 127
Antony a Burgundia — Mundi Lapis Lydius — C. 4° 20
S. Antonini — Confessionale — 4° 21
— Item — 4° 29
— De Sacramentis

Fig. 26 A page from the catalogue of the library in the Irish Franciscan college in Prague, post 1752 (NK).

arranged alphabetically according to author (Fig. 26). The title is always in Latin. It is always shown in its Latinised version if the book was in another language and a note of the language is added in brackets. This admittedly means that, in a number of instances, there is a brief characterisation of the contents rather than the title. This is true to an even greater extent with the anonymous works. The beginnings of the alphabetical sections (under each letter, though it is never arranged according to the second letter but the next vowel, for example, "Anselmus" precedes "Adrichomia") are all in one handwriting (evidently Hackett's), and then new works have been added by other hands. A rough calculation shows that there are about ten thousand books in the catalogue. The books are recorded as follows: author's name (if shown in the book); title; manuscripts rarely had a specification of the type of document (*Ms*); and the shelf mark thus – capital letter + format + Arabic numeral (for example, E 4° 176). The final column contains numerical entries, admittedly only for certain books, and we have been unable to determine exactly what purpose these served.

We can consider the Bible as the absolute basis of the library of a religious institution (as well as the directly connected biblical concordances and commentaries), along with books required for the celebration of the liturgy, constituent documents of the order (the Rule, interpretations and commentaries on the Rule, statutes and so on) and the theological writings of the order's authors and schools of thought. In the extensive collection of bibles, with practically indistinguishable examples, identification is impossible, with perhaps the exception of the folio New Testament in Czech, which we can guess may be the first volume of the St. Wenceslas Bible (*Svatováclavská bible*), and the Gospels in Greek, Czech, German and Latin may be *Evangelia et epistolae* published in Bremen in 1616.[52] A number of bibles were in English. Of the later commentaries, we could name the standard work by Cornelius a Lapide, the commentary by Alfonso Salmerón or the one by the Carmelite, Joannes de Sylveira. Books used in the liturgy understandably did not belong to the library or the catalogue, but were in the hands of the friars. So it can come as no surprise that we can only find in the catalogue what was in some way superfluous, whether out-of-date and unusable in terms of Church precepts, or belonging to another order or Church province or rarely used locally for language or other reasons. Among the few surviving examples of breviaries are a Roman one and a Benedictine one, and, preserved in the Strahov library from the Irish Franciscan collection, there is a breviary from the Salzburg archdiocese, printed in Venice in 1518.[53] There is also a *Caeremoniale*

---

52   In SK there have been preserved a Latin bible printed in 1510 by Jacques Mareschal in Lyon (BZ VIII 16), the third part (Prophets) of the Greek-Latin bible published in Basel by Nicolaus Brilynger 1500 (BB VIII 15, the original shelf mark in the Irish Franciscan library was K 8° 101), a Latin bible printed by George Gruppenbach in Tübingen in 1606 (BY V 2; the original shelf mark in the Irish Franciscan library was A fol. 8) and a Latin edition of several Books of the Old Testament without the place and date of publication from the turn of the sixteenth and seventeenth centuries (possibly part of a multi-volume bible; BB IX 38). After the dissolution of the college, the Greek-Latin New Testament published in Lyon in 1600 appeared in the Franciscans' library in Dačice. Vladislav Dokoupil, *Dějiny moravských klášterních knihoven* [*The History of Moravian Monastery Libraries*] (Brno: Musejní spolek; Universitní knihovna, 1972) 274. *Euangelia et epistolae ... Bremae 1616*, see Zdeněk Václav Tobolka and František Horák eds., *Knihopis českých a slovenských tisku od doby nejstarší až do konce XVIII. století* (Praha: Komise pro knihopisný soupis českých a slovenských tisků, 1925–1967), no. 2280. Further quoted as *Knihopis* [*A Bibliography*] plus number of entry.

53   *Breviarium secundum ritum almae ecclesiae Saltzburgensis...*, Venetiis 1518, SK, ACh X 23–24.

missalis in Spanish, wedding ceremonies in French, several *caeremoniale epis-coporum* and *caeremoniale* of the Carmelites and Barnabites, then the *Graduale romanum* and *Martyrologium romanum*. One example of martyrology, Czech and understandably Franciscan, is shown, but in a different place in the catalogue under the author Arthur Du Monstier. There is also an unspecified Olomouc missal. With the basic documents of the order, the same situation occurred as with the liturgical books; there was good reason for them not to be in the library. It was a different case with the collected works of the saints and distinguished men of the Order of Friars Minor: examples include the collected writings of St. Francis of Assisi (including the Rule, his life and a volume entitled *Opuscula Varia*) and St. Bonaventure,[54] an unspecified work by St. Anthony of Padua or the collected writings and sermons of St. Bernardine of Siena.[55] Of the older distinguished Church authors, the library contained a considerable number of works by St. Augustine (the collected twelve-volume edition and a number of other individual titles, in German and French as well), the collected edition of the writings of St. Albert the Great, St. Anselm, St. Bernard of Clairvaux, St. Cyprian (with a commentary by Erasmus of Rotterdam), St. Cyril of Alexandria, St. John Chrysostom, St. Gregory the Great and others.

For the Franciscan library, the primary theological texts were the writings of John Duns Scotus. Although even in this case we cannot identify the particular edition, we can confidently assume that it was the edition published by Luke Wadding. Besides the works by Wadding himself, the author of *Annales*, the magnificent work on the history of the Franciscan Order, and his colleague John Punch (often called Poncius in the literature), two copies of whose extensive philosophical and theological commentaries on Scotus were owned by the college, Wadding's nephew, Bonaventure Baron, is also to be found there. (Wadding's edition of works by St. Francis of Assisi entitled *Opuscula* was in the library.) Although we cannot be certain, hiding under the titles *De Deo Trino* and *De angelis* are most probably Scotist theological tracts first published in Lyon in 1668, or in Florence in 1676, as the case may be; under the title *Cursus philosophicus* is a three-volume work published in Cologne in 1664; and shown as *Annales ordinis Sanctissimae trinitatis* is the first volume (no further ones were published) of a history of the Order of the Holy Trinity, published in Rome in 1684.[56] A digest in two volumes of Wadding's *Annales*

---

54 In the library were his complete works and, in particular, a number of editions of his *Speculum disciplinae ad novitios* in various European languages.

55 In SK is preserved a general index to the work of St. Bonaventure by Bartholomaeus de Barberiis *Tabula seu index generalis...*, Lugduni 1681, BG III 46.

56 Benignus Millett, *The Irish Franciscans 1651–1665* (Rome: Gregorian University Press, 1964) 474–475 and 469–473. Antonín Podlaha ed., *Český slovník bohovědný I* [*The Czech Dictionary of Theology I*] (Praha: Cyrillo-Methodějská knihtiskárna and V. Kotrba, 1912) 932.

was published by Francis Harold, who was also in Prague, and this work, too, was owned by the library. Other students at the college were Francis Bermingham and the above-mentioned Bonaventure O'Connor Kerry, who wrote, among other things, the apologetical work *Lumen orthodoxum*.[57] One of the Louvain authors in the library was, understandably, John Colgan, who had been in charge of the demanding project, *Acta sanctorum Hiberniae*. We do not know whether the library had, in particular, a rare print of the text on St. Patrick's Purgatory, which Andrew MacVeigh (Vitalis) had drawn up in 1652 in a revised form from another of Colgan's works, *Trias Thaumaturga*. It is not to be found in the catalogue, but, nevertheless, it is notable that a copy was owned by the library of the Franciscan friary in Votice.[58] Raymond Caron, friend and supporter of Peter Walsh, was represented here by *Apostolatus missionarium*, *Controversiae generales fidei* and other minor works.

Based on the catalogue, traces of the literary activity of members of the college are not very significant, but there is an explanation for this. The annual printed theses were regarded more as consumer goods and only some of them sometimes found their way into the library and were recorded in the catalogue. Perhaps the most important work by an Irishman in Prague was *Collectanea sacra* by Patrick Fleming, and they naturally possessed the writings of Anthony Bruodin, including the polemic with Thomas Carve, although the writer was a member of the Bohemian Franciscan province for most of his life. The books in the catalogue which originated in teaching were primarily the work of James Griffin. There were also many copies of Anthony Murphy's *Theologia dogmatica*, published in Prague in the mid-1750s.

Among the remaining contemporary Scotists in the catalogue are: John Bosco (1613-1684), a member of the Franciscan branch of Recollects and teacher at Louvain; the Minorites, Jean Gabriel Boyvin (died c.1680), who taught in the order's schools, and Bartholomeus Mastrius (1602-1673); the Franciscan Francis Lychet; Claude Frassen (1620-1711), whose first entry in the catalogue is *Disquisitiones biblicae*, then later *Scotus academicus*, one of the main works of the Scotist school; Philip Faber (died 1630). It is impossible to determine from how they were recorded whether the books by Mastrius in the library were either in various editions or multiple copies of one edition. Local authors are represented by Vilém Antonín Brouček, whose *Domus sapientiae* was the first Scotist philosophical handbook to be printed in Bohemia; the philosophical, theological and historical works of the most significant scholar of the Bohemian Franciscan province, Bernard Sannig; and the complete works of Anthony Bruodin. Another Scotist author connected with the

---

57 Millett, *The Irish Franciscans*, 478–479.
58 Millett, *The Irish Franciscans*, 488. *Tractatulus de purgatorio S. Patricii...*, Venetiis 1652. Votice's copy is now in SK, F II 360.

Bohemian Franciscan province was Amandus Hermann, whose *Ethica sacra* (published in Würzburg in 1698) and *Tractatus theologici in sententiarum libros Joannis Dunsii Scoti* (Cologne, 1690) are recorded in the catalogue. The author, however, is shown for the first time in the catalogue as "Amandus" and then other works are shown, such as *Capistranus triumphans*, under "Hermann" Other Franciscan theologians are to be found, such as Patrick Sporer or Francis Henno (like Mastrius, in various editions or multiple copies of the same one).

To represent Scotus appropriately, the library included Thomas Aquinas, whose extensive writings occupied many lines of the catalogue. Unfortunately, in this case as well, it is impossible to provide even an approximate identification, as with the Thomists of the Dominican Order (and not only them); we can mention individual authors but we cannot find specific editions of their works at all.[59] Jesuit authors, too, make up an extensive entry in the catalogue.[60] Roderigo Arriaga, who served in Prague, was represented in the library by *Cursus philosophicus* and *Disputationes theologicae in Summam D. Thomae*, but it is not possible to determine which editions. We could also mention the commentaries on Aristotle from the Jesuit college in Coimbra. Works by Carmelites are also represented: apart from the above-mentioned Sylveira, there were Philippus a S. Trinitate, Dominicus a S. Trinitate, Gabriel a S. Vincentio, Didacus a S. Antonio, Joannes a Jesu Maria and again commentaries on Aristotle, this time by Carmelite scholars from the college at Alcalá.

The Irish evidently obtained the basic modern hagiographical work of the Catholic Church, *Acta Sanctorum*, over a period of time: they had the volumes for April of the Antwerp edition and in part those for June and July, but they obtained the Venice edition (it began to appear in 1734) up to September; the Antwerp September volumes appeared in the middle of the seventeenth century. Individual volumes can, however, be found under author. Besides these, they had the hagiographies by Laurentius Surius. Contemporary Church histories appear in the catalogue, such as the notable work by Caesar Baronius, and those by Alexander de Natalis, Antoine Godeau and Claude

59 Here we can find Pedro de Godoy, Domingo de Salazar and Vincent de Contenson, Antoine Goudin, Bartolomé de Medina, Marco Antonio de Serra, one of the last great commentators on Thomas Aquinas, Joannes a S. Thoma, and a representative of strict Thomism, Jean Gonet.

60 Here we can find Francisco Suárez, Théophile Raynaud, Martin de Esparza, Leonard Lessius, Luis de Molina, a leading representative of Spanish scholasticism, Gabriel Vásquez, the moralists Enrique Henríquez, Tirso Gonzáles de Santall, Paul Laymann, Tomás Sánches, Ildefonso de Peñafiel and Honoré Fabri, the preacher, Antonio Vieira and Gian Paolo Oliva (there are also his biblical commentaries), the historian, Pedro de Ribadeneira and the historian and humanist, Dionysius Petavius, and other popular authors such as Roberto Bellarmino, Luis La Puente (there were numerous copies of his *Meditationes* in the library, also in German, Italian and Czech), Juan Eusebius Nieremberg (the list of his works fills one and a half pages), Cristóbal de Vega or Franz Coster, and one Irishman, the author of a repeatedly republished practical handbook listed here as *Theologia tripartita polemica* by Richard Arsdekin.

Fleury. There are also numerous works by Louis Maimbourg, Jesuit Church historian and keen opponent of Jansenism.[61] We do not intend to detail the occurrence of authors popular at the time; it may suffice to mention Cardinal Giovanni Bona or the popular moralist Hermann Busenbaum. In contrast, a fixed star in the sky of ascetic literature is *The Imitation of Christ* by Thomas à Kempis, still read many centuries later, and which was in the library in Latin as well as German, French and Spanish.

However, even theologians whose teachings the Church had not approved found their way into the library. There were numerous works by Cornelius Jansen; in the catalogue, his commentaries on the Pentateuch appear six times, those on the Gospels five times and his *Augustinus* once. It is worth mentioning here the suspicion Malachy Fallon aroused with his lectures and his relatively close contacts with Louvain. Among other Jansenist theologians was Louis Ellies du Pin (the library contained several volumes of his *Bibliothecae auctorum ecclesiasticorum*), but there are also opponents of Jansenism, provided the Tournelius shown in the catalogue is in fact Honoré de Tournély. There is also one work by Miguel de Molinos, one of the chief representatives of Quietism.[62]

To what extent were the past and present of the Irish Franciscans' distant homeland and England and Scotland reflected in the profile of the library? Political and historical works connected with the islands are well represented in the catalogue, often in editions in German or French. With anonymous works, it is impossible to recognise from the greatly simplified titles (*Relatio...* or *Historia...*) which language it was. There were even surprises: a volume of Spanish romances from the sixteenth century was hidden under the title *Historia Hispanica*. Anonymous biographies of English sovereigns are quite common. While one copy of the topographical work on Great Britain by William Camden is preserved in the Strahov library,[63] elsewhere, with a title such as *Antiquitates Universitatis Oxoniensis*, we can only guess that it was by Camden. Some copies have been preserved in the National Library in Prague, including Maurice Conry's *Threnodia hiberno-catholicae* on the persecution of Catholics in Ireland, which he published under the pseudonym of

---

61   Among works describing more recent Church history, there was, for example, Pallavicino's history of the Council of Trent, but this author was also represented by other works.

62   For example, a copy of *Guida spirituale, che di sinuolge l'anima, e la conduce per l'interior camino ...*, Roma 1677, now in NK in Prague. However, the copy was originally in the Šternberk library.

63   *Britannia, sive florentissimorum regnorum Angliae, Scotiae, Hiberniae ... descriptio*, Amstelredami 1617, SK, AQ XVII 34. According to the provenance inscriptions on the title page, it was obtained by Father Bernard O'Neill for Brother (*frater*) Anthony Donnelly in 1660, the same year that it was appropriated (*applicatur*) by the college. In the part dedicated to Ireland, there are some marginal notes in Latin, sometimes pointing out the errors of the author; especially telling is a note in the part *Angli in Hibernia: malum omen proh dolor.*

Morison.[64] There was also MacMahon's *Jus primatiale Armacanum*, which was obtained for the library by the guardian, William Hogan, in 1739, along with Richard Cox's *Hibernia anglicana: or, The History of Ireland* from 1689.[65] Carve's works, so criticised by Bruodin, are there. In the "English circle" could be included the collection of poetry by Elizabeth Jane Weston, who lived and died in Prague. While in these cases we mainly have the titles of the works, although the copies have been lost, sometimes it is the other way round. There are no doubt books without the mark of provenance of the college library which clearly arrived in Prague through the Irish Franciscans; for example, a basic Irish language textbook in English, published in 1728 in Louvain, which originally belonged to Father Thomas Mahon and later became the property of Brother Terence Maguire.[66]

Today, thanks to rapidly developing Internet resources, we can trace more books than was possible with the Czech edition just over a decade ago. The library collection included a general edition of *The Present State of England* by Edward Chamberlayn. Hugh MacCurtin was the author of *The Elements of the Irish Language* alluded to above and he also wrote *A brief discourse in vindication of the antiquity of Ireland collected out of many authentic Irish histories and chronicles*. A book described in the library catalogue as *Monasticon Hibernicum anglice* could perhaps be identified as John Weever's *Ancient funerall monuments within the united monarchie of Great Britaine, Ireland and the islands adiacent, with the dissolued monasteries therein contained*, the first edition of which was released in London in 1631. *Florum Historiae Ecclesiasticae gentis Anglorum libri septem* was written by Richard Smith, titular bishop of Chalcedon and, from 1625, vicar apostolic of England, Wales and Scotland. A history of English monasteries of Benedictines, Cistercians, and Carthusians by William Dugdale and Roger Dodsworth was published under the title *Monasticon Anglicanum* in the years 1655 to 1673. The volume registered as *Errington Missionarium* probably referred to the life and work of Catholic priest William Errington. It was obviously entered in the catalogue subsequently because Errington's mission in England began in 1748 and did not achieve anything important until 1763.

The Irish did not limit themselves to imported literature. From the catalogue it is clear that they also paid attention to the book production of the

---

64   See note no. 25 in Chapter 3. *Threnodia hiberno-catholica sive planctus…*, Oeniponti 1659, now in NK, 21 J 214.

65   *Jus primatiale Armacanum … S.l.* 1728, now in NK, 24 J 51, *Hibernia anglicana: or, The History of Ireland…*, London 1689, NK, 22 B 179.

66   H. MacCurtin, *The Elements of the Irish Language…*, Lovain 1728, SK, AC XI 4. A similar case is undoubtedly a book by Edmund Dickinson *Physica vetus et vera sive tractatus de naturali veritate Hexaemeri Mosaici…*, Hamburgi 1705, which Francis Fleming obtained for himself in 1724, now in SK, BC IX 31.

Bohemian Crown Lands, and not only works in Latin and German, languages accessible to them, or those, such as the above-mentioned authors of philosophical and theological writings, whose subjects were of interest to them, but also works in Czech. We naturally need to ask to what extent this was a case of planned purchasing and to what extent they were, for example, gifts or, as we have shown, the Šternberk acquisition.[67] In formulating a hypothesis, caution is called for, although it would be tempting to prove from the stock of the library that the community was not so isolated in the Czech environment, that its members were interested in finding out about the country they were in, or even, in the case of Czech writings, some of them, to a certain extent at least, mastered Czech. Contemporary authors, especially those who had something to do with the college, the archiepiscopal seminary or the Franciscan Order as such, may have dedicated one or more copies of their work to the library.

More precise specification is, however, impossible, especially in relation to works published more than once. With Bohuslav Balbín, we find ourselves puzzled as to whether it is his historical work; that is, we can find three copies of a book entitled *Historiae Bohemiae*, one of just *Historiae*, two of *Epitome ejus* (meaning *historiae*), one of *Miscellanea Bohemia* and, surprisingly, one of the precisely specified sixth book of the ten-part *Miscellanea* (on the Prague Archbishopric). In any case, however, the library of the Irish Franciscans was well supplied with the works of the leading Bohemian Baroque historiographer. Besides these, we can also find all three of Balbín's works on the Marian places of pilgrimage (Svatá Hora – let us not forget the reverence for the Virgin Mary in the church of the Irish Franciscans, Varta and Tuřany), biographies of the first Archbishop of Prague, Arnošt of Pardubice, and the Jesuit Mikolaj Lenczycki as well as a book on the family of the Counts of Guttenstein.

Also notable is the appearance of the Czech-German language textbooks by Ondřej Klatovský of Dalmanhorst, which were published for an entire century from 1540 to 1641 entitled *Knížka v českém a německém jazyku složená, kterakby Čech německy a Němec česky čísti, psáti ... učiti se měl* [A book written in the Czech and German languages, how a Czech should read, write ... and study German and how a German should read, write ... and study Czech]. There were two copies in the library, with the author shown as "Andreas," together with the difficult to determine *Proverbia bohemica et latina*.[68] On the same subject, there is *Lima linguae Bohemicae tj. brus jazyka českého* (Prague 1667) by Jiří Konstanc and *Grammatica linguae bohemicae* by Václav Jan Rosa.[69]

---

67   Zdeněk Tobolka states that the Šternberk library contained very few works in Czech, but Petr Mašek proves that it is necessary to revise this opinion. See note no. 38.
68   *Knihopis*, nos. 3938–3949.
69   Ibid., nos. 4307 and 14884.

Less surprising is that, among the numerous works by the then popular Jesuit ascetic writer, Paul de Barry, is a Czech translation of *La Solitude de Philagie* (*Poušť Svatomila*), published in Prague in 1674 or a work by another French Jesuit often found in the library, Nicolas Caussin, given in the catalogue as *Dies christianus*, but translated into Czech as *Dobrý den* (*Good Day*) and published in 1660 in Litomyšl.[70] The Czech translation of a work by another very frequently published Baroque author, Jeremias Drechsel's *Zodiacus christianus*, found its way into the library. It is listed in the catalogue under the translator, Václav František Celestin of Blumenberk, and there are a number of Latin titles under Drechsel's own name.[71] Apart from this more or less ascetic literature, which provided the reader with spiritual guidance according to the conceptions of the time, the library also contained the writings of Ondřej Fromm, who, following his conversion to Catholicism, wrote a work entitled *Smysl a zdání sektářův a Luthera učení* [*Ideas and Understanding of Lutheran Sectarians*]. In view of the fact that Fromm later became a Premonstratensian in Strahov, the good relations between the Irish college and the members of Strahov monastery may have played a role in obtaining this book.[72] We could presume a similar connection with the writings of another Strahov Premonstratensian, Amandus Fridenfels, on St. Romedius and the chapel consecrated to him in the Thun chateau in Choltice[73] or the numerous publications by the Abbot of Strahov, Kaspar Questenberg, (for example, *Digitus Lazari, Ex annotationibus abbatis Strahoviensis*) and Hieronymus Hirnhaim (*De typho generis humani, Meditationes*). Another author who also had intensive relations with the college, as shown above, was Christian Pfaltz of Ostritz, whose works were plentiful in the library.

Much more interesting than this very often ordinary and in any case procurable religious literature are the writings of John Amos Comenius, not only *Janua linguarum*, which even came out in the Bohemian Crown Lands, but also *Unum necessarium* and, above all, the work shown in the catalogue as *Opera didactica* in folio form, which we can presume was the Amsterdam edition of 1657 to 1658. Among the rarer Czech publications was the one shown in the catalogue as *Joannes Aquensis: Vocabularium Lat.-Boh.*, which we can justifiably consider to be Guarinus's Latin-Czech dictionary, *Vokabulář Lactifer*, published by Jan Vodňanský in 1511 and printed in Plzeň by Mikuláš Bakalář.[74] Also noteworthy is the otherwise unspecified work by Michna in the catalogue called simply *Cantilenae bohemicae*.

---

70   Ibid., nos. 960 and 1499.
71   It was published three times in Czech, twice in Celestin's translation – 1674 and 1761. Ibid., nos. 2114 and 2115.
72   Ibid., no. 2604.
73   *Gloriosus sanctus Romedius ... nec non gloriosa domus comitum de Thun...*, Pragae 1699.
74   Ibid., no. 2801.

Various works connected in some way with Czech history can be found in the catalogue, beginning with Aeneas Silvius Piccolomini, additional works of whose appear here; *Historia Bohemica* by the Bishop of Olomouc and humanist, Johannes Dubravius, in various editions; *Ephemerides* by Prokop Lupáč of Hlaváčov; to "contemporary" authors such as the above-mentioned Bohuslav Balbín, Jiří Crugerius or Tomáš Pešina of Čechorod (his *Mars Moravicus* even appears twice). We cannot, however, claim to be able to deduce from the library's stock that the Franciscans were greatly interested in this subject: only a few individual volumes of Crugerius's *Sacri Pulveres* are to be found, Hájek and Beckovský are missing and Hammerschmid, for example, is represented only as a preacher. Of the historians of the Bohemian Franciscan province, whose works may have arrived in the library as gifts, we can also find, apart from Sannig, *Nucleus minoriticus* by Severin Vrbčanský (listed, however, under Severin) and multiple copies of minor works by Jindřich Labe, who wrote about the Franciscan friaries in Bechyně and Hájek.

With regard to the fates of some of the benefactors of the college, the first published response to the betrayal and death of Albrecht of Valdštejn, which came out under the title *Alberti Fridlandi perduellionis chaos*, is somehow indicative. Bohemian topography is represented by Merian's *Topographia Bohemiae, Moraviae et Silesiae* or by *Knížka obsahující v sobě kratičké poznamenání měst, zámkův...* [*A Booklet Containing Short Notes on Towns, Chateaux...*] by Václav Lebeda of Bedrštorf (again, it is impossible to be certain which edition it is). Among the professors of Prague University, the name Jan Marek Marci of Kronland occurs numerous times, and among the lawyers, Christoph Kyblin of Waffenburg, Johann Christoph Schambogen or Václav Xaver Neumann of Puchholtz. Understandably, there are also the works of more and less important Prague theologians (besides those already mentioned), largely from the archiepiscopal seminary and the university, but also from the Minorite college, Ferdinandeum, at the Friary of St. James.

As far as we can judge from the one preserved catalogue and several copies, the Šternberk bequest enriched the Irish Franciscan library with works on the natural sciences, militaria, politics and *belles lettres*. For a friary library, some of the titles are rather unusual.[75] There are the works of Jacob Bernoulli, Pierre Gassendi and others in the natural sciences.[76] Some of the books of this sort did not come from the Šternberk library: in 1707, when Anthony O'Neill was guardian, the Irish Franciscans obtained Ludolph van Ceulen's *De circulo*

---

75 For example, the Italian *Documenti militari del Colonello...*, Padua 1668 by Niccolo Volo, SK, AN III 43.

76 Jacob Bernoulli's *Conamen novi systematis cometarum*, Amsterdam 1682, SK, AG XIV 86, Pierre Gassendi's *Institutio astronomica*, Amsterdam 1680, now in SK, AG XVI 41. Other examples are provided by Bohumil Ryba in *Soupis rukopisů Strahovské knihovny*.

et adscriptis liber, published in Leyden in 1619; its previous owner had been a Doctor O'Farrell, probably the above-mentioned Bernard Farrell, a chantry priest in St. Vitus's.[77] The *belles lettres* the Irish Franciscans gained from the Šternberk library included *Les oeuvres de M. Francois Rabelais*, published in Amsterdam in 1675, the first volume of Racine's works and the 1661 *Poemes dramatiques* by Thomas Corneille, brother of the famous Pierre Corneille.[78] Religious literature also came from the Šternberk library, such as Minetti's meditations and spiritual exercises dedicated to members of the Italian congregation in Prague. On the other hand, far from all of the definitely secular subjects came to the Irish Franciscans only through the aristocratic library, such as de Strada's *Epitome thesauri antiquitatum*, which contained portraits of Roman emperors as they were preserved on old coins.[79]

From today's point of view, the rarest book in the Irish library was a unique Spanish one. There were otherwise plenty of Spanish works in the library.[80] In obtaining some of these books, it is probable that contacts with the order in Spain and the Spanish Netherlands played a role, but it is impossible now to be sure how the library acquired the most notable example of this group. In the Irish library under the vague designation *Historia Hispanica* is in fact a volume of *pliegos sueltos* (chapbooks), Spanish romances from the sixteenth century, many of them unique. The romances were in the form of pamphlets with only a few pages, sometimes decorated with woodcuts. Several similar volumes can be found in various distinguished European and American universities. It is possible to deduce, on the basis of older manuscript foliation, that the Prague volume is not quite complete. However, it does contain eighty-two printed items with more than four hundred romances, fifty-three of which are the only copies in the world. The majority of them were printed in the years 1540 to 1550 in Burgos, Sevilla, Medina del

---

77 Today SK, AG XIII 30.

78 François Rabelais, *Oeuvres...*, Amsterdam 1675, now in NK in Prague, Jean Racine, *Oeuvres ... Tome premier*, Paris 1682, now in SK, EU XIII 26, Thomas Corneille, *Poemes dramatiques...*, Paris 1661, now in SK, AE XI 46.

79 Giacomo Minetti, *Raccolta di orationi con diversi avvertimenti spirituali...*, Pragae 1696, now in NK in Prague. Jacobus de Strada, *Epitome thesauri antiquitatum, hoc est impp. Rom. orientalium et occidentalium iconum...*, Lugduni 1553, now in NK in Prague.

80 It is possible to point out *Libro de la historia y milagros, hechos a inuocacion de nuestra Señora de Montserrate...*, Barcelona 1627 and the popular work by Pedro Mejía *Silva de varia lección...*, Leon de Francia 1556, which was obtained for the library by the guardian, Louis MacNamara, both now in NK in Prague, *Las obras que se hallan Romancadas ... Anvers s.a.* by Hieronymus Savonarola, now in SK, BD II 47 or the Antwerp publication from 1557 *Historia de las cosas de Etiopia* by Francisco Álvares, originally from the library of the Spanish ambassador at the Imperial court in 1581 to 1608, Don Guillén de San Clemente. The copy of Álvares's book was researched by Jaroslava Kašparová, "Příspěvek k působení španělských vyslanců Juana de Borja a Guilléana de San Clemente na dvoře Rudolfa II." [A Contribution to the Activity of the Spanish Ambassadors Juan de Borja and Guilléan de San Clemente at the Imperial Court of Rudolf II], *Miscellanea oddělení rukopisů a starých tisků* 15 (1998): 141–161.

Campo and Alcalá de Henares. On the title page, there is the mark of provenance of the Irish Franciscan library, unfortunately completely lacking any kind of date or other detail.[81]

To conclude this very cursory look at the Irish Franciscan library, we might still mention one aspect which is lacking from the outset. The question is whether it is possible to determine the quantity and value of manuscripts and incunabula in the library. The answer is no: the structure of the catalogue entirely excludes this analysis of incunabula and almost entirely that of manuscripts. In the case of manuscripts, it is often possible to be guided by means of catalogues. Truhlář's catalogue of Latin manuscripts includes an illuminated copy of *Opera* by Pseudo-Dionysius the Aeropagite from 1392 (which could be identified as the manuscript listed as *Theologicum MSS. B Fol II 87*, although none of the older shelf marks on the inside front cover match), an interesting collection of heraldic manuscripts of the Scottish nobility from the seventeenth century, *Psalterium Davidicum* of Polish origin, also from the seventeenth century, which the library acquired in 1657 as a gift from Franz Eusebius, Count of Pötting (perhaps *Expositio in Psalmos man. scr. A Fol I 16*), and a list of Latin inscriptions from Italy, Germany and Hungary (perhaps *Abbreviationes Vetust. Monumen. [MSS] G 4° 14*), the probability of which is supported by the initial alphabetical list of abbreviations. The catalogue of Czech manuscripts then shows the spiritual novel *Solfernus*, originally from the library of Ignác of Šternberk.[82] The library's own manuscript catalogue shows some inclination to classification – by the titles *Scarron cum sua uxore Maintenon* in French and *Tractatus de angelis* there is the note *Ms*, as well as *Liber in membrana pro choro*, and some German manuscripts are marked as *Ars equestris*, *Pathaviensis Ecclesiae jura*, *Pauli V. Epistolae*, *Praxis devotionum*, *De causa regaliae* and non-identified *Politica*. It would, however, require a thorough analysis of the entire catalogue for it to be possible to reveal how

---

81   Basic literature, for example, Antonio Rodríguez Moñino, *Diccionario bibliográfico de pliegos sueltos poéticos (siglo XVI)* (Madrid: Castalia, 1970) 58–60, R. Foulché-Delbosc, *Les Cancionerillos de Prague* (New York and Paris: n.p., 1924). A facsimile of the Prague volume of *Pliegos Poéticos Españoles en la Universidad de Praga. Prólogo de … don Ramón Menéndez Pidal* was published in 1960 in Toledo. A short report by Vít Urban, "Los pliegos sueltos de Praga" in *Ibero-Americana Pragensia* 5 (1971): 210–205 was published in Czechoslovakia, although it contained some inaccuracies about the Irish Franciscans.

82   Truhlář, *Catalogus codicum manu scriptorum latinorum* … nos. 74, 1340, 2247, 2381. Manuscript Pseudo-Dionysia (NK, I B 18) is accessible online at http://www.manuscriptorium.com, edited 28.12.2012. Ibid., *Katalog českých rukopisů c. k. veřejné a universitní knihovny pražské* [*A Catalogue of the Czech Manuscripts of the Imperial and Royal Public and University Libraries in Prague*] (Praha: Česká akademie císaře Františka Josefa pro vědy, slovesnost a umění, 1906) no. 256. As far as the other three manuscripts originally from Šternberk are concerned (the travel writings by Ignác of Šternberk, the legal collection from 1666 and a list of the social groups (estates) and peasants in the Kingdom of Bohemia subjected to taxes in 1557 … see nos. 25, 154 and 303), it is impossible to prove that they were in the Irish Franciscan library.

consistent this classification system was and how many manuscripts are still hidden among the entries. Apparently, no Irish handwritten literary relics are to be found in the library catalogue. The word *hibernice* is explicitly used only for the following titles: printed editions of *Lucerna fidelium* by Francis Molloy and *Clerii Vocabularium Hibernicum* and what is obviously *Foclóir nó Sanasán Nua* by Mícheál Ó Cléirigh. The third volume is easily recognisable as *Hibernici Flores Bibliorum*. Even the work *Grammatica Anglo-Hibernica, or a brief introduction to the Irish language* by Francis Walsh, who had been ordained a priest in Prague in 1677 and later moved to Louvain and Rome, is not to be found in the college library.[83]

It was not by chance that Václav Vojtěch, Count of Šternberk, chose the Irish Franciscans to realise his intention of turning his library into a collection accessible to the public. He was aware that he would enrich one of the very good Prague libraries, whose stock was adequate to the demanding task of educating young men in formation and was indicative of active contacts with colleges in other European countries. His plan was never completed because of an unwillingness on both sides; however, while he could not have envisaged the opposition of his heirs during his lifetime, the question is to what extent he had assessed the ability, the possibility and the wish of the Irish to re-establish themselves in Prague's intellectual society, from whose public sphere they had had to withdraw shortly before his decision, for which they were certainly not blameless. Perhaps it was the library, whose stock, despite the distribution of the Šternberk books, only slightly exceeded the more narrowly specialised and smaller collections of average monastery libraries, which could help to renew the lustre of the name of the college. The possibly not too exact comparison with the Strahov library is unavoidable. Thanks to its liberal acquisitions, the Strahov library became a unique collection of books. The Irish Franciscans, however, were in an altogether different situation and Šternberk's gift and the construction of the library wing were exceptional events which, to all appearances, ultimately brought them, at the very least, as many problems as benefits. Patrick Hackett did not perhaps anticipate that, some twenty-five years later, his library would be scattered, partly entrusted to the university library, partly sold at auction or in bulk to Jewish shopkeepers in Prague[84] and partly irretrievably lost.

83   Robert Welch ed., *Oxford Concise Companion to Irish Literature* (Oxford: Oxford University Press, 2000) 379. Joseph MacMahon OFM, "The silent century, 1698–1829," 99.

84   Frequent notes in the books refer to second-hand shopkeepers, who were almost exlusively Jewish at the time (e.g. "I bought this booklet from the Jew Koranda for 25 kreutzer").

5. THE DISUNITED CREW
OF A FORGOTTEN SHIP (1730–1786)

The symptoms of disruption and crisis are always the same: a gradual relaxation of discipline, a questionable interpretation of the rules and deviation from them, a negligent overlooking of transgressions, leading in the end to the impossibility of a community reforming itself by its own efforts. Also, the schemata of such crises are never very diverse, so that anyone who has at their disposal simply a final list of deficiencies will, as a rule, only need general statements. Regular visitations of the religious communities (for example, during a change of guardian) were a means of maintaining the life of the order at the required level. If, however, inadequacies appeared, high representatives of the Church could intervene and subject the college to an inspection outside the scheduled term. The papal nuncio, Domenico Passionei, decided on such an extraordinary visitation of the College of the Immaculate Conception at the end of 1736. After a description of the course of the visitation, we can attempt, using various testimonies, to reconstruct

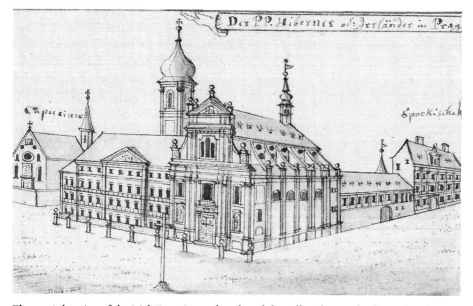

Fig. 27 A drawing of the Irish Franciscan church and the college by Friedrich Bernhard Werner (Before the mid-18th century) (NPÚ).

the approximate development of the community in the years immediately preceding it (Fig. 27).

THE COURSE OF EVENTS

At about half past nine on the morning of 16 February 1737, drawn by six horses in hand, the coach of the Archbishop of Prague, Johann Moritz Gustav, Count Manderscheid-Blankenheim, pulled up outside the College of the Immaculate Conception of the Virgin Mary. The Archbishop proceeded into the church, on whose threshold he was welcomed by the Irish Franciscans. Inside, for perhaps an hour, Manderscheid's chaplain and master of ceremonies checked whether the interior of the church was prepared as befitted the coming occasion. The canonical visitation had begun.

We are indebted for the detailed description of this *entrée*, possibly not so much to the meticulousness of a clerk, but rather to the hesitancy aroused, by all accounts, among the delegated visitators by the task at hand and which can be read between the lines of the introductory pages of the minutes of the visitation, recorded with the greatest possible exactitude. The document, as we will call it, is in fact a bundle of decidedly varied content: apart from the minutes of the visitation in the proper sense of the word, namely, records of the meetings of the commission and of discussions with individual friars, it contains *depositiones*, that is, written statements on the state of the college given to the visitators by a majority of the friars, the originals of the nuncio's credentials, the draft of the archbishop's speech and admonitions, copies of the internal regulations of the college, the concluding reports of the visitation commission, the originals and copies of the correspondence between the archbishop and the nunciature and the Irish college, plus other, less important writings only loosely connected with the actual visitation. Documents relating to the visitation of 1690 are attached to the back of the bundle.

The first announcement of the visitation had arrived in Prague sometime at the end of November the previous year. It was the authorisation from Domenico Passionei, the nuncio at the Imperial Court (1731–1738), dated 24 November 1736, for the Archbishop of Prague to carry out as his representative, together with the vicar general of the Archdiocese of Prague and the provincials of the Dominicans, Franciscans and Jesuits, a visitation of the Irish Franciscans.[1] In a further decree, dated 12 December 1736, the nuncio,

---

1   The authorisation is dated 24.11.1736. All the facts mentioned below are based mainly on the visitation protocol, NA, APA, book no. B 65/13. A part of the visitation protocol – a list of the members of the college on ff. 386–389 – was published by Benignus Millett, "Some lists of Irish

with a view to the health of the archbishop, nominated the Abbot of Strahov, Marian Hermann, as his second representative during the impending visitation. The first official preliminary meeting of the visitators took place at the archbishopric on 6 February. It began at about nine o'clock in the morning and those present were the vicar general of the archdiocese, Jan Mořic Martini, the provincial of the Dominicans, Kajetán Burger, the provincial of the Franciscans, Valerián Humer, with his confrère, the former provincial, Severin Vrbčanský, for the Jesuits, Jan Seidel (who was rector of Prague's Old Town college from 1732 to 1736) in place of the provincial, the archbishop's chancellor, Antonín Jan Václav Vokoun, and the vice-chancellor, Jan Richter, as secretary. The archbishop appeared later.

One of the vital questions resolved by the commission was its right to carry out the visitation. In other words, its members feared that the Irish Franciscans would not accept the nuncio's undoubted authority without protest. The actions of the visitators would be assured by a papal brief and they therefore decided to start by trying to obtain one from the nuncio. During the proceedings, however, they changed their mind, believing that it would be better in the meantime to begin the visitation and if anyone objected to anything, they would apply for it then; the document could be obtained from Vienna within eight days.

After the archbishop had been welcomed, formal and practical matters were resolved, for example, the order in which the friars would be questioned during the visitation or how the questions would be arranged. The commission decided on the following categories. 1. Are there any documents from the last visitation recording which had not been adhered to? 2. Observance of liturgical obligations. 3. The quality and observance of choral worship. 4. Piety during divine worship and reverence for the Eucharist. 5. Observance of the statutes. 6. Behaviour of the superiors. 7. Punishment of disorders. 8. Good mutual relations among the superiors and between superiors and subordinates. 9. Observance of the vow of poverty. 10. Observance of the vow of chastity. 11. Observance of the vow of obedience. 12. Is the Rule observed? 13. Participation in prayers at mealtimes. Readings at mealtimes. 14. Financial matters. 15. Is the purpose of the college actually to prepare missionaries for England, Scotland and Ireland? 16. The numbers of missionaries sent annually to those countries. 17. The obtaining of means for the running of the college without troubling the kingdom. 18. The numbers of friars, how many are in the college, how many gather alms? If we are not to regard the final draft of the questions as a mere formality, then it must occur to us that the archdiocesan dignitaries and the superiors of the Bohemian religious orders

Franciscans in Prague, 1656–1791," *Collectanea hibernica* 36–37 (1994–5): 67–71. This list, however, is not complete.

had their doubts about the purpose of the college. The date of the visitation was also set at the meeting of the commission because the announcement to the Irish Franciscans was written the following day and delivered by the vice-chancellor on 8 February.

The opening of the visitation with the usual ceremonies took place in the church. After the blessing, the visitators inspected the ciborium, the purificator and the altar to discover how the Eucharist was stored. Then the commission and the friars went into the refectory, where the nuncio's decrees were read and participation assured. The archbishop then dismissed everyone and directed only the guardian to remain, reminding him "solemnly and emphatically" in Italian (!) to reveal everything and conceal nothing that might be of interest to the visitation commission. The guardian replied with an assessment of the current situation of the college: it was in good condition, the debts which it had had when he was elected had been paid. He had introduced several new measures to improve discipline (friars were not allowed to eat or drink anywhere in the city) and particularly incorrigible disturbers of the peace had been sent to other colleges. He complained, however, about his extremely unfavourable reception after attaining office, when he had had to spend thirteen weeks in Vienna as if in exile, about his limited authority and about his troublesome accord with the discreets. It must have been clear to the visitation commission that his authority with his confrères was not very great. With that, the introductory obligations ended and a further meeting was set for 20 February.

The visitation protocol basically contains two types of information. The first type is statistical data on the members of the college: name, age, number of years in the order and in the Prague college itself, country (in the case of lay brothers not from Ireland) or province (in the case of the Irish) of origin, and position or function within the college. The process of compiling this collection of data, unique for the college, is entirely clear. The second type – or possibly, in terms of its importance, the first, for it concerned what happened during the visitation – is much more problematic. After several introductory questions, individual friars began talking incessantly and presented to the visitators reality as it appeared to them and as they wanted the commission to perceive it. They elaborated, obfuscated and interpreted reality according to their own aims, sympathies and antipathies, doubtless, too, in good faith. They almost all agreed that existing relations in the college were untenable. The causes of this crisis, to name a few, were in no way unusual: two strong personalities, neither of whom could boast of integrity in the eyes of his colleagues, a mutual aversion between them and a guardian too weak and without enough support to resolve the accumulated problems. If to this we add faltering communication with higher authorities, Irish vehemence and malice, then the picture of relations pieced together from the individual

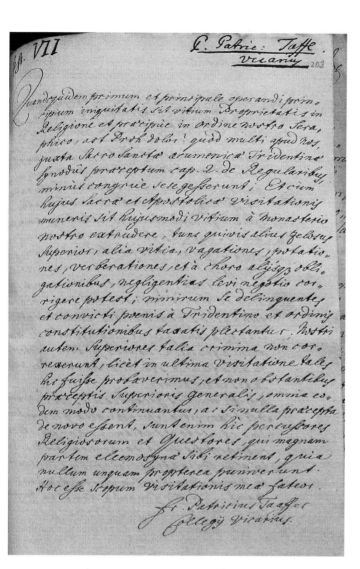

Fig. 28 Patrick Taaffe's utterance in the visitation protocol of 1737 (NA).

statements, however harsh and unflattering, does in fact reflect the realities of life in the Prague college (Fig. 28).

At the time of the visitation, the college had sixty-seven members, of whom eleven were lay brothers and nine were clerics, that is, not yet ordained priests. At that time, there were no novices at all in Prague, which accounts for the absence of the office of novice master. There were seventeen friars from Munster, including the guardian, then fourteen from Connaught, thirteen from Leinster and twelve from Ulster. Two young teachers, Anthony Deleny and William O'Brien, had only been in Prague for a few months and left for Rome during the visitation. Apart from the friars, there were also an unspecified number of secular students.

Among the lay brothers, there was only one Irishman and two Bohemians, while the rest came from German regions: one from the Rhineland-Palatinate, two from Swabia, two from Bavaria and one each from the Tyrol, Austria and Mainz. Twenty-seven-year-old Anton Kauser from Swabia had spent the least time in the order; just three months. The sixty-five-year-old Irishman Paul Jordan, who was the oldest lay brother of all, had spent the most time; thirty-four years, of which twenty-nine had been in Prague. In terms of age, Kauser was an exception, followed by the thirty-three-year-old Jakob Obermayer from Bavaria and the forty-three-year-old Bohemian, Bonaventura Weyr. Among the younger brothers was perhaps Paschal Ochetz from the Rhineland-Palatinate, who did not give his age but had been in the order just nine months. The ages of the remaining lay brothers were between forty and fifty-five. Their original occupations had been joiners, cobblers, cooks, tailors, fishermen and soldiers, and in the college they worked as kitchen assistants or served in the infirmary or the sacristy. Gabriel Pichler retained his original occupation of cobbler, Jordan served as nurse in the infirmary and Weyr was a gatekeeper together with the tertiary, Johann Kroner.

There were nine clerics altogether. Further information is lacking on one of these, Brother Didacus, who clearly made his statement to the visitation commission at a later date. Their ages were between nineteen and twenty-one and they had been in the order for between eighteen months and six years; this means that most had entered the Franciscan Order at about seventeen. They were studying philosophy and all of them were, understandably, Irish.

There are three instances where we lack more precise details concerning full members of the community: firstly, Daniel Confiden, who was Johann Michael, Count Sporck's chaplain and was absent at the beginning of the visitation; secondly, Anthony O'Neill, who showed that he had been in the order for fifteen years, so was more a member of the younger generation; and finally, which is especially annoying, the current guardian, about whom we know only that he was from Munster.

The community as a whole was relatively young; only seven members (not including the guardian, who was probably not one of the younger ones) out of forty-five were over forty. The oldest of all, Peter Jones, was sixty-five years old. This age range would correspond to the purpose of the college as a centre of study. For some of them, joining the Franciscans was not straightforward. Some friars, already ordained priests, had been in the order for only two years so it can be ruled out that they had entered the order as youths of seventeen or eighteen. How many actual students were there? There were four who specifically stated that they were studying philosophy, another four who did not specifically state what they were studying and ten students of theology. Four students stated that they had completed their study of theology. Apart from these, there were other young men who did not say that they were studying or that they were preparing for missions or that they had any kind of function in the community; at most, within the community they enjoyed the title *lector habitualis*, that is, they could teach when required. The necessary offices were otherwise occupied for the most part by older members of the community: the guardian, two discreets with the title *lector jubilatus* (Peter Jones from Leinster and the fifty-eight-year-old Rudolph O'Neill), the forty-two-year-old lector in theology Anthony Murphy from Connaught as the third member of the discretorium, and the thirty-seven-year-old lector in theology Nicholas Dalton from Leinster as the fourth member. There were two further lectors in theology, forty-one-year-old James Griffin from Munster and thirty-four-year-old Joseph Donnelly from Ulster, so that the proportionality of individual provinces was preserved. Twenty-eight-year-old Francis Fleming from Leinster and his contemporary, Michael Keogh from Connaught were lectors in moral theology. Two lectors in theology are to be found in the protocol: Anthony Magennis from Ulster and Anthony Wallis from Munster both twenty-eight. Fifty-six-year-old Patrick Taaffe was vicar. Forty-seven-year-old Francis Allin from Connaught, who had been serving as preacher and confessor for seventeen years, looked after wood for the college. The position of preacher and confessor was also held by sixty-four-year-old Bartholomew Fitzgerald, who had come from Lorraine to Prague eight months previously to train the friars in Gregorian chant, and the former sacristan, Laurence Crowe. The current sacristan had only been in the college for nine months and was, according to one statement, little suited to his position because he did not speak German. Among the other members of the college, Thomas Magdonon had been serving as chaplain to Count Herberstein for nine months.

On 20 February 1737, the visitation recommenced, with the lay brothers making their statements first. The visitators had been given information beforehand about the previous visitations in 1664, 1714 and 1735. At the archbishopric, they clearly remembered Pfaltz's indignation in 1690, because preserved documents were attached to the visitation protocol. They also added regulations for the tightening of college discipline, which the commissary visitator, Peter Jones, formulated as notes to the college statutes. In 1714, the commissary visitator, MacHugo, had also implemented changes in the college statutes during the visitation.

There were eleven sessions of the visitation and it ended officially only in July, the visitation protocol being completed on 1 October. In the college, during this long period, there were more and less stormy reactions to the visitators' investigations, as some of those who made statements informed the commission and as the commission rebuked the college for its inappropriate behaviour. Some of the friars gave the visitators their own statements on the condition of the college and these were appended to the protocol.

There was nothing that was praiseworthy. The impression gained on the spot by the commission was undoubtedly even worse than that gained by the reader from the visitation protocol. The visitators could not be accused of inexperience or a lack of knowledge of the monastic environment, nor of partisanship or using stricter criteria because the community stood entirely outside the local church structure and its members were foreigners. Roughly on the basis of the above questions, the visitators drew up a summary and came to the following conclusions. Meditation, discipline, college Masses and spiritual exercises were all very much neglected. Only three or four friars sang in the choir, which, for a friary with almost seventy members, was inexcusable. It is, however, interesting that, apart from lay brothers, more than twenty of those who made a statement complained about the poor attendance at the choir. Monastic discipline and subordination had simply deteriorated, subordinates had little respect for their superiors, and the superiors hardly offered their subordinates a good example by which to retain their authority. Community life was not maintained, there was always more than enough to eat on the superiors' table, while their subordinates went hungry. All the friars saw the reasons for the lack of adequate food as being due to too many secular students being fed at the college, some of the students serving as lectors' assistants. The statements vary principally in their numbers: some speak of five or six, others of as many as eleven. One of the friars stated that aristocratic students were invited to meals and regaled to the detriment of the brothers. The superiors added items of clothing to the habit of the order, in contravention of the regulations (those on footwear and head coverings), the subordinates were dressed in tatters, dirty and driven to providing themselves with the requisite clothing by their own efforts.

Peace and tranquillity did not prevail in the college and the community was divided into factions. It even went as far as violent excesses. The superiors were negligent towards this state of affairs, punishing only according to which faction the person involved belonged; sometimes the injured party was punished more than the guilty party. Sins against the vow of poverty, which were not even regarded as sins, had firmly established themselves. In its final report, the commission made the bitter declaration that "some can be reproached for being more in contact with money than with a consecrated chalice and paten." The main reason for this misconduct was the rather unfortunate practice, introduced at the college several decades before, which allowed those who gathered alms to keep part of the collection for their own needs. None of the friars specified what proportion of the money collected this amounted to (allegedly from one third to one half), but, in any case, there was a shortage of funds that could have been used, for example, for repairs to the college or the equipping of missionaries travelling to England, Scotland and Ireland. This college practice undoubtedly made alms gathering more attractive, so that even lectors who should not have absented themselves from their students devoted themselves to it. The majority of friars denounced this practice before the visitation commission. Some members of the college even incurred debts and, in order to evade their creditors, applied successfully for a transfer. Not even the observance of the vow of chastity was impeccable, not to mention vulgar speech and songs. There was relatively little criticism of studies. Apart from complaints against the lectors who went out to gather alms, the visitators criticised the poor knowledge of the students sent from Ireland (lacking the basics of Latin, they really were problematic), the inadequacies in the study of moral theology and the sometimes over-lengthy exposition of those teaching, which prevented the gathering of the necessary material from theology in three years.

THE PROTAGONISTS: VIEWS FROM WITHIN

Sometime in the autumn of 1733, Michael MacCullin, then guardian of the college and lector in theology, fell ill during his period of office. His illness was considered so serious that it seemed necessary to appoint the praeses as the guardian's deputy. On 11 November, Nicholas Dalton was appointed *pro interim*, and because the guardian's condition did not improve but further deteriorated, after two months he was confirmed in office.

Nicholas Dalton was born around 1700 in Leinster and had entered the order at about the age of nineteen. At the beginning of the 1730s, he most likely occupied the position of lector in philosophy at the college. Without this preparation, it would have been difficult for him to take over the lectures in moral theology after Bernard Molloy's death at the beginning of 1733 and, although unexpectedly, in the correct manner. Because it was the turn for someone from Leinster, the discreets put his name forward to the general, who then confirmed Dalton in office in May 1733. Dalton's professional qualifications were good and later, during the visitation, despite all the complaints, no-one seriously cast doubt on them (the reservations of the unquestionably excellent James Griffin must be attributed to a mutual antipathy). On the contrary, he was praised by the students and one of them even flatteringly called him *aquila scholasticae*. He was, however, a complex character, not without ambition, with a tendency to severity and a quick temper which, under the pressure of circumstances, manifested itself as aggression. He was decidedly not the man for a superior position. Dalton's confrères characterised him with the attributes furious, impatient, hypochondriac or bilious. Under normal circumstances, however, these traits remained hidden.

Michael MacCullin the guardian, died on 16 January 1734. It was then necessary to select suitable candidates immediately for the two vacant positions – lector in theology and guardian. For the former, the discreets decided on Dalton, for the latter it was more difficult to come to an agreement and the circumstances that ensued are not too clear even from the statements in the protocol. James Griffin stood as candidate against Dalton.

James Griffin was four years older than Dalton, he came from Munster and had entered the order at about seventeen. He was a learned and able theologian with a gregarious and sociable nature; he did not shun female company and sometimes amused himself in town, he maintained contacts with a number of aristocrats, both Irish emigrants and local nobility. His knowledge of worldly behaviour gained him a number of followers and admirers as well as some more or less intractable adversaries who rightly blamed him for the too lax discipline, the very casual conception of the vow of poverty and intimate contacts with secular persons. His critics, however, in their discontent, let themselves slip into pettiness: in the statements, there were constant references to Griffin's close relationship with an Englishwoman named Bishop, which had been discussed during the previous visitation, during which Griffin had been reprimanded for his conduct. According to several statements, in certain ways Griffin's behaviour had recently improved, but suspicion of financial machinations had arisen and, in particular, the burden of his old reputation remained with him which, in the eyes of his adversaries, could only be rectified with difficulty. He definitely could not improve his reputation in the eyes of Nicholas Dalton.

Measured in terms of his publishing activity, in the first half of the eighteenth century, Griffin was a star of the first magnitude in the Prague college. It is not, however, only a matter of quantity (we know nothing of Dalton's own work) but also of a critical attempt in his philosophico-theological works to connect the old with what was useful in the new tendencies.[2] In 1727, together with the thesis James O'Byrne defended under Griffin's chairmanship, his *Nucleus celebriorum fidei controversiarum* was published. The copy preserved in the Strahov library is interesting, among other things, for its provenance. In 1727, Griffin gave this to the then seventeen-year-old Johann Anton Kajetan of Wunschwitz, son of the genealogist and heraldist, Gottfried Daniel of Wunschwitz. It is one of the proofs of Griffin's relations with a family of the nobility, though one far from the noblest. He also knew the Countess of Martinice and her daughter Aloisie, Countess of Šternberk, Count Filip Kinský, Countess Pötting and Count Browne, whose estates he is said to have temporarily managed. Griffin's editorial work is evidence of his relations

---

2   Stanislav Sousedík, *Filosofie v českých zemích mezi středověkem a osvícenstvím* [*Philosophy in the Bohemian Crown Lands between the Middle Ages and the Enlightenment*] (Praha: Vyšehrad, 1997) 282 and in more detail in his *Jan Duns Scotus. Doctor subtilis a jeho čeští žáci* [*John Duns Scotus. Doctor Subtilis and His Bohemian Pupils*] (Praha: Vyšehrad, 1989).

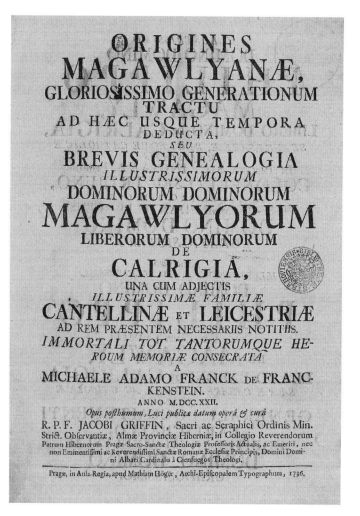

Fig. 29 The title page of the work about the descent of the MacAwley family by M.A. Franck. Prague 1736 (SK).

with the Irish emigrant nobility; that is, the publication of a genealogy of the MacAwley family, written by Michael Adam Franck von Franckenstein in 1722. Two years later, confirmation of the trustworthiness of its contents was shown by, among others, the then superiors of the college including the guardian, Francis Fitzgibbon. In 1736, when the treatise was published, it was also opportune for another reason because Philip MacAwley had just been made a Count of the Holy Roman Empire (Fig. 29; Fig. 30). Griffin's main literary area was, however, theology. In 1732, his *Tractatus theologicus de ultimo fine hominis* and *Tractatus theologicus de tribus naturae humanae statibus* were published, and, then in 1735, *Tractatus theologicus expendens quaestiones prologeticas Libri primi sententiarum, juxta mentem Joannis Duns Scoti*, which was the edition, with an up-to-date title page and dedication, still in use (as far as we know) in 1739 and then again in 1741, this time during Anthony

Fig. 30 The superiors of the Prague Irish Franciscan college testify to the noble descent of the MacAwley family. Michael Adam Franck of Franckenstein, *Origines Magawlyanae*, Prague 1736 (SK).

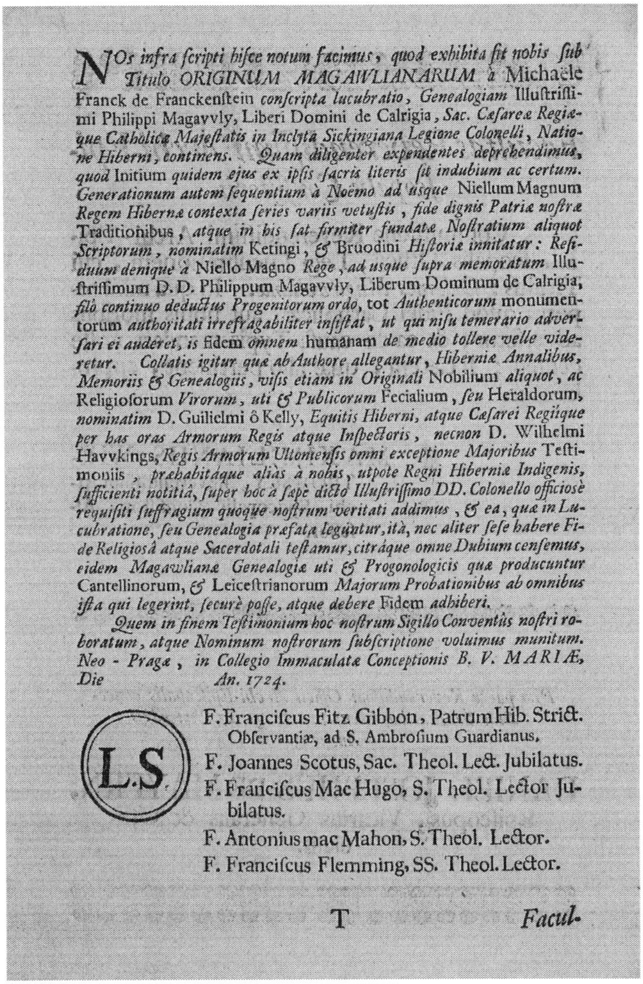

NOs infra ſcripti hiſce notum facimus, quod exhibita ſit nobis ſub Titulo ORIGINUM MAGAWLIANARUM à Michaële Franck de Franckenſtein *conſcripta lucubratio, Genealogiam* Illuſtriſſimi Philippi Magavvly, Liberi Domini de Calrigia, *Sac. Cæſareæ Regiæque Catholicæ Majeſtatis in Inclyta Sickingiana Legione Colonelli, Natione Hiberni, continens. Quam diligenter expendentes deprehendimus, quod* Initium *quidem ejus ex ipſis ſacris literis ſit indubium ac certum. Generationum autem ſequentium à Noëmo ad uſque* Niellum Magnum *Regem Hibernæ contexta ſeries variis vetuſtis, fide dignis Patriæ noſtræ* Traditionibus, *atque in his ſat firmiter fundatæ Noſtratium aliquot Scriptorum, nominatim* Ketingi, *&* Bruodini *Hiſtoriæ innitatur: Reſiduum denique à* Niello Magno *Rege, ad uſque ſupra memoratum* Illuſtriſſimum D. D. Philippum Magavvly, Liberum Dominum de Calrigia, *filò continuo deductus Progenitorum ordo,* tot *Authenticorum* monumentorum *authoritati irrefragabiliter inſiſtat, ut qui niſu temerario adverſari ei auderet, is* fidem *omnem* humanam *de medio tollere velle videretur. Collatis igitur quæ ab Authore allegantur, Hiberniæ Annalibus, Memoriis & Genealogiis, viſis etiam in Originali* Nobilium *aliquot, ac* Religioſorum *Virorum, uti & Publicorum* Fecialium, *ſeu* Heraldorum, *nominatim* D. Guilielmi ô Kelly, *Equitis Hiberni, atque Cæſarei Regiique per has oras Armorum Regis atque Inſpectoris, necnon* D. Wilhelmi Havvkings, *Regis Armorum Ultonienſis omni exceptione Majoribus* Teſtimoniis, *præhabitâque aliàs à nobis, utpote Regni Hiberniæ Indigenis, ſufficienti notitiâ, ſuper hoc à ſæpè dicto Illuſtriſſimo DD. Colonello officiosè requiſiti ſuffragium quoque noſtrum veritati addimus, & ea, quæ in Lucubratione, ſeu Genealogia præfata leguntur, ità, nec aliter ſeſe habere Fide Religiosâ atque Sacerdotali teſtamur, citràque omne Dubium cenſemus, eidem Magawlianæ Genealogiæ uti & Progonologicis quæ producuntur* Cantellinorum, *&* Leiceſtrianorum *Majorum Probationibus ab omnibus iſta qui legerint, ſecurè poſſe, atque debere* Fidem *adhiberi.*

Quem in finem Teſtimonium hoc noſtrum Sigillo Conventûs noſtri roboratum, atque Nominum noſtrorum ſubſcriptione voluimus munitum. Neo - Pragæ, in Collegio Immaculatæ Conceptionis B. V. MARIÆ, Die An. 1724.

L.S.

F. Franciſcus Fitz Gibbon, Patrum Hib. Strict. Obſervantiæ, ad S. Ambroſium Guardianus.
F. Joannes Scotus, Sac. Theol. Lect. Jubilatus.
F. Franciſcus Mac Hugo, S. Theol. Lector Jubilatus.
F. Antonius mac Mahon, S. Theol. Lector.
F. Franciſcus Flemming, SS. Theol. Lector.

T *Facul-*

MacNamara's disputation under the chairmanship of Nicholas Dalton! His *Tractatus theologicus de Deo uno* was published in 1736 and *Tractatus theologicus de intellectu et voluntate Dei* in 1738. The last publishing achievement by Griffin that we know of was the publication of *Tractatus catholicus de divino opificio hexameron* by Bonaventure Baron, which was, according to the title page, part ten of Griffin's works. At that time already *lector jubilatus*, Griffin, brought out the book in Prague in 1744 and dedicated it to the abbot of the Cistercian monastery in Žďár nad Sázavou, Bernard Hennet, who, judging by the foreword, contributed financially to its publication.[3]

3 On the list of Griffin's printed works, see Hedvika Kuchařová and Jan Pařez, "On the trail of Irish émigrés in the collections of the Strahov Abbey Library in Prague," *The Ulster Earls and Baroque Europe. Refashioning Irish Identities, 1600–1800*, eds. Thomas O'Connor and Mary Ann

Let us, however, return to 1734. Immediately after MacCullin died, Dalton became the guardian of the college. He tried to reform those friars whose discipline was lax (most likely Griffin and his followers), but he also aroused opposition to himself by his quick-tempered and unmanageable behaviour. The conflict came to a head in July, when there was an ugly scene between Dalton and a student, Thomas Bruodin, who was agitating the students against the guardian. The leader of those who were dissatisfied was Griffin, and the following day he summoned Dalton to account before the discreets and accused him of being insane, psychologically unbalanced and incapable of managing his appointed office. What happened then is not too clear (if we do not take into consideration the subjective description of the intrigues con-nected with Dalton's dismissal in his writings), but, in the end, the superiors of the order decided on a change of guardian. As we can only deduce from the mutually contradictory statements, William Hogan from Munster was proposed to the college by the superiors, although he was evidently not in Prague at the time. Dalton was behind the selection of Hogan, though some members of the college's discretorium obviously proposed Griffin. Finally, the general of the order confirmed Hogan's appointment, which affected the majority of the members of the college who were now united at least in that their right to choose the next guardian had been restricted. Hogan's appoint-ment immediately became a political affair when somewhere the suspicion was voiced that he had been recommended by the Spanish *infante*, Don Carlos, and that, consequently, in the heart of the Habsburg Monarchy, he had to be considered "politically unreliable." This time, Griffin's clique had turned to the secular authorities. That was, then, the reason for Hogan's exile in Vienna and his cold reception after his arrival in Prague. His situation was indeed unenviable: at first neither Griffin's nor Dalton's supporters had any reason to welcome him. Although after a time the antagonism lessened, ex-tremely tense relations with James Griffin continued and some members of the college were under the suspicion that the somewhat better relations with Dalton had been, on the part of the guardian, bought by concessions to the detriment of justice, motivated by fear. In the meantime, Dalton's psycholog-ical condition and behaviour worsened. He began to slacken in the fulfilment of his college responsibilities and his uncouth behaviour culminated in him striking the vicar, Patrick Taaffe, allegedly due to a dispute over a friar. The college was torn between Dalton, Griffin and the guardian, and those who would perhaps have liked to remain neutral were identified, whether they liked it or not, with one or other faction. This was the community that the visitators had entered and were supposed to reform.

Lyons (Dublin: Four Courts Press, 2010) 208–211. *Tractatus theologicus de tribus naturae humanae statibus* ... Pragae 1732, now in NK in Prague, is not shown here.

A VAGUE RESOLUTION: THE QUESTION OF EDUCATION AND AUTHORITY

In choosing the means of reform, the visitators mainly accepted proposals by members of the college themselves. Above all, they recommended that the regulations be confirmed by the sacred congregation *De propaganda fide*, in order for the members of the college to be supported by the law and to halt and eliminate the deterioration in the awareness of what should be adhered to. This proposal was well founded: directly attached to the visitation protocol are two different copies of the internal regulations, which differ in detail from the official version which was approved later. The differences were decidedly not just peripheral matters: while the copy which is close to the later official version envisages an eight-member council of discreets (excluding the guardian), the other version, which was put into practice, explicitly speaks only of a four-member council. The archbishop, at least temporarily, attempted to prevent these inconsistencies in such a basic matter as the organisation of the college when he drew up the instructions which were obviously intended to guide the members of the college into approving their own regulations. Another reform was more frequent visitations: once every three years, the college should have a visitation by the commissary general of the *natio Germano-Belgica*, under the control of other Irish Franciscan colleges "in these lands," while in the intervening two years, it would be under the control of a suitable man dedicated to the work and appointed by the commission. It seemed to the commission entirely inappropriate for the guardian, along with the discreets, to decide who to send to another college, or who to ask to come to the Prague college from somewhere else. The general of the order would decide how this practice should be changed. In the college, there should only be as many friars as there were cells (for example, Rudolph O'Neill proposed that the number of friars be reduced to ten from each province). The laity, whether famous or not, should not be invited to table (the guardian proposed reducing the number of secular students to four, or five at the very most) and there could be only two *lector habituales* in the college as substitute teachers. Hogan, the guardian, had a particularly low opinion of this post: his proposal was that everyone who graduated in theology should be sent to Ireland for a year because, for the most part, *lectores habituales* were of no use to the college: they were companions to lectors in their ceaseless wanderings or they acted as chaplains on country estates, where, instead of books, they concerned themselves with firearms (*sclopetis*) and fowling and forgot about their calling as missionaries.

In general, the visitators demanded that the regulations of the order and the college be observed and that there be regular supervision of the college. The statement that they would not tolerate disputes between natives of the various parts of Ireland is one that was easier said than done. They proposed, however, to dismiss Hogan the guardian, Dalton, Griffin and also Franz Summer, a somewhat problematic lay brother. Besides these hot-tempered members, others were discovered who had to depart. The superiors of the order were evidently in no hurry; William Hogan was still guardian in 1739 and James Griffin and Nicholas Dalton, as discreets, confirmed the wording of the regulations in 1744.

The friars themselves had reservations about their studies. Above all, they recommended extending the study of philosophy to three years because the lack of preparation of the new arrivals from Ireland did not allow the material to be mastered in two years. They also found deficiencies in the study of moral theology, which was adversely affected by poor time-keeping in daily study. One precondition for a high standard was, of course, that the lectors remained within the college during the school year.

William Hogan submitted a paper with proposals for reform. He suggested a reduction in the powers of the discretorium in favour of a strengthening of the powers of the guardian (possibly, he himself had had the experience that if the discreets did not want to agree with the guardian, then he was practically powerless) and the reduction of the discretorium to four members including the guardian instead of four without the guardian. However, the guardian should not be allowed to be a lector who actually taught. In terms of study, he recommended the same reforms as his confrères, apart from the prolongation of the study of theology to four years, with the division of the material in theology so that two lectors would teach speculative theology, one biblical theology and one canon law. He also asserted the obligatory nature of Scotism and forbad attacks on the theological schools of other orders. The opportunity of going into the city was to be limited, the number of secular students was to be reduced and the exact amount of money a friar could have with him was to be stipulated. Once every three years, there must be a visitation, and the visitator would not be from the college but nevertheless from the Franciscan Order.

The Irish Franciscans indicated their willingness to reform, the visitation commission compiled its final report and submitted the papers to the nunciature in Vienna. As evidenced by the preserved documents, further development was somewhat drawn out and clearly without major convulsions. As stated above, the visitation protocol was finished on 1 October 1737, and the final report sent to the nunciature in Vienna. In February 1738, the archbishop informed the college that, until further notice or another decree was issued, the sacred congregation *De propaganda fide* had forbidden the sending of friars to other friaries or outside the archdiocese without his written permission. In April, the papal nuncio ordered that, until further decisions were made by *De propaganda fide*, the college should maintain the same conditions as during the visitation or immediately after it. At the beginning of May, *De propaganda fide* again demanded all the documents connected with the visitation and, at the end of the month, they were transferred from Prague to Rome via the Vienna nunciature. Several documents from the spring of that year have been preserved, confirming that the archbishop did indeed temporarily supervise the college.

At the beginning of March 1741, after their decision of 27 February had been ratified by Pope Benedict XIV on 1 March, the sacred congregation *De propaganda fide* issued a decree. It confirmed that the college fell directly within the jurisdiction of the general of the order and also the wording of the statutes from 1664.[4] On this occasion, what was prepared was clearly a copy of the statutes confirmed in 1665, into which the above decree had been inserted. In the college, however, this measure was not met with a favourable response and, almost two years later, *De propaganda fide* discussed a request, presented by the commissary visitator, Fr. Daniel Toole, the guardian and the council of discreets, for the reforms which had been introduced into the statutes in 1714 by the then commissary visitator, MacHugo. The sacred congregation approved the revision but forbad the superiors to introduce further reforms. The revised wording of the statutes was confirmed in Prague on 12 August 1744. The guardian at the time was Rudolph O'Neill (Fig. 31),[5] the discreets were James Griffin, Nicholas Dalton, Anthony Murphy and Anthony Magennis. In view of the incompleteness of the college papers, the question is whether all the deleted passages are the result of this revision. The greatest changes were made in the chapters on the guardian and the lectors. The deleted passages were on the following subjects: the selection of friars to be presented to the general of the order for the office of guardian, the punishment for the suppression of edicts of superiors, the relationship of the temporary commissary to the superiors of the college, the choice of commissary visitator and practically the whole of the chapter on lectors (apart

---

4   We have an undated manuscript of the statutes. It was last amended in 1741. It records the wording of the statutes of 1664, confirmation of this wording of 1665, and additions from 1741. For the period before the additions from 1741, we are not able to paleographically distinguish individual time layers of text. In future it would be appropriate to carry out a differential analysis of the Prague and the Roman copies.

5   Rudolph O'Neill is the only Irish Franciscan in Prague whose portrait has been preserved. A pen drawing of the guardian was made by Johann Rudolph Count Sporck, Prague auxiliary bishop and canon of the chapter house at St. Vitus at Prague Castle, and included in Sporck's sketchbook, now saved in the SK, MS DE III 19, f. 52r. For this seven-volume work, see Pravoslav Kneidl, "Šporkiana kreseb hraběte Jana Rudolfa Šporka," *Strahovská knihovna* 20–21 (1985–1986): 183–214. Rudolph O'Neill was mentioned in the last will of John Louis O'Devlin who was a major in the Austrian army and uncle of another renowned Irish Franciscan Francis O'Devlin who is however not the renowned Prague one. According to this testament of 1729, Rudolph O'Neill received 50 florins to buy books, see Anselm Ó Fachtna, "The last will of John Louis O Devlin (1729)," *Journal of the South Derry Historical Society*, 1.4 (1983–84): 349, 353, 354.

Fig. 31 A portrait of Rudolph O'Neill, guardian of the Irish Franciscan college in Prague. A drawing by Prague Auxiliary Bishop Johann Rudolph Sporck (SK).

from two articles). The powers of the discreets were restricted. The deletion of the articles concerning lectors may have been connected with the end of the public activity of the Franciscan teachers at the archiepiscopal seminary, following which these passages were regarded as unnecessary. The reform concerning the selection of the guardian could indicate that next time he was to be appointed directly by the general of the order. In 1740, the general chapter in Valladolid attempted to resolve the business of the property of the college, possibly even under the influence of the Prague visitation, when it decided that the general would appoint two commissaries for the Prague and Louvain colleges who would inquire into and determine the limits of the income necessary to maintain the colleges. Exceeding these limits or accumulating property would be punishable. This measure was not so much aimed at friaries who were too rich as at the attitude of some of its members, as witnessed by the visitation commission in Prague. Complaints against the Irish Franciscans due to the gathering of alms were also brought by the Bohemian province.[6] The Irish evidently resolved these complications, not

---

6   Vigilius Greiderer, *Germania franciscana, seu chronicon geographo-historicum ordinis S. P. Francisci in Germania. Tomus I.*, Oeniponte 1777, 787.

specified in further detail, by means of the Empress, as verified by a rescript by Maria Theresa dated 9 May 1746, which permitted them to gather alms in the towns of Prague from the beginning to the middle of Advent and during Lent. It is possible to judge from this that Leopold I's charter of 1659 on the gathering of alms in Prague no longer served any practical purpose and that the friars had again to obtain permission for this source of income.[7]

THE FADING FLAME OF SCOTISM

We can learn about study activities from the thesis published by the teaching staff on the occasion of a thesis defence. Besides Griffin's literary output, naturally there were other theologians in the college. One was Peter Archdekin, Bishop of Killala, who occupied quite an important position in the college. From fragmentary annotations to documents of the visitation protocol, it is possible to estimate how long he stayed at the college, but he was no longer there at the time of the visitation. A document dated February 1736 has, however, been preserved, in which Johann Moritz Gustav, Count Manderscheid, granted him the right to (once again) consecrate the Church of the Immaculate Conception of the Virgin Mary, during which the remains of the martyrs Clementia and Amadeus were embedded in the high altar.[8] His philosophical work, published on the occasion of the defence by František Ferdinand, Count Novohradský of Kolovraty, in 1732, shows that the teachers at the college still had secular students.[9] Apart from the previously mentioned Michael MacCullin and Bernard Molloy, Archdekin's colleagues also included Francis Maguire and, in 1736, Francis Higgin. Among the teachers in the preceding period were also the late guardian Francis Fitzgibbon (recorded as a lector in moral theology in 1718), and, from the visitation protocol, the well-known senior member of the community Peter Jones (recorded as a lector in theology in 1715).[10]

---

7   NA, L2, ŘH sA, no. 1229. In 1718, Charles VI confirmed all the previous privileges of the college, ibid., no. 1228.

8   NA, ŘHyb Praha, carton no. 45.

9   Kuchařová and Pařez, "On the trail of Irish émigrés," 195. In May 1736, Archdekin was in Vienna and he asked Friedrich August, Count Harrach, to support him in obtaining some benefices in the Spanish Netherlands which had been promised to him by the Emperor. A year later, he was in Brussels but was unsuccessful because, in March 1738, he wrote to Harrach from Dublin that "he is eating the bread of adversity," and he asked him for financial support. The correspondence between Count Harrach and Archdekin is stored in 'ÖSW, FA Harrach, carton no. 482.

10   In both cases, the prints of the theses have been preserved. Under the chairmanship of Peter Jones, Anthony MacMahon defended his theological thesis; the theme of the unsigned sheet dedicated to Baron Račín was Christ Crucified (SbR, inv. no. 233). Under the chairmanship of Francis Fitzgibbon, Bernardine Murphy defended his thesis; the engraving was dedicated to Count Vratislav of Mitrovice and it showed an allegorical celebration of John of Nepomuk (at

Works by Griffin's and Dalton's colleagues that have been preserved in-clude Anthony Murphy's four-part *Theologia dogmatica* from 1755, a polemical textbook primarily concerning a systematic refutation of the views and ar-guments of non-Catholics and non-Christians in the basic teachings of the Catholic Church.[11] The names of other teachers whose works dating from the 1750s have been preserved are not, however, mentioned in the visitation protocol. The only exceptions are Peter Fullum from Leinster, eighteen at the time of the visitation, who was a student and evidently a supporter of Griffin, and Michael Keogh, a lector in moral theology. Twenty years later, Fullum was a lector in theology in Prague, while Keogh became guardian and is re-corded as being the oldest member of the college in 1765.[12] We would search in vain in the material connected with the visitation for Louis MacNamara, lector in theology in 1751, or Anthony O'Brien, a long-serving teacher at the college who was recorded as a lector in philosophy in 1750, lector in moral theology in 1752 and lector in dogmatic theology three times – first in 1756, then in 1762 and again from 1765 to 1770 when he was also a discreet.[13] He was still alive when the college was dissolved. His namesake, Bonaventure O'Brien, taught philosophy at the college in 1758. In 1756, one of the lectors in philosophy was Christopher Fleming, who later became lector in theol-ogy in Prague (1760) (Fig. 32; Fig. 33).[14] In 1750, Bonaventure Managhan was recorded as a lector in philosophy and it was under his chairmanship that Francis Davett defended his philosophy thesis in July. The thesis was in the form of a single sheet with a depiction of St. Francis under a palm tree with portraits of Franciscan saints, blesseds and popes. This was, however, most probably the second time the copperplate had been used because its creator, Balthasar van Westerhout, had died in 1728 and also the hairstyle of the pa-tron portrayed (although there is no dedication whatever on the thesis) is in the fashion of about thirty years previously.[15] James Griffin evidently died in Prague in the first half of 1758 and both Anthony Murphy and Peter Fullum in 1762.[16]

that time, he had not yet been canonised) signed "Balt. v. Westerhaut vendit Pragae" (NA, SbR, inv. no. 239).

11   The high evaluation of Blaise Pascal, who was a Jansenist, is interesting here. Anthony Murphy, *Theologia dogmatica*, Pragae 1755, 170. The work mentioned is *Pensées*. In the chapter dedicated to *Writing and Tradition*, especially to the authorship of the Pentateuch, Murphy lists Herbert of Cherbury or Spinoza as among the opponents of Thomas Hobbes.

12   Kuchařová and Pařez, "On the trail of Irish émigrés," 207.

13   Ibid., 212 and 215–217.

14   Ibid., 217 and 206–207.

15   SK, without a shelf mark.

16   At least, this is indicated in the record of the money sent to some Franciscans by their relatives and friends to cover expenses related to their return to Ireland. However, the recipients died in Prague and the money was left with the college. NA, APA, carton no. 2101, Millett, "Some lists of Irish Franciscans in Prague," 74.

Fig. 32 An engraving with scenes from the life of St. Patrick by Jan Kryštof Smíšek (after the mid-17th century). The engraving was used again 1752 for the thesis print (SK).

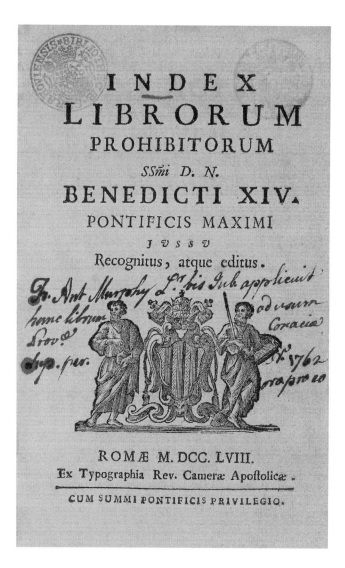

Fig. 33 The title page of the copy of *Index librorum prohibitorum* which was owned by Anthony Murphy the younger (Rome 1758, SK).

In the subsequent decade, lectors in dogmatic theology at the college included Patrick Brady (recorded in 1765) and Anthony Coskran (1766 and 1770), while Patrick O'Brien (1766 and 1770) was lector in bible studies. Thomas O'Donoghue (1770), who had defended his theology thesis four years earlier under the chairmanship of Coskran, and Bartholomew Fagan (1772) were lectors in philosophy in the 1770s. The final decade saw the lector in philosophy James O'Flynn (1780) and Thomas Clancy who, besides defences of traditional Scotist views, inveighed emotionally against the Enlightenment.[17]

---

17   Sousedík, *Filosofie v českých zemích mezi středověkem a osvícenstvím*, 285-286. In the Strahov library, there are, for example, *Theses theologicae ex tractatibus de Deo Uno Trino et Incarnato*

If we want to examine the personnel of the college in the final twenty years of its existence, we are dependent on the documents in the archives of the Prague Archbishopric, which originated as a rule in connection with the problems the college encountered. For this reason, the superficial impression may easily be that the friars were unable to disentangle themselves from complaints and scandals. Nevertheless, in the early 1770s, when a further volume of records was preserved at the archbishopric, more than thirty years had passed since the visitation described above and we have no information, either positive or negative, from this period. In 1771, a certain James Murphy began to study at the college. He did not get on with the guardian, Michael Tipper, towards whom he obviously felt a strong personal antipathy and rather stereotypically accused him of bad administration of the college, bad management of the finances, questionable personal characteristics and the contravention of the directives of his superiors. Murphy differed from the usual chronic complainer in his determination to take the matter higher, and when he was unsuccessful at the Prague Archbishopric and punished with confinement to the college, which became close confinement after an attempt to escape, he eventually (in about autumn 1772) set out for Rome to see the general of the order. The question of how he managed his departure remains unanswered in the available material. What is clear is that the Congregation of Bishops and Regulars passed the investigation of the case to the Archbishop of Prague, who entrusted the whole affair to the Suffragan Bishop of Prague, Jan Ondřej Kayser of Kaysern, in May 1773. Within a week, an investigation began in the college. Its conclusions were not at all surprising: some spoke in the guardian's support, some spoke against him, and Kayser himself recommended his dismissal. In March 1774, Tipper was in fact no longer guardian, but this was because his period of office had elapsed. On the subsequent fate of James Murphy the documents are silent. At the time of the investigation, there were twenty-eight priests, sixteen clerics and seventeen lay brothers in the college, one of the priests being in the Prácheň region at the time. Lectors in philosophy were then Thomas O'Hogan and James O'Reilly, and lectors in theology were Bartholomew Fagan, Bonaventure O'Kelly, Peter Cornen and the already mentioned Anthony Coskran and Patrick O'Brien. Anthony O'Brien and Peter Kelly, a former guardian, are

---

from 1783 defended by Bonaventure Smith, EZ II 51/18. The *Theses philosophicae* from 1780, preserved by O'Flynn and defended by James Connolly and Peter Brady, FG V 2/11. Kuchařová and Pařez, "On the trail of Irish émigrés," 200 and 219. The disputation from 1786, in which theses in theology were defended by James Collins, Peter O'Dolan and Bonaventure Smith, all under Clancy's chairmanship, may well be the last occasion from which prints from the college have been preserved. See Kevin MacGrath, "The Irish Franciscan Library at Prague," *Franciscan College Annual 1951*, (Multyfarnham 1951): 29, note no. 1.

recorded as *lectores jubilati*. The lay brothers, whose number had considerably increased since the visitation, all came from the Bohemian Crown Lands.[18]

The agenda of the Irish Franciscan college intensified at the archiepiscopal office from the beginning of the 1780s. That is, on 29 March 1781, a court decree was issued which, if interpreted strictly, would almost have placed the college outside the law. All religious institutes in the hereditary (i.e. Habsburg) lands had to sever their connection with their foreign counterparts and superiors (apart from purely spiritual contacts, that is, prayers and supplications). If a religious institute was under the control of a general of the order who was not based in the monarchy, it had to be placed under the control of the local provincial, supervised by the local diocesan bishops. Religious were forbidden to travel to general chapters and congregations abroad, and, by the same token, visitations and the visits of spiritual reformers from abroad to religious institutes in the monarchy were also forbidden. Foreigners were not allowed to be superiors and the necessity for private journeys by religious to Rome and other foreign countries would also be restricted by this measure.[19] The college passed into the administration of the archbishop, who now supervised the selection of the guardian, confirmed new superiors and new lectors, carried out visitations and adjudicated in disputed matters. It was clearly impossible to implement the regulation's statutes to the letter, and the college obviously enjoyed certain privileges (for example, the regulation about local superiors was impractical) but nevertheless, in the light of this decree and similar ones, the idea of a missionary centre managed from above turned into a farce. In 1783, Bonaventure Killdea completed his period of office as guardian and in his place Michael Fullum was elected and confirmed in the post, but he died most probably in early 1785. Fullum's successor was James O'Kelly, elected in May 1785. Even before his election, the representatives of the college were demanding that the powers of the discreets be strengthened and checks on the (primarily financial) affairs of the college be carried out.

The increasing interference of the state in the field of education had, however, been felt by the Franciscans much earlier. The uniform method of teaching theology imposed on the university had admittedly initially been ignored by the mendicant orders, but from 1770 onwards had been imposed on all the schools of the mendicant orders without exception.[20] Anthony

18   NA, APA, carton no. 2101. Here is preserved a letter by the Irish Franciscans dated 27.3.1774 concerning the fact that the former guardian, Tipper, and his supporters spread rumours to the effect that Tipper had been unjustly deprived of office following intervention by the Archbishop. The list is published in Millett, "Some lists of Irish Franciscans in Prague," 77–79.
19   Peter Karl Jaksch, *Gesetzlexikon im Geistlichen, Religions- und Toleranzfache, wie auch in Güter-Stiftungs- Studien- und Zensurssachen für das Königreich Böhmen von 1601 bis Ende 1800. Bd. 4* (Prag: K.K. Gubernial registratur, 1828) 257–259.
20   Jaksch, *Gesetzlexikon*, Bd. 4, 531–532 and 533–534.

O'Coskran's thesis, which he defended at Prague University, came only from the second half of the eighteenth century (1756). The Imperial decrees directly demanded greater participation of non-Jesuits in academic life and, from the 1750s, the representation of teachers from different orders and colleges was enforced for the teaching of theology.[21] The college avoided these attempts at unifying the education of future priests, which were crowned in 1783 by the opening of a single general seminary for all clergy without exception, but it was not due to the diplomacy of its superiors but rather because of the state officials' conviction that the Irish were "unuseable" in local spiritual administration and possibly also due to the secret opinion that the college would, sooner or later, be dissolved. The court decree of 1 December 1783 permitted the Irish Franciscans to complete their studies with their own lectors, while simultaneously forbidding them to serve in religious administration with this qualification.[22] Teaching at the college continued as normal until its dissolution in 1786.

In the spring of 1786, clouds were already gathering over the college. During April, Emperor Joseph II was considering the dissolution of the college and raised the question with the burgrave, Count of Nostitz of how the building could be used for military purposes. Despite its uncertain future, however, community life went on, and practically at the same time, led by Erasmus Dionysius Krieger, vicar general and official of the Archbishop of Prague,[23] a canonical visitation took place, the report from which was preserved at the archbishopric and during which the last guardian of the Prague college, Thomas O'Hogan, was elected.[24]

To conclude, we should also mention the departure of missionaries to Ireland, those of the second half of the eighteenth century being recorded on a register, now in the archives of the Prague Archbishopric, which was published by Benignus Millett. The register appeared in connection with the use of alms to pay for clothing, books and other necessities for departing missionaries. In the years 1756 to 1783, forty-five friars received this, but a note at the end of the register adds that about another seventy were not allowed the viaticum. It seems that the college was not as bad in the fulfilment of its calling as some reports would suggest.[25]

---

21   Josef Tříška, *Disertace pražské univerzity 16.–18. století* [*The Dissertations of Prague University in the Sixteenth to Eighteenth Centuries*] (Praha: Univerzita Karlova, 1977) 128.

22   NA, APA, carton no. 2101.

23   On Krieger, see Podlaha, *Series praepositorum, decanorum, archidiaconorum aliorumque praelatorum et canonicum, S. Metropolitanae Ecclesiae Pragensis a primordiis usque ad praesentia tempora* (Praha: Metropolitní kapitula u sv. Víta, 1912) 291–293.

24   NA, APA, carton no. 2101.

25   Millett, "Some lists of Irish Franciscans in Prague," 71–73.

6. ITE, MISSA EST[1]

In the 1780s, during the reign of the enlightened Emperor Joseph II, the Bohemian religious institutes were sunk in gloom accompanied by slight nervousness, in places unconcealed panic, caused by the Church policy of the monarch, which dealt the final blow to the lush Baroque way of life which was coming to an end in the monasteries, friaries and colleges. It is not the purpose of this study to describe the broad political background which caused, among other things, the dissolution of the college of the Irish Franciscans; this has been done elsewhere and better by others, above all by Eduard Winter,[2] but let us at least mention some of the significant moments in the process of reform.

The Josephine reforms affected the monasteries of Bohemia and Moravia, as well as those in the hereditary (Habsburg) lands. The sovereign's decree of the Imperial office from the end of 1781, for the registration of all houses of mendicant and contemplative orders which served no practical purpose, boded no good. With the legal backing of the Patent of 12 January 1782, the first wave of dissolutions of monastic houses took place in the years 1782 to 1784. At the same time, further steps were taken; monasteries were brought under the influence of the state, exemptions in particular were abolished (monasteries were removed from the judicial power of local bishops) as were the orders' own colleges, general seminaries being introduced for all orders. The second wave, that is, the one that also swept away the College of the Immaculate Conception of the Virgin Mary in Prague's New Town, began in 1786.

Accounts of life in the college, hidden in transalpine Prague from the general definitory as well as the leadership of the Irish province, reveal that monastic precepts had been taken out of the control, not only of the order, but also of the Catholic Church itself. It is no coincidence that, as early as the

---

1   "Go forth, the Mass is ended."
2   Mainly Eduard Winter, *Josefinismus a jeho dějiny. Příspěvky k duchovním dějinám Čech a Moravy 1740–1848* [Josephinism and its History. Contributions to the Religious History of Bohemia and Moravia 1740–1848] (Praha: Jelínek, 1945). The dissolution of the monasteries has been dealt with recently by Ondřej Bastl, see, for example, his "Rušení klášterů v Čechách a na Moravě za Josefa II." [The Dissolution of the Religious Institutes in Bohemia and Moravia under Joseph II], *HG* 28 (1995): 155–173.

visitation of 1737, we can guess at the visitation commission's suspicion that the college was losing its original vocation; how can we otherwise understand one of the questions they put to the friars, asking whether the education of missionaries was in fact the main purpose of the college?

Dissolution was consequently just a logical step in the historical decline and fall of the Franciscan college of Irish exiles.

CONVENTUS

On 12 September 1786, commissioners arrived at the Irish college to announce to its members that, by the will of the sovereign, Emperor Joseph II, in accordance with the court decree issued on 7 September, the college was dissolved. At the same time, the physical liquidation of the college began.[3] This is the date to be found in the report for the Clerical Commission at Court (*geistliche Hofkomission*), in particular for Karl, Count Clary, president of the commission.[4]

It relates that the former librarian, Father Anthony O'Brien, handed over the catalogue and the key to the (unsigned) commissioner and, continuing in accordance with the decree, he had a list made of the members of the college. The treasury was doubtless sealed and other measures taken. The clerics, the teachers and the lay brothers were allocated a daily sum of forty kreutzer, while the last guardian, Thomas O'Hogan, was awarded one florin. The latter also verified the document with his signature.

On the same day, a list was made of the friars in the college. From a total of fifty people (of whom thirteen were lay brothers), only a few were missing, for example, Fr. Anthony Coskran, Fr. Francis Conelly and Fr. John Commins, who were acting as tutors in aristocratic families.

It cannot be supposed that, after everything that had happened, the news that the college was being dissolved came like a bolt from the blue. The report of the finding of 132 "lost" florins, a full quarter of the alms gathered from the Litoměřice region, on 19 September can be understood as a reaction to the pressure by the state officials for all the cash in the college to be secured. On 3 October, the guardian, O'Hogan, and the vicar, Farrell, issued a confirmation that the gatherers had handed all of the alms over to the college. As early as 2 October, the Chamber Accounting Office (*Kammeral Zahlamt*) transferred the total capital of the Irish college, amounting to 38,977 florins

---

3   Records are in NA, ČG Publ, 1786–1795, 145/111/1786-7, carton no. 2729. Because individual documents do not have their own reference number, there is no point referring constantly to a carton number only. If we have used information from other sources, these will be cited.

4   See Bastl, "Rušení klášterů v Čechách a na Moravě," 157.

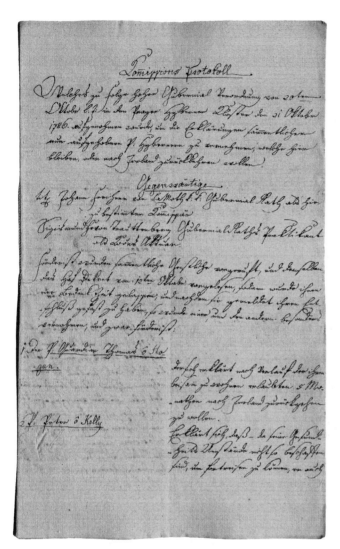

Fig. 34 A protocol of interrogation from the year 1786. Irish Franciscans declared whether they want to stay in Bohemia, or to go back to Ireland (NA).

24 kreutzer, to the Religious Fund (*Religionsfond*) that was established to administer the assets of abolished monasteries.

The liquidation progressed systematically and quite quickly. On 21 October, in the presence of the regional counsellor and *ad hoc* commissioner Baronet de la Mothe-Fénelon and his assistant Baronet of Trauttenberg, a commission register was compiled which recorded the attitudes of the members of the college to their own futures. This means that, in contrast to the members of other monastic institutions, who received a pension, the Irish were asked whether they would agree to accept this pension and therefore remain in Bohemia or whether they would like to return to Ireland. In addition, there was even a court decree issued on 25 November offering the priests and lay brothers who were unable, due to old age or ill health, to undertake the long and arduous return to Ireland the possibility of applying to the diocesan bishop for secularisation. Let us look a little more closely at the prevailing mood among the members of the college and forget for the moment the fate of the college's property.

As has already been stated, there were thirty-seven Irishmen in the college (Fig. 34). Of these, a full twenty-six, including the guardian, O'Hogan, and the former vicar, Farrell, expressed a determination to return home. During the writing down of the protocol, the remainder decided to stay in Bohemia. This mainly concerned the older members; sixty-six-year-old Peter O'Kelly, who had general rheumatism, as can also be seen from the shaky signature on his request of 14 October for a pension, and who proved by a confirmation dated 26 October from MUDr.[5] František Giesele that the illness required daily bathing and care. It also concerned seventy-two-year-old Anthony O'Brien, who was suffering from gout and therefore could not travel, although, as he put it, he would gladly have returned to Ireland. Several of those who were ill considered staying in Bohemia: the stone-deaf lector in theology, Peter Cosgrave, who evidently had long-term health problems,[6] and Denis Martin, who had had a stroke, gone deaf and could only communicate by signs. Even the mentally ill (*wahnsinnig*) Thomas O'Cornen, who was at this time in the hospital of the Brothers of Mercy, counted on staying permanently in Bohemia. Philip Cosgrave, a relative or even possibly a brother of the above Peter Cosgrave, expressed an interest in staying in Prague, evidently because of this relationship. However, there were also other reasons why some of the Irish did not wish to leave the Bohemian Crown Lands. Anthony Coskran was serving as a tutor with the Lobkovic family, which enabled him, in contrast to some of his confrères, to establish a real connection with the local population. The young James Collins and Patrick Conway wanted to complete the course in theology in order to be ordained priests. Documents characteristically give an account of the official proceedings: the regional government checked up on their requests at the archbishopric.[7] Another friar, Anthony O'Dolan, stated in his request that he had served for ten years as chaplain with Imperial troops of French and English origin and would like to continue doing so.

It seems, however, that wounded vanity played a significant role in the initial decision-making, causing the Franciscan Order to lean demonstratively towards a return home. In the course of time (quite a short time) many of the Irish realised, not only how far away home was, but also the difficul-

---

5   MUDr. is an abbreviation of the academic title *medicinae universae doctor*, i.e. Doctor of Medicine.
6   He stated that at the age of 36 his fontanelle had to be open.
7   NA, APA, carton no. 2101.

ties they might again meet with there, despite the fact that the situation in Ireland had improved dramatically in 1782,[8] now that the Penal Laws had been partially repealed and Catholic clergy were again allowed to live in the country.

The case of the forty-one-year-old[9] Thomas Clancy, who was a *lector primarius*, could serve as an example. He had told the commission that within five months he intended to travel to Ireland, but as early as 6 January 1787 he applied for secularisation and a pension. The Archbishop of Prague, Antonín Petr, Count Příchovský of Příchovice, quickly granted his application for secularisation on 25 January. He later, on 22 May, received a pension of 200 florins in accordance with the court decree. One month later, however, he accepted a further 200 florins as a grant towards his journey to Ireland (*Reisegeld*), which indicates that the state authorities took his original decision as binding. The following year, however, they could still have come across Clancy in Prague, as he had applied for his pension to be extended due to his poor state of health, substantiated by a certificate from MUDr. Josef Kašpar Šťastný.[10] This was also repeated in 1789, with a certificate from the same doctor attached to the application and, for greater credibility, yet another from a MUDr. Müller.[11] After that, when nothing was heard of Clancy for several years, at the very end of spring 1796, he was applying to the archbishopric for a letter of discharge (*litterae dimissoriales*) because he was leaving for Ireland.[12] Not even that was his final word: on 9 August 1798, the regional government was asking the consistory under what conditions Thomas Clancy and Thomas O'Hogan would be given an annual pension of 200 florins, and calling for the consistory to create a commission to determine whether the above-named were at all suitable persons to undertake the office of secular priest.[13]

Anthony Geraghty went through a similar process. On 25 October 1786, he declared[14] that he wished to return to Ireland. On 30 March 1787, he applied for a pension accompanied by a certificate from the same MUDr. Šťastný, saying that at the age of thirty-one he had rheumatism.[15] On the basis of this, he received the pension on 14 June, together with permission to stay in the

---

8   Theodore W. Moody and Francis X. Martin eds., *Dějiny Irska* [*The Course of Irish History*] (Praha: Nakladatelství Lidové noviny, 1996) 160–170.

9   On 25.4.1788, he stated that he was forty-one years old and enclosed a certificate of ordination to the priesthood in Rome on 19.12.1772, see NA, ČG Publ, 1786–1795, 145/111/1789-93, carton no. 2731.

10   Ibid.,1786–1795, 145/111/1788, carton no. 2730.

11   Ibid., carton no. 2731.

12   NA, APA, carton no. 2101. The request was received on 16.6.1796.

13   Ibid.

14   He was not present at the initial commission hearing. The guardian stated that he would like to return.

15   NA, ČG Publ, carton no. 2731.

country for one year. At the end of January 1788, he attempted, with a certificate referring to rheumatism (from MUDr. Josef Jindřich Bauer), to gain a pension for a further period[16] and evidently achieved his objective because the following year he applied again, on the basis of the medical opinion of (none other than) MUDr. Müller and MUDr. Šťastný.[17]

As mentioned above, the guardian, Thomas O'Hogan and the oldest Father of the community (*senior pater*), James O'Kelly, also eventually applied for a pension.[18] Together with Thomas Clancy, they received this in accordance with the above-mentioned decree of 22 May. Thomas O'Hogan then, together with Clancy, applied for a letter of discharge in 1796.

Francis Crowley also wished to be pensioned off, but his repeated requests were not granted, so that he finally received 300 florins travelling expenses and left for Vienna to see *Platz-Major* O'Sullivan, as Thomas O'Hogan informed the authorities on 20 August of that year.[19] In May 1788, proceedings began regarding Crowley's transfer to the diocese of Linz.[20]

John Fitzpatrick, who had originally committed himself to return to Ireland within five months, entered into the service of Count Marcolini as a tutor and began to teach his children. In 1792, therefore, he applied for secularisation,[21] but, in February 1799, the regional authorities were dealing with his pension, so it seems likely that in the end he remained in Bohemia.

Those who had decided to return to Ireland already began to leave Bohemia in December 1786. O'Hogan always informed the regional authorities of departures; for example, Father F. Fitzgerald and Brother J. Plunkett departed on 10 December, Father J. Collins (he clearly, like Father Conway, did not complete the course in theology) and Father A. O'Brien on 15 December,[22] and then Father P. Conway and Brother B. O'Donell on 27 December.[23] According to Bílek's unverified account, twenty-one Irishmen left Bohemia.[24]

---

16   Ibid., carton no. 2730.

17   Ibid., carton no. 2731.

18   He is signed as *senior pater* on the commission protocol from 21.10.1786. In the protocol, he stated that he wished to return to Ireland but only after he had confirmed an "inventory" (he may have meant a transfer protocol). According to the same document, he had lived in the college for thirty-four years. On 13 February, he requested secularisation. In the certification of ordination dated 20.9.1767, attached to the second request from 16.4.1787, the Archbishop of Prague A.P. Příchovský of Příchovice confirmed that James O'Kelly had been ordained a priest in the archbishopric chapel on 21.9.1754.

19   At that time, O'Sullivan possibly knew that he would be sent to the city garrison in Prague as is stated in *Schematismus für das Königreich Böheim 1789*, Prag 1789, 124.

20   NA, APA, carton no. 2101

21   Ibid., request dated 23.8.1792.

22   Report dated 21.12.1786.

23   Report dated 25.1.1787.

24   Tomáš V. Bílek, *Statky a jmění kollejí jesuitských, klášterů, kostelů, bratrstev a jiných ústavů v království českém od císaře Josefa II. zrušených* [*The Property and Assets of the Jesuit Colleges, Monasteries, Churches, Fraternities and Other Institutions in the Kingdom of Bohemia Dissolved by*

As regards the friars, we know about fourteen who went to other Irish Franciscan religious institutes. James Connolly,[25] Anthony O'Reilly, John Commins,[26] and James Plunkett[27] headed to Boulay college. We have no idea what happened to them after this friary had been closed down. Bonaventura O'Donell went to Rome in 1786 to be ordained a priest there the next year.[28]

Nine friars from the Prague college returned to Ireland. Francis Gallagher went to St Anthony's college in Louvain[29] and then served as guardian of Donegal friary up until 1804.[30] Anthony Collins is mentioned as guardian of Ennis house in 1788.[31] Patrick Harty was vicar of Boulay in 1787,[32] then moved to Roscrea in 1790 to be guardian there,[33] Nenagh was his next house from 1791 to 1806[34] and finally he was guardian of Bantry in 1815.[35] Michael Egan was ordained a priest in Prague in 1786.[36] He was subsequently guardian of a number of friaries: Ennis in 1790,[37] Roscrea in 1793,[38] Ennis in 1794[39] and again in 1796[40] and finally Castlelyons from 1800 to 1801.[41] In 1802, he relocated to the United States and in 1808, he was appointed the first Bishop of Philadelphia.[42]

Emperor Joseph II] (Praha: Frant. Bačkovský, 1893) 229. Some of the other data in Bílek's report is not reliable: the number of persons in the Irish Franciscan college (only forty-nine) and the date of the dissolution of the college (12.2.1786).

25   Anselm Faulkner O.F.M. ed., *Liber Dubliniensis. Chapter documents of the Irish Franciscans 1719–1875* (Killiney: Franciscan Friars 1978) 167, 171 reports on his stay in Boulay in 1787 to 1788. His death is announced in the chapter bill of 23 July 1793, ibid., 182. He defended his thesis in Prague in 1780, and in 1782 was a student of theology there. Hereinafter quoted as *Liber Dubliniensis.*

26   *Liber Dubliniensis,* 167. Mentioned on 9 May 1787 as an instructor of youths and novices. Benignus Millett, "Some lists of Irish Franciscans in Prague, 1656–1791," *Collectanea hibernica* 36–37 (1994–5): 80–81. The first information about him in Prague says he was a vicar in 1782.

27   Ibid., 171. Mentioned on 14 July 1788 as a lector of moral theology in Boulay.

28   Matthäus Hösler, "Irishmen ordained at Prague, 1629–1786," *Collectanea hibernica* 33 (1991): 53. Tonsure and minor orders 10 June 1786, subdiaconate 2 December 1786.

29   *Liber Dubliniensis,* 175. Mentioned on 18 May 1790 as a lector of theology. According to Millett, "Some lists of Irish Franciscans in Prague," 81, he was already a lector of theology and discreet in Prague in 1782.

30   Ibid., 185. Mentioned as guardian, *lector iubilatus* of theology and *ex-custos.* Also in 1796, ibid., 189; 1800, ibid., 192; 1801, ibid., 196; 1803, ibid., 199; 1804, ibid., 203. In 1806, Gallagher is listed among the deceased members of the Irish province, ibid., 206.

31   Ibid., 170. Anthony Collins came to the Prague college as a student in 1782. Two years later, he was a lector of philosophy.

32   Ibid., 167.

33   Ibid., 174.

34   Ibid., 177, 181, 184, 188, 191, 195, 198, 202, 205.

35   Ibid., 208.

36   Hösler, "Irishmen ordained at Prague," 53. On 10 June 1786.

37   *Liber Dubliniensis,* 173.

38   Ibid., 181.

39   Ibid., 184.

40   Ibid., 188.

41   Ibid., 192 and 195.

42   Maelísa Ó Huallacháin, OFM., "Notebook 36 of Father Laurence Browne, O.F.M.," *Collectanea hibernica* 44–45 (2002–2003): 281.

Ambrose Cassidy[43] was guardian of Bonamargy from 1800 to 1803[44] and Derry from 1804 to 1824.[45] Joseph Joyce, who had been ordained a priest in Rome in 1783,[46] went first to Prague and then probably back to Ireland although we have no reliable information about this. Perhaps he became guardian of Dromahaire friary from 1819 to 1825.[47] Francis O'Neill is mentioned as guardian of Dromore in 1788,[48] of Armagh in 1791,[49] and of Dungannon from 1793 to 1815.[50] Thomas Lorcan[51] was guardian of Kinaleghin from 1800 to 1804.[52]

Anthony O'Brien left Prague back in 1786.[53] The chapter bill of 1791 lists two Anthony O'Briens: the first was guardian of Youghall, the second of Galbally.[54] Which of them was in Prague still remains a mystery.

In the Irish college, however, there were still thirteen lay brothers, but they were all Czech or German. Three of them, evidently the oldest, were accepted at their own request by the Franciscans of Our Lady of the Snows.[55] According to the protocol, the others favoured secularisation and a pension.[56]

Here, the Irish Franciscans vanish from the sources. How many of them actually remained in Prague or Bohemia till the end of their lives we have not been able to discover. We may suppose that it was difficult for the oldest members of the college to succeed in embarking on the arduous journey across the whole of Europe and that they found eternal rest in the Bohemian Crown Lands.[57] One Irish Franciscan of whose further religious activity we

---

43 Hösler, "Irishmen ordained at Prague," 53. On 14 June 1783, Cassidy received tonsure and four minor orders.
44 *Liber Dubliniensis*, 192, 196, 199.
45 Ibid., 203, 209, 212, 216, 219.
46 Ibid., 282.
47 Ibid., 212, 215, 218, 222. Dromahaire is listed under its Latin name Petrae Patricii.
48 Ibid., 171.
49 Ibid., 178.
50 Ibid., 182, 186, 189, 192, 196, 199, 203, 206, 209.
51 Hösler, "Irishmen ordained at Prague," 53. Lorcan received tonsure and minor orders on 17 December 1785 and he was ordained a subdiacon on 10 June 1786.
52 *Liber Dubliniensis*, 192, 195, 199, 202.
53 His biographical data see below in the section *Members of the Franciscan College of the Immaculate Conception of the Virgin Mary in Prague (1629–1786)*. He already defended his thesis in 1772.
54 *Liber Dubliniensis*, 177.
55 On 17 February 1787, the provincial Fr. František Bartoň notified the regional government that at Our Lady of the Snows they had accepted three lay brothers from the Irish Franciscan college, namely, Anton Gasser (83), Josef Martini (78) and František Raab (60).
56 Otto Reschka, Benevenut Král, Josef Kasseker, Dominik Smrčka, Bonaventura Phlimbl, Jan Handel, Pacificus Spirrman, Damián Kuželka, Kilián Mess and Paschal Finck.
57 Bílek, *Statky a jmění kollejí*, 229, states that twenty-one priests returned to Ireland. It is noteworthy that the interest of the Irish in the fate of the lay brothers did not die down for a long time after the dissolution of the college, as evidenced by a report on the death of three of them – Dominik, Damián and Otto – in the record from the provincial chapter in 1803 (*Liber Dubliniensis*, 200).

have indisputable proof is Francis Conelly, who was chaplain in the private chapel of Baron of Hildebrand in Slabce.[58]

Apart from the friars, several other people, whom we could call civilian personnel, worked within the college. They are referred to in the sources by the German expression *"die weltliche Dienstleute."* We can learn about them from a document dated 27 November 1786, containing the outstanding amounts owed by the Irish Franciscans to these seven secular employees (a total of 16 florins 52 kreutzer). Their trades correspond to the needs of the college; organist, cook, assistant in the sacristy, gardener, tailor, laundress and bookbinder.[59]

Thus, after one hundred and fifty-seven years in the heart of Europe, concludes the history of the Franciscan College of the Immaculate Conception of the Virgin Mary by St. Ambrose. Now let us examine what the college was like in the period when the friars were leaving it and what exactly its assets were during its liquidation.

BONA: MOBILIA ET IMMOBILIA[60]

The 1791 application[61] by three merchants in the dyeing industry, Piccard, Euler and Compaque, to buy the former Irish Franciscan college also included a description of the building which had been recorded in their estimate at the beginning of 1787[62] by four Prague specialists in this field, the builders Filip Hejer and Jan Želnický and the gardeners Václav Ryšlánek and Jan Adamec According to their testimony, the two-storey building of the college measured fifty-three Viennese fathoms on the side facing Dlážděná street and twenty-five Viennese fathoms on the front side facing towards the Old Town. The garden with two *altans* and a stable with one stall and a small chamber extended over 1,546 square Viennese fathoms and the area of the two courtyards was 528 square Viennese fathoms. On the ground floor of the building above the vaults was a kitchen with all the requisite tableware of copper and iron utensils and several small rooms, including a pantry, a

---

58   Conelly is mentioned as late as 1789, see *Catalogus universi cleri archi-diaecesani Pragensis in cura animarum existentis*, Vetero-Pragae 1789, 5.

59   NA, ČG Publ, carton no. 2729, the following names are given: Antonín Čermák, organist; František Biba, cook (*Kucheling*); Prokop Hřebíček, assistant (*Bedienster*) in the sacristy; Jakub Hartig, gardener; Matyáš Rašek, tailor; Kateřina Kuncová, laundress; Bernard Poslušný, bookbinder.

60   "Assets: movables and immovables."

61   NA, ČG Publ, carton no. 2731. The document arrived at the regional government 14.11.1791.

62   The estimate is dated 18 January. Another document which described the college in detail was the inventory, NA, CSÚ, carton no. 293. *Inventarium über das Vermögen des aufgehobenen Klosters des P. P. Hiberner in der Neustadt Prag adjustiert 7. August 1787.* The following picture of the college is a combination of information taken from these two sources.

corn store and cellars, a refectory with a small storeroom for tablecloths, brass and tin tableware and a billiard room (*Piliard Zimmer*) with various furnishings such as a billiard table, one four-sided and one five-sided playing table, a small glass table, ten leather chairs, three benches, six coffee cups, a porcelain punch bowl with a tin dipper and an old gun with a broken trigger, probably used as a decoration. On the first floor, there were eight rooms with heating and thirty-six small cells without. In the other wing of the second floor was the library, the archives and another nine rooms with heating, and fifteen cells. The library consisted of an anteroom with a cabinet for books, two shelves and a chair, and the library hall with shelves along all four walls. On the second floor was a guest room furnished with book shelves, a chair, a sofa, a table, a kneeler, a bed with green hangings, and a washstand. Then there was an infirmary building which included a cabinet maker's workshop, a theological school with a pulpit and benches, and a philosophical school which has not been used for some time. On the second floor was a pharmacy with two big apothecary cabinets full of glass and earthen utensils, a large oil painting of St. Patrick and a ceiling painting of the Birth of the Virgin Mary. On the third floor was a sick bay with two rooms, each with two beds, a chapel for the sick with a small wooden altar and a painting of St. Didacus, a Marian picture under glass, and a room for convalescents. The rest was reserved for another guest room which was more lavish than the above-mentioned quarters, a pharmacist's room, a tailor's room, a workshop and a depository.

The wing facing Dlážděná street also had a second floor with twenty small rooms and a vaulted corridor. Here on the first floor there was also a space, belonging to Count Sweerts-Sporck, with two rooms and a passageway to the church. The estimated value of the assets, including the church, the garden and the courtyard, was 18,500 florins.

When drawing up the initial inventory, for understandable reasons, the state authorities had to commence sealing the treasury and taking over the property extremely quickly and efficiently. We have already mentioned the detailed financial inventory of 2 October 1786, carried out by the Chamber Accounting Office, as well as the overall sum of 38,977 florins 24 kreutzer. The library was also closed and the keys handed over. On 2 and 10 November, the state librarian, Rafael Ungar, received the endowment deeds (*Stiftung-briefe*) from the Irish Franciscans.[63] There were fifty-three Mass endowments altogether, among them also those which had been arranged by other Irishmen: O'Byrn, O'Farrell, Kavanagh, Plunkett, Hamilton and Taaffe.[64] The documents from the archive sorted out by Ungar, of which one archive car-

---

63   Librarian Rafael Ungar to the regional government, 11.11.1786.
64   The list of Mass endowments from 5.8.1787.

ton has been preserved, were stored in the Clementinum and only in this century added to the archives of other dissolved monasteries in the National Archives in Prague.

The protocol recording the assets of the college on 13 December 1787[65] gives the following figures:

cash – 1,092 florins 56 kreutzer
assets – 989 florins 24 kreutzer
endowment capital – 35,033 florins
4% annual interest on the capital sum of 3,537 florins 30 kreutzer amounts
    to – 141 florins 30 kreutzer
various arrears and money withheld for the college – 1,623 florins 45 kreutzer
real estate value – 12,500 florins
from the sale of wine – 527 florins 8 kreutzer
from the sale of eggs – 80 florins
from the sale of vinegar – 3 florins 8 kreutzer
from the sale of other items – 25 florins 15 kreutzer
from the sale of goods after the deduction of auction fees – 908 florins
    41 kreutzer

This all came to a total of 56,320 florins 47 kreutzer, and then, after the deduction of liabilities, 55,002 florins 7 kreutzer. The protocol goes on to say that 4% interest from the total amount would bring in 2,200 florins 12 kreutzer annually. However, if annual pensions for nine priests of 200 florins each and for thirteen lay brothers of 150 florins each were taken into account, then the aggregate sum would come out at 3,750 florins per year, which would be 1,549 florins 48 kreutzer more than the calculated interest. To this would also have to be added the alms granted to the college by state institutions, originally in kind, later in cash (for example, the Salt Office paid 98 florins instead of fourteen casks of salt). In total, these "*Almosen von Aerario*" amounted to 2,313 florins.

An inventory of the friars' cells gives us an interesting, though humdrum, insight into everyday life in the college. Let us look at three examples of these cells. The first is that of the last guardian, Thomas O'Hogan, who had in his room a sofa, six armchairs, eleven other chairs of different kinds, three small tables, a book shelf, a glassed-in cabinet for books, a wardrobe, a bed, a washstand, a cupboard, a clavichord, a counter, a kneeler, a grandfather clock, various books of his own and several pictures. Anthony Geraghty's

---

65   During the process of secularisation of the college, the estimated amounts of money changed. This is the last assessment we know about.

room contained two tables, a clavichord, a cupboard, a cabinet, a kneeler, a sofa, a suitcase, six seats, an armchair, two other chairs, a bed, various books of his own, two crucifixes. Anthony Dolan had three small tables, an armchair, a washstand, three other chairs, a book shelf, a bed, various books of his own, a terrestrial globe and a celestial globe. Most of the friars owned books or had book shelves in their cells, which completes the picture of the intellectual background of the college.

Valuables and other objects from the church were initially left to the friars so that they could conduct divine worship. In the spring of 1788,[66] an inventory of church vessels, Mass vestments and church textiles was made. It mainly concerned less valuable items, that is, silver ciboriums, four silver chalices with patens, pewter candlesticks, lamps and jugs. These objects should have been transferred to the garrison church (that is, to the former Seminary Church of St. Adalbert), where they were also stored, but some of them ended up in the main depository in the Minim friary. A document from September of the same year has been preserved which lists the church's gold, silver, copper, brass and pewter valuables, plus fabrics and rare furniture. Not even this inventory is complete and the main inventory (*Hauptverzeichnis*) to which it refers has unfortunately not been preserved. According to the inventory, the item estimated as most valuable was a monstrance with six diamonds, a silver stand and a golden lunette (533 florins), then nineteen silver chalices with patens (778 florins). Books are also recorded in the list; six good large missals, five large old missals, two small missals, one sacramentary and twelve old books containing the requiem. The overall estimated value was 4,386 florins 24 kreutzer. Again, the objects were transferred to the Minim friary, the valuable gold and silver items were handed over to the Imperial and Royal Assay Office (*k. und k. Gold und Silber-Einlösungsamt*) for official valuation, a smaller quantity passed on to the consistory of the Prague Archbishopric for redistribution and some were sold off (at the estimated value plus a 10% surcharge). Among the buyers were, for example: František Zikan, canon of the Vyšehrad Chapter house, who bought an altar frontal, Mass vestments and canopies; the Irish Franciscan O'Dolan who thus obtained three silver chalices with patens; or Karel Rocker who bought a chasuble for the church in Plzeň.

The last mention of objects from the church comes from 26 November 1791, when an inventory was made of items from the Irish Franciscan church, up to fifty florins in estimated value, which were transferred to the archdiocesan consistory to be divided among various parts of the diocese. The list consisted of a silver ciborium with a lid, silver chalices with patens, pewter

---

66   22.4.1788, see NA, ČG Publ, carton no. 2730.

Fig. 35 The interior of the Irish Franciscan church during structural adaptations between the two world wars (NPÚ).

lamps, Mass jugs, salvers, vestments in various liturgical colours and linen to
the value of 362 florins.[67]

We can follow the fate of the individual college buildings for longer. As
we know, the Franciscans continued to live in the college for a time. In 1791,
the three dyeing merchants, Piccard, Euler and Compaque, wanted to purchase the building. The following year, the State Banking Office expressed
an interest, wanting to establish a customs and excise office.[68] Eventually,
however, the Church put up the buildings, including the consecrated church,
for public auction. Johann Franz Christian, Count Sweerts-Sporck, was successful at the auction. He owned the neighbouring palace and also claimed
priority right to the college, thanks to the long-term contacts his predecessors had had with the Irish Franciscans. He paid 25,587 florins 33⅓ kreutzer
for the whole complex.[69]

The Count may have intended to build a theatrical stage in the former college church (Fig. 35); from as early as 1789, for that matter, the Czech Patriotic
Theatre (České vlastenecké divadlo) played here – in the former refectory – in
Czech. With this objective in mind, Sweerts-Sporck had a substantial portico,
later demolished, built in front of the church. A year after his death, that is,
in 1803, Jan Rudolf, Count Chotek of Chotkov, bought the former college for
60,000 florins. Sweerts-Sporck's investment of 15,000 florins was included
in the price. Chotek of Chotkov's plans were linked with the original idea of
creating a customs and excise office in the building. Preparations, in particular the designs, dragged out for some time, so that they were not completed
until 1807. The professor of architecture at Prague Polytechnic, Jiří Fischer,
became the author of the plans for the adaptation, with the assistance of the
Vienna court architect, Louis Montoyer. Fischer was also entrusted with
management of the construction. To carry out the building alterations, he
chose the Prague builder Josef Zobel, while Jan Želnický was charged with
the carpentry (he had been involved in the 1787 estimate of the value of the
building). The alterations, above all to the decorations, were also carried out
by the stonemason Ludvík Kranner and the stucco artist František X. Leder-
er. The reconstruction was definitively completed in 1813. Due to rising prices
during the Napoleonic Wars, the original budget doubled and ultimately exceeded half a million florins.

Up to the present day, the new customs and excise office has not under-
gone any significant alterations.[70]

---

67 Ibid., carton no. 2731.
68 Růžena Baťková ed., *Umělecké památky Prahy. Nové Město, Vyšehrad, Vinohrady* [*The Artistic
    Monuments of Prague: New Town, Vyšehrad and Vinohrady*] (Praha: Academia, 1998) 548.
69 Alois Kubíček, "Adaptace kláštera hybernů na celnici" [The Adaptation of the College of the Irish
    Franciscans into a Customs and Excise Office], *Umění 3* (1955): 41–42.
70 Ibid.

The college of the "Hybernians" once gave the name to the square its façade looks out on – "Hybernské náměstí" – whereas the northern part of the square now called náměstí Republiky was named after the friary of the Capuchins, with whom the Irish had quarrelled in the early period. After 1870, the name was changed several times, but only returned to its original form during the German Protectorate.[71] At the beginning of the nineteenth century, but not before 1816,[72] Dlážděná ulice [Dlážděná street] which then led East from the former Irish Franciscan college towards the ramparts and fortification of St. Nicholas (where the Masaryk Railway Station is now), was renamed "Hybernská ulice" [Hybernian street]. This name has remained to the present day,[73] as with the exhibition hall in the former church called "U hybernů" [The Hibernians], even though most inhabitants of Prague have no idea where the name originated.

In 2006, the conversion of the church to a music theatre was completed.[74] The building was reverted to its first profane function, but its name *Divadlo Hybernia [Hybernia Theatre]* refers to much older times.

So before long only the name of the street will reflect those times when, in the very centre of Prague, in the streets around the Powder Gate, Irish could be heard and its reverberations mixed with the footsteps of men who had undertaken the long pilgrimage from Erin's green isle, with the Latin and German words of the sermons on their celebrated patron saint, St. Patrick, and with the murmur of students who were learning theology according to the interpretation of John Duns Scotus from his learned successors.

---

71   See Jiří Čarek, Václav Hlavsa, Josef Janáček and Václav Lím, *Ulicemi města Prahy od 14. století do dneška [Through the Streets of Prague from the Fourteenth Century to the Present Day]* (Praha: Orbis, 1958) 65; later Marek Lašťovka ed., *Pražský uličník. Encyklopedie názvů pražských veřejných prostranství, 1. díl (A–N) [Prague Street Guide. An Encyclopedia of the Names of the Public Spaces in Prague, Volume 1 (A–N)]* (Praha: Libri, 1997) 577ff.

72   Jütter's plan from 1816 still shows Hybernská ulice as "Pflastergasse," i.e. Paved Street (Dlážděná ulice). See a facsimile edition with commentary and explanatory notes: *Plán Prahy z roku 1816 [The Plan of Prague of 1816]*. Prepared for publication by F. Roubík, K. Kuchař and V. Hlavsa (Praha: Kartografie Praha, 1972).

73   Čarek, Hlavsa, Janáček and Lím, *Ulicemi města Prahy*, 65, and Lašťovka ed., *Pražský uličník*, 228ff.

74   On the reconstruction, see Richard Biegler's article, "Rekonstrukce kostela Neposkvrněného početí Panny Marie (tzv. Paláce u Hybernů) na muzikálové divadlo" [The Reconstruction of the Church of the Immaculate Conception of the Virgin Mary (the Palace of Hybernians) into a Musical Theatre], *Za starou Prahu. Věstník klubu za starou Prahu* 30.3 (2000): 7–9. The author criticised the approach of the investors and officials involved in the reconstruction as insensitive and even uncivilised, and mentioned that the demolition work was extensive.

7. ARCHIVES AND LIBRARIES

MANUSCRIPT SOURCES

The archive of the College of the Immaculate Conception of the Virgin Mary by St. Ambrose in Prague,[1] where we would expect to find the most important written sources, is unfortunately in disarray. When the college was dissolved in 1786, its archive and library were, like many other archives and libraries belonging to the houses of other orders, passed into the hands of Rafael Ungar, the State Librarian. All that remains here as a testimony to more than one hundred and fifty years of the Irish Franciscans in this country can fit into just one archive carton in the National Archives in Prague (NA, I. odd., archive group AZK – ŘHyb Praha, Spisy 2726–2727, carton no. 45). There are more than two hundred items of particularly heterogenous material, which is only in part preserved in the original. The bulk of it comes from the golden period of the college in the second half of the seventeenth century; the scant documentation from the following century speaks tellingly of the gradual decline in the importance of the community. As for the surviving deeds, these are deposited in archive group AZK L 2, ŘH sv. Ambrož; admittedly, this collection amounts to a mere ten items, but it contains almost every important privilege granted to the Prague college by the Pope or the emperors up to 1746.

A minor source was provided by the archive group Stará manipulace (SM, ref. no. SM H 99 1, 3, 4, 8, carton no. 912), containing references to the compulsory purchase of houses for the needs of the college; these can be complemented by Lancinger's topographical research in the Prague Historical Review.[2]

---

1.   The Irish Franciscan Friary was built in place of an earlier St. Ambrose monastery of the Benedictines, which perished during the Hussite Wars in the first half of the fifteenth century. The history of the location was known to the Irish Franciscans, who respected the previous foundation by including a reference to St. Ambrose in the name of their college. In Latin, the official name was *Collegium Immaculatae Conceptionis Beatae Marie Virginis ad sanctum Ambrosium*, in Czech *Kolej Neposkvrněného Početí Panny Marie u svatého Ambrože*. Both the Latin *ad* and the Czech *u* mean "by" in English. On the St. Ambrose monastery, see Jan Pařez, "Kláštery na Novém Městě pražském do husitských válek a jejich právní a ekonomické postavení v městském prostředí" [Monasteries in Prague's New Town up to the Hussite Wars and Their Legal and Economic Status in the City], *DP* 17 (1998): 75–91.

2.   Luboš Lancinger, "Z místopisu Nového Města pražského v 15.–19. století – Hybernská ulice I" [On

In the archive group Nová manipulace there are also some records which enable a closer examination in particular of the maintenance of the college or the building activity in relation to the Bohemian authorities (NM, ref. no. NM K2 H1 1).

In the archive group of the Franciscan Friary of Our Lady of the Snows in Prague (archive group ŘF in the same archives), under serial number 13, there is a book, written in the Irish Franciscan college, which is important for the understanding of the internal structure and functioning of the community, namely the Statutes of the Prague college (*Statuta domestica pro religio regimine fratrum minorum strictoris observantiae provinciae Hiberniae, collegii Immaculatae conceptionis B.V. Mariae Praqae*). In the archive group there are also other documents from which can be learnt the names of the Irish Franciscans (ŘF, carton no. 22), and also *Archivum seu protocollum conventus Otticensis ad s. Patrem Franciscum* (ŘF, book no. 46) which comes, as the title suggests, from the Franciscan friary in Votice. In the part of the latter entitled *Memorabilia conventus* there is, for one thing, a description of the death of Patrick Fleming which was copied from a less well-known Bruodin publication, as well as references to the alteration of Fleming's tomb from the eighteenth century.

In the same place, the Archives of the Prague Archbishopric (Archiv pražského arcibiskupství) contains some materials relating to the Irish Franciscan college. There are less important documents on the history of the college, for example, information on tuition in the 1630s and 1640s (APA, 2014), documents which originated in communications with the consistory from the 1630s to the 1650s (APA, ref. no. C 119/2, carton no. 2100), ordination registers for the 1620s to the 1640s containing Irish names, (from APA, book no. B 3/4, the ordination register by Šimon Brož for the years 1627 to 1643), documents relating to the sale of Franz Anton Sporck's garden (APA, carton no. 2166), but, above all, there is a volume of written material concerning the visit by the Archbishop's commission in 1737 (APA, book no. B 65/13). This detailed record allows us, not only to reconstruct the personnel of the house, but also to understand the atmosphere which governed the community at that time. It is a unique opportunity for a detailed examination of the functioning of the college in the eighteenth century.

From the same period, there is a catalogue of the library entitled *Catalogus librorum bibliothecae Patrum Hibernorum ad sanctum Ambrosium Pragae*

the Topography of Prague's New Town in the Fifteenth to Nineteenth Centuries – Hybernian Street I], *PSH* 20 (1987): 138–180. The author based his contribution not only on city records but also on the records in the Šternberk-Manderscheid family archive in the archives of the National Museum, see below.

inceptus … 1752 a me Fratre Patricio Hackett which is in the National Library in Prague.[3]

The personal archive of Archbishop Ernst Adalbert, Cardinal Harrach, contains details which complement and illuminate life in the college up to the 1660s. This is in the archive group Familienarchiv Harrach in Allgemeines Verwaltungsarchiv in the Austrian State Archives in Vienna.

There are further documents from the period of the dissolution of the college which predate the material which will be discussed in the next paragraph. This concerns mainly the time of the college's subordination to the Prague Archbishopric (APA, carton no. 2101 – the 1770s and 1780s).

The sad end of the Irish Franciscan community is recorded in another archive group in the National Archives, in that of the Bohemian Governorate (ČG Publ, 1786–1795, 145/111/1786-7, carton no. 2729–2731) and also in the Bohemian State Exchequer (CSÚ, carton no. 293). In studying this material it is possible to follow not only the dissolution of the college but also the fates of its members in subsequent years.

Bernard Jennings collected and published sources, primarily in Franciscan archives, connected with the founding and early years of the Prague college. The work contains correspondence and other documents from the years 1629 to 1639, mainly in Latin, but also in English, Spanish and German. The material came from the archives of St. Isidore's College in Rome, the friary on Merchants' Quay in Dublin, the current National Archives in Prague and the Franciscan friary in Schaerbeek in Brussels.[4]

In the 1990s, two important new publications have appeared in the Irish Franciscan journal devoted to historical research, *Collectanea hibernica*: a list of the Irishmen ordained in Prague in the years 1629 to 1786 by Matthäus Hösler (with additions by Benignus Millett) and several lists of Irish Franciscans drawn from various archive groups in the archives of the Prague Archbishopric, the Prague City Archives and from the Strahov library, which we have mostly taken from the originals.[5] We have used documents related to

3   NK, MS IX I 2. See Josef Truhlář, *Catalogus codicum manu scriptorum latinorum qui in c.r. Bibliotheca publica atque universitatis Pragensis asservantur.* Vol. 2 (Pragae: Regia societas scientiarum Bohemica, 1906) 30.

4   Brendan Jennings ed., *Documents of the Irish Franciscans College at Prague. I*, Archivium Hibernicum or Irish Historical Records. Volume IX, Maynooth 1942, 171-294. In the front page and the contents of the volume it is quoted incorrectly *Irish Franciscan Documents: Prague, I,* (further quoted as *IFD*).

5   Matthäus Hösler, "Irishmen ordained at Prague, 1629-1786," *Collectanea hibernica* 33 (1991): 7-53. Benignus Millett, "Irishmen ordained at Prague, 1628-1700: additions and corrections to Matthäus Hösler's lists," *Collectanea hibernica* 39-40 (1997-8): 23-31. Ibid., "Some lists of Irish Franciscans in Prague, 1656-1791," *Collectanea hibernica* 36-37 (1994-5): 59-84. *Collectanea hibernica* has unfortunately ceased publication.

the Irish province, principally to the provincial chapters, but more marginally connected to the Prague college.[6]

We have exploited two further archives: that of the Šternberk-Manderscheid family, stored in the archives of the National Museum, which contains detailed documents clarifying the part played by the Šternberk family in the founding of the library of the Irish Franciscan college,[7] and the Franciscan archives in Rome, from which Augustin Neumann presented his extracts.[8] These records relate to the Irish Franciscans and especially the period during which they were deprived of the possibility of teaching at the archiepiscopal seminary in Prague.

To conclude, we will mention our listing of handwritten and printed sources. In it we have presented a survey of the literary production of the humanities by Irish emigrants in Bohemia in the seventeenth and eighteenth centuries found in the Strahov library. Although with the passage of time it has become clear that the work is not entirely exhaustive, it is the only essay of its type which has been published by Czech scholars.[9] It also includes,

---

6   Cathaldus Giblin ed., *Liber Lovaniensis. A Collection of Irish Franciscan Documents, 1629-1717* (Dublin: Clonmore and Reynolds, 1956). This work provides the names of several guardians of the Prague college. Anselm Faulkner ed., *Liber Dubliniensis. Chapter documents of the Irish Franciscans 1719-1875* (Killiney: Franciscan Friars, 1978). The deaths of some Prague lay brothers are mentioned in this work. The most recent general list was published in *Liber Killiniensis. Irish Franciscan chapter bills 1876-1999 and other lists, including a catalogue of friars on lists already published*, ed. Ignatius Fennessy OFM. (Killiney: Franciscan Library, 2001). See "Appendix 3. A catalogue of Irish Franciscans found on published lists," 230-341 and also Maelísa Ó Huallacháin, OFM., "Notebook 36 of Father Laurence Browne, O.F.M.," *Collectanea hibernica* 44-45 (2002-2003): 246-311.

7   Alžběta Birnbaumová, "Příspěvky k dějinám umění XVII. stol. z archivu Šternbersko-Manderscheidského" [Contributions to the History of the Art of the Seventeenth Century from the Šternberk-Manderscheid Archive], *PA* 34 (1925): 492-497.

8   Augustin Neumann, "Výpisy z menších řádových archivů římských" [Extracts from Smaller Archives of Roman Catholic Religious Orders], *ČKD* 73.1 (1932): 92-97.

9   Hedvika Kuchařová and Jan Pařez, "Po stopách irských emigrantů ve fondech Strahovské knihovny v Praze (Z literární produkce irských emigrantů v Čechách v 17. a 18. stol.)," *Migrating Scholars. Lines of Contact between Ireland and Bohemia*, ed. H. Robinson-Hammerstein (Dublin: Navicula Publications, 1998) 116-208. Since the publication of this contribution, we have discovered the following prints: *Theses theologicae ex tractatu de opera sex dierum, et notis theologicis, cum continuatione operis de divina revelatione, quas praside P.F. Antonio Ô Brien, ord. min. strict. observ. almae provinciae Hiberniae, ss. theologiae lectore actuali ... defendas susceperunt P.F. Joannes Prendergast et P.F. Franciscus Kirwan, ejusdem ordinids, nationis, ac collegii alumni*, Pragae 1762, SK, MS JN I 43; and also the engraved thesis (signed "Bal. V. Vesterhaut"): *Theses philosophicae ad mentem doctoris subtilis Joannis Scoti ... praeside P.F. Bonaventura Managhan ... in collegio Immaculate Concep. B. V. Mariae P.P. Hibernorum Pragae ad S. Ambrosium actuali philosophiae lectore, propugnanda suscepit P. F. Franciscus Davett, ejusdem ordinis, collegii, nationisque alumnus*, Vetero-Pragae 1750, SK, without ref. no. Here, we also need to correct the attribution of a small work by Cornelius O'Mollony *Anatomicum examen* – this was a pseudonym of the famous Scotist theologian, Anthony Bruodin. English version: Hedvika Kuchařová and Jan Pařez, "On the trail of Irish émigrés in the collections of the Strahov Abbey Library in Prague," *The Ulster Earls and Baroque Europe. Refashioning Irish identities, 1600-1800*, eds. Thomas O'Connor and Mary Ann Lyons (Dublin: Four Courts Press, 2010) 183-222.

of course, works by Irish authors who were not Franciscans. Clearly, it cannot record every work, but the close contacts with the Premonstratensians, whose college, Norbertinum, was close to the Irish college and whose students attended lectures on theology and philosophy by the Irish teachers at the archiepiscopal seminary, account for the inclusion of prints and manuscripts (though primarily lists of lectures) by the Irish in the Strahov library.

PERIOD PUBLICATIONS

When the Irish college in Prague still existed, works were printed which today enable us to look into its history, in particular *Propugnaculum catholicae veritatis* by the most important Irish representative of Scotism in Bohemia, Anthony Bruodin.[10] Although this work was dedicated to the history of heresies, in it the author not only dealt with the Church history of his people and acquainted Europe with the oppression by the English to which his people were subjected at that time but also described the arrival of the Irish Franciscans in Bohemia and their impact there. Jan Florian Hammerschmid undoubtedly drew on Bruodin's work for his own survey of the history of the Church and a description of the Church and its endowments in his *Prodromus*.[11]

The final important contemporary printed work is a list of the lectors and students of Irish origin, members of the College of the Immaculate Conception, who taught and studied in the archiepiscopal seminary in the years 1635 to 1692. This detailed list also recorded some biographical information. Besides the Franciscans of the Irish province, it also contains lists concerning some of the other orders working in Bohemia.[12]

Other printed works can be found in the above-mentioned listing of Irish literary production in the stock of the Strahov library.

---

10   Anthony Bruodin, *Propugnaculum catholicae veritatis... Pars prima historica...*, Pragae 1669. SK, BCh VIII 35. Stanislav Sousedík researched A. Bruodin in his exceptional work *Jan Duns Scotus. Doctor subtilis a jeho čeští žáci [John Duns Scotus. Doctor Subtilis and His Bohemian Pupils]* (Praha: Vyšehrad, 1989) and was so interested in Bruodin's *Propugnaculum* and his other work *Armamentarium theologicum* (see below) that in the conclusion of his book he used extracts from historical works and memoirs, which he translated into Czech.

11   Jan Florian Hammerschmid, *Prodromus gloriae Pragenae*, Vetero-Pragae 1717, 297–303.

12   *Quartum quod incedit feliciter seu numerus quaternarius, celeberrimo collegio archi-episcopali Pragensi, felix, faustus, et fortunatus, discursu panegyrico deductus*, Pragae 1697, including the part *Catalogus admodum reverendorum, eximiorum, ac doctissimorum patrum professorum ex diversis religionibus, scilicet RR.PP. hibernorum, praemonstratensium, cisterciensium, benedictinorum, conventualium, franciscanorum Nivensium, tam philosophiam quam theologiam & controversias in celeberrimo collegio archi-episcopali Pragensi, ab anno 1635 usque ad Annum 1697 docentium;* a list of students then contained in the part called *Nomina aliquorum qui in collegio archi-episcopali Pragensi, ex collegio PP. Hibernorum studuerunt*, SK, AP VIII 95, duplicate HK VIII 3/1.

LITERATURE

The fate of the Irish Franciscan province[13] was described by Canice Mooney[14] and Benignus Millett,[15] and important correspondence from the beginning of the Prague college was published by Brendan Jennings.[16] Millett's work covers almost exhaustively a fifteen year period; the author used a variety of sources stored in Bohemia in the current National Archives, and, naturally, Irish sources too, as well as Vatican, Italian, Austrian (for example, the Harrach family archive), English and Spanish sources. This book provided us not only with excellent biographical information and a list of valuable sources but also with a basic understanding of the structure of the Irish province and its activity. Millett devoted a not inconsiderable part of his work to the Prague college and not only dealt in detail with its fortunes but also noted some of the literary works of its members, in particular Anthony Bruodin. He devoted one of the more detailed essays to James Taaffe, who attended the Prague college.

The Irish were the first to take scholarly note of the Franciscans in Prague. A detailed article, symbolically entitled *Ireland and Bohemia*, written in 1907 by Richard J. Kelly, admittedly lacks annotation and is rather an account of the author's time in Prague, in which he "discovers" for Ireland the Prague College of the Immaculate Conception, but it nevertheless contains a considerable amount of information.[17] Kelly followed this up with an account of the literary activity of the Irish Franciscans in Prague that contained a comparatively extensive introduction and a list of two hundred works published by the Irish.[18] At the end of the 1930s, Brendan Jennings, a Franciscan from the order's college in Louvain, visited Prague, and the result was a similar but better informed article about the Irish Franciscans in Prague.[19] In the Franciscan Library in Killiney, there is correspondence between Jennings and his Prague associate Karel Mušek who obtained excerpts from the Archives of the Ministry of the Interior (now the National Archives in Prague). There are also copies of related documents saved in Killiney.

---

13   Basic information about the history of the orders is provided by the ten-volume dictionary *Dizionario degli istituti di perfezione I–X* (Roma: Paoline, 1974–2003).

14   Canice Mooney, "The Golden Age of the Irish Franciscans, 1615–1650," *Measgra i gCuimhne Mhichíl Uí Chléirigh*, ed. S. O'Brien (Dublin: Assisi Press, 1944) 21–33; and by the same author, "The Irish Franciscans 1650–99. Rough and Uncultured Men?," *Catholic Survey* 1.3 (1953): 378–402.

15   Benignus Millett, *The Irish Franciscans 1651–1665* (Rome: Gregorian University Press, 1964). Benignus Millett, "The Papal Mission to Ireland of James Taaffe in 1668," *Dún Mhuire Killiney 1945–95* (Dublin: Lilliput Press, 1995) 102–126.

16   See above the footnote 4, Jennings, *IFD*.

17   Richard J. Kelly, "Ireland and Bohemia," *The Irish Ecclesiastical Record*, 4th series, 21 (1907): 355–360.

18   Richard J. Kelly, "The Irish Franciscans in Prague (1629–1786): Their literary labours," *Journal of the Royal Society of Antiquaries of Ireland* 52 (1922): 169–174.

19   Brendan Jennings, "The Irish Franciscans in Prague," *Studies* 28 (1939): 210–222.

In the 1950s, Kevin MacGrath, who had visited Prague in autumn 1949, wrote some critical essays. He had met the Strahov abbot, Jarolímek, who allowed him to study in the Strahov library. In 1951, in his first article, devoted to the Strahov library, MacGrath commemorates Abbot Jarolímek, who had in the meantime died in a Communist prison, briefly recounts the history of Strahov monastery and its library and presents a survey of the literary works by Irishmen which he had been able to see.[20] This work had no annotation, obviously because it was commemorative, in contrast to his next essay, published in the same year, on the Irish Franciscan library in Prague.[21] A further study was devoted to Anthony Bruodin and his cousin, Bonaventure.[22]

Among the most important titles published in Ireland over the last decade are several collections edited by Thomas O'Connor and Mary Ann Lyons, in particular *Irish Migrants in Europe after Kinsale, 1602–1820*, also including an article about the literary activities of the Irish Franciscans in Prague by Mícheál MacCraith and David Worthington.[23] *The Irish in Europe, 1581–1815* and *Irish Communities in Early Modern Europe* provide an overview of the comparative studies on Irish exiles in Europe.[24] *The Ulster Earls and Baroque Europe. Refashioning Irish Identities, 1600–1800* is the most recent volume of this kind. A new edition of a collection of older works by various authors compiled by Nollaig Ó Muraíle is also noteworthy.[25] The most comprehensive and outstanding work is undoubtedly *The Irish Franciscans 1534–1990* by various authors, edited by E. Bhreathnach, H. MacMahon OFM and J. McCafferty, an in-depth study on the history of the Irish province of the Franciscans.[26]

In the Bohemian context, if we ignore Polišenský's monograph from 1982,[27] Kovář's work on England in the second half of the seventeenth

---

20 Kevin MacGrath, "The Library of Strahov Abbey in Prague," *Irish Library Bulletin* 12 (1951): 46–48.
21 Kevin MacGrath, "The Irish Franciscan Library at Prague," *Franciscan College Annual 1951*, (Multyfarnham 1951): 29–33.
22 Kevin MacGrath, "The Bruodins in Bohemia," *The Irish Ecclesiastical Record*, 5th series, 77 (1952): 333–343.
23 Mícheál MacCraith and David Worthington, "Aspects of the literary activity of the Irish Franciscans in Prague, 1620–1786," *Irish Migrants in Europe after Kinsale, 1602–1820*, eds. T. Connor and M.A. Lyons (Dublin: Four Courts Press, 2003) 118–134.
24 Thomas O'Connor ed., *The Irish in Europe, 1580–1815* (Dublin: Four Courts Press, 2001); Thomas O'Connor and Mary Ann Lyons eds., *Irish Communities in Early-Modern Europe* (Dublin: Four Courts Press, 2006).
25 Nollaig Ó Muraíle ed., *Mícheál Ó Cléirigh, His Associates and St Anthony's College, Louvain.* (Dublin: Four Courts Press, 2008).
26 E. Bhreathnach, H. MacMahon, OFM and J. McCafferty eds., *The Irish Franciscans 1534–1990* (Dublin: Four Courts Press, 2009).
27 Josef Polišenský, *Dějiny Británie* [*The History of Britain*] (Praha: Svoboda, 1982). Apart from this, it is worth mentioning a popular book by the same author, *Britain and Czechoslovakia* (Praha: Orbis, 1966), dedicated to British-Czech relationships which also include the most important Irishmen in Bohemia.

century,[28] and a survey of British history[29] which only deals with Irish history when it interconnects with British history, then the only general work on Irish history which has been published in the Czech Republic is a translation of *The Course of Irish History* (1994), edited by T.W. Moody and F.X. Martin.[30]

Some basic facts about the College of the Immaculate Conception can be found in *Encyklopedie českých klášterů*,[31] which also refers to older literature and focuses on the historical development of the college's construction. If we are to mention a more general work, the volume on Prague's New Town entitled *Umělecké památky Prahy*[32] does so in greater detail, as does the above-mentioned article by Luboš Lancinger (which deals more with historical topography) and that by Alžběta Birnbaumová. Developments after the dissolution of the college are dealt with by Alois Kubíček.[33]

A survey by Miroslav Baroch and Ludvík Schmid of certain families, mainly ones serving in the Imperial Army, can be found in the almanac *Heraldická minucí 1987-1988*.[34] Much biographical information is provided by the quite extensive prosopographical study by Ludvík Schmid which was published in two annual volumes of *Sborník historický* [*Historical Review*] in the years 1985-1986.[35] Professor Schmid will be referred to again in the text, *inter alia*, with biographical information connected with the question of Irish emigrants to Bohemia.

A book by Stanislav Sousedík[36] on Scotism in the Bohemian Crown Lands, which also included the fate of the Irish college, was published, but because of the main theme of the work the author was unable to provide more detailed research into the history of the college. J. Polišenský also touched on the Irish in Bohemia, understandably again only marginally, in his work *Tisíciletá*

---

28   Martin Kovář, *Anglie posledních Stuartovců 1658-1714* [*England under the Last Stuarts, 1658-1714*] (Praha: Karolinum, 1998).

29   Kenneth O. Morgan ed., *Dějiny Británie* [*The Oxford History of Britain*] (Praha: Nakladatelství Lidové noviny, 1999).

30   Theodore W. Moody and Francis X. Martin eds., *Dějiny Irska* [*The Course of Irish History*] (Praha: Nakladatelství Lidové noviny, 1996).

31   Pavel Vlček, Petr Sommer and Dušan Foltýn, *Encyklopedie českých klášterů* [*The Encyclopedia of Bohemian Religious Institutes*] (Praha: Libri, 1997).

32   Růžena Baťková ed., *Umělecké památky Prahy. Nové Město, Vyšehrad, Vinohrady* [*The Artistic Monuments of Prague: New Town, Vyšehrad and Vinohrady*] (Praha: Academia, 1998).

33   Alois Kubíček, "Adaptace kláštera hybernů na celnici" [The Adaptation of the College of the Irish Franciscans into a Customs and Excise Office], *Umění 3* (1955): 41-47.

34   Miroslav Baroch and Ludvík Schmid, "Irská a skotská emigrace do střední Evropy" [Irish and Scottish Emigration to Central Europe], *Heraldická minucí 1987-88* (1988).

35   Ludvík Schmid, "Irská emigrace do střední Evropy v 17. a 18. století" [Irish Emigration to Central Europe in the Seventeenth and Eighteenth Centuries], *SH* 32 (1985): 189-254; *SH* 33 (1986): 247-293. Another work summarising the history of the Irish in Bohemia by the same author together with J. Polišenský is "Irové ve střední Evropě a Universita Karlova" [The Irish in Central Europe and Charles University], *AUC-HUCP* 16.2 (1976): 53-66.

36   See footnote 10.

Praha očima cizinců.[37] The final works are by the authors of this monograph and are, understandably, closely connected with it: the lecture by Hedvika Kuchařová at the conference on monasteries in Poland in 1999 and Jan Pařez's lecture at the conference on the Irish abroad in Maynooth in 2000.[38]

Then the Czech edition of the present volume was published in 2001, followed by several articles and lectures which focused on particular related subjects. Relations between Irish and Bohemian Franciscans were described in an article dated 2005[39] and an updated version of the study on books in the Strahov library by Irish exiles was published in English.[40] Then the educational work of the Irish Franciscans was mentioned in passing in the monograph on the Norbertinum, College of Premonstratensians in Prague.[41] Most recently, the fate of the Irish Franciscans after leaving their college was the topic of a conference paper presented at the Metropolitan University Prague in autumn 2012.[42]

Additional information about the Irish Franciscans in the first decades of the college in the period of archiepiscopal office of Cardinal Harrach was published in *Die Diarien und Tagzettel des Kardinals Ernst Adalbert von Harrach (1598-1667)*[43] (in German only) and in the monograph by Alessandro Catalano, originally in Italian and later published in Czech as *Zápas o svědomí* [*A Struggle for Conscience*], which is based on the above-mentioned source.[44]

---

37 Josef Polišenský, *Tisíciletá Praha očima cizinců* [*The Thousand-Year History of Prague through the Eyes of Foreigners*] (Praha: Academia, 1999) 63-65.

38 Hedvika Kuchařová, "Pražští hyberni – exilová komunita v novověkém městě" [The Irish Franciscans of Prague – an Exile Community in a Modern City], *Klasztor w mieście średniowiecznym i nowożytnym*, eds. M. Derwich and A. Pobóg-Lenartowicz (Wrocław and Opole: LAHRCOR, 2000) 329-336; Jan Pařez, "The Irish Franciscans in Prague: Their Position in the Prague Society of the 17th and 18th century [sic]," lecture at the conference entitled "Irish in Europe" held at the National University of Ireland, Maynooth on 25 November 2000. The latter was published as "The Irish Franciscans in seventeenth- and eighteenth-century Prague," *Irish Migrants in Europe after Kinsale, 1602-1820*, eds. T. O'Connor and M.A. Lyons (Dublin: Four Courts Press, 2003) 104-117.

39 Jan Pařez, "Irští františkáni (hyberni) a česká provincie františkánského řádu" [Irish Franciscans and the Bohemian Province of the Franciscan Order], *Historia Franciscana II*, eds. Petr Regalát Beneš and Petr Hlaváček (Kostelní Vydří: Karmelitánské nakladatelství, 2005) 144-150.

40 Hedvika Kuchařová and Jan Pařez, "On the trail of Irish émigrés in the collections of the Strahov Abbey Library in Prague," *The Ulster Earls and Baroque Europe. Refashioning Irish Identities, 1600-1800*, eds. Thomas O'Connor and Mary Ann Lyons (Dublin: Four Courts Press, 2010) 183-222.

41 See note no. 9.

42 Hedvika Kuchařová and Jan Pařez, "The Fate of Irish Franciscans After Leaving Their Prague College. The Last Community." Lecture at the conference "Ireland and the Czech Lands: Connections and Comparisons" at Metropolitan University, Prague, 18 October 2012. Published as "The Last Community: Irish Franciscans after the Dissolution of the Prague College, 1786," *Ireland and the Czech Lands. Contacts and Comparisons in History and Culture*, eds. Gerald Power and Ondřej Pilný (Bern: Peter Lang, 2014) 85-99.

43 Katrin Keller and Alessandro Catalano eds., *Die Diarien und Tagzettel des Kardinals Ernst Adalbert von Harrach (1598-1667)*, 7 vols. (Wien: Böhlau, 2011).

44 Alessandro Catalano, *La Boemia e la riconquista delle coscienze. Ernst Adalbert von Harrach e la*

Czech art historians Radka Tibitanzlová, Martin Mádl and Štěpán Vácha recently published works on the subject of the furnishings and decoration of the college church.[45]

Other sources and literature are refered to in the text in passing.

Controriforma in Europa centrale (1620-1667) (Roma: Edizioni di Storia e Letteratura, 2005). Czech version was published as *Zápas o svědomí. Kardinál Arnošt Vojtěch z Harrachu (1598-1667) a protireformace v Čechách*, trans. Petr Maťa (Praha: Nakladatelství Lidové noviny, 2008).

45 Martin Mádl, "Kresba Stigmatizace sv. Františka z Assisi a Šternberská kaple v kostele pražských hybernů" [Drawing Stigmatisation of St Francis of Assisi and Šternberk chapel in the Irish Franciscan church in Prague], *Ars linearis II. Grafika a kresba českých zemí v evropských souvislostech*, ed. Alena Volrábová (Praha: Národní galerie, 2010) 58-65. Radka Tibitanzlová, "Osudy obrazů z hybernského kostela na Novém Městě pražském" [The Fate of the Irish Franciscan Church in Prague's New Town], *Karel Škréta (1610-1674): dílo a doba. Studie, dokumenty, prameny*, eds. Lenka Stolárová and Kateřina Holečková (Praha: Národní galerie, 2013): 69-70. Radka Tibitanzlová and Štěpán Vácha, "Nově nalezené dílo Karla Škréty. Sv. Antonín Paduánský s Ježíškem a obrazová výzdoba kostela hybernů na Novém Městě pražském" [A Newly Discovered Painting by Karel Škréta: St Anthony of Padua with the Infant Jesus and the Painting Decorations in the Church of the Irish Franciscans in the New Town of Prague], *Umění* 62 (2014): 118-140.

MEMBERS OF THE FRANCISCAN COLLEGE OF THE IMMACULATE CONCEPTION OF THE VIRGIN MARY IN PRAGUE (1629–1786)

Join	entering the order
Arr	entering the college
Dep	leaving college
Lit	literary activity
Con	Connaught
Lei	Leinster
Mun	Munster
Uls	Ulster

Functions and titles

Arch	archivarius
As	archiepiscopal seminary
Br	brother and cleric
CC	commissary for the college
Cf	confessor
Cs	custos
CTD	chairman at a thesis defence
CVis	commissary visitator
D	deacon
Def	definitor
Dis	discreet
DT	defendant of a thesis
DTU	defendant of a thesis at Prague University
em	emeritus
Exam	examinator of future confessors of secular persons
fG	former guardian
fLPh	former lector in philosophy
fLPhAs	former lector in philosophy at the archiepiscopal seminary
fLTh	former lector in theology
fLThA	former lector in theology "actualis"
fLThAs	former lector in theology at the archiepiscopal seminary
Fr	Father
fSacr	former sacristan
fV	former vicar
G	guardian
Grad	graduated
GradTh	graduated in theology
J	jubilarius (50 years after the professional vows)
L	lector
LAs	lector at the archiepiscopal seminary
LBr	lay brother
LG	lector generalis

LH	lector habitualis
Lib	librarian
LPh	lector in philosophy
LPhA	lector in philosophy "actualis"
LPhAAs	lector in philosophy "actualis" at the archiepiscopal seminary
LPhAs	lector in philosophy at the archiepiscopal seminary
LPr	lector primarius
LPrPh	lector primarius in philosophy
LPrTh	lector primarius in theology
LTh	lector in theology
LThA	lector in theology "actualis"
LThAs	lector in theology at the archiepiscopal seminary
LThH	lector in theology habitualis
LThJ	lector in theology jubilatus
LThM	lector theologiae moralis
MP	minister provincial
N	novice
NM	novice-master
Ord	ordained
Ph	philosopher
PNAp	protonotary apostolic
PP	pater provinciae
Prae	praeses
PraeC	praeses of the chapter
Preach	preacher
Prof	professed
Prov	provisor (actualis ligorum provisor)
PrPS	procurator senior of the province
PTh	professor of theology
S	student
Sacr	sacristan
SAs	student (including former) at the archiepiscopal seminary
ScP	scriptor provinciae
SPh	student of philosophy
STh	student of theology
Th	theologian
V	vicar
Vis	visitator
VisP	visitator of the Irish province

When revising the list of the members of the College of the Immaculate Conception of the Virgin Mary in Prague, we primarily intended to place individual religious in the broader context of the Irish Franciscan province and – where possible – determine basic vital data. The main sources for this complementary part were editions of *Liber Lovaniensis*, *Liber Dubliniensis*, Laurence Brown's notebook and, to a lesser extent, the list in *Liber Killiniensis* which is in fact only a list of other lists.

The basic problem was to accurately identify some people. We did not attempt to do so even hypothetically in the cases when

1. several people of the same name appear in the same period and their biographical data do not allow unambiguous identification;
2. the time span in which a name occurs significantly exceeds the presumed length of productive age;

3. the phases of a person's individual career contradict the normal rules (for example, if the office of guardian appears to precede novitiate).

The list has to serve as the next comparative resource. Dates without geographical location refer to the Prague college.

For the key to the sources see *Abbreviations*.

Adelius, John (O'Dell?) (SPh, Uls – 1653-4: Millett 137)

Allin, Francis (Allen) [* c. 1690 Con] (Fr, Preach, Cf, Prov, Join c. 1716 – 1737: APAp)

Archbold, Francis (Archibald, Archepold) [†6.10.1635 Louvain] (Fr, Arr – 1633: Hammerschmid 301; Preach, Cf – Browne 90)

Archdekin, Francis [* c. 1717 Mun – a. 1755] (Join c. 1735, Ph, SPh – 1737; APAp)

Archdekin, Peter (Arcedeckne, Archedeckne, Arsedeckne) [† a. 1739] (Fr, LTh, CTD – 1732: Kelly 173; Fr, LThA, CTD, Lit – 1732 : Kuchařová/Pařez 195; 1736: AZK; Dep 1736: FA Harrach; LJ 1736: LD)

Aspol, ? (Fr, Arr – 1633: IFD 270)

Aylward, Anthony (Br, D, Arr – 1692: AZK)

Babe, Patrick [† a. 1746] (DT – 1704: SbR; G at Drogheda, Preach, Cf – 1714: LL; G at Dundalk – 1716: LL; G at Dundalk – 1720, 1736: LD)

Ballesty, Laurence [† a. 1791] (S – 1770: Lists 75, Dep – 1772: Lists 72; Preach – 1772: LD; G at Multyfarnham 1779, 1781: LD)

Barnavall, John (Barnwall, Barnevall) (Arr, LBr – 1635: AZK; Fr, Prov, LPhAs, LThAs, LJ: SIAS; MP – 1639, G at Dublin – 1645: LL)

Barry, Bernardine (G at Louvain – 1647, 1648: LL; LJ, CC? – 1659: AZK; Preach – 1659: APA; MP – 1666: LL)

Barry, John [* c. 1709 Con – † a. 1751] (Fr, Join c. 1735 – 1737: APAp; Preach, Cf – 1745: LD)

Barton, James (1773; APA)

Belein, Barnabas (Arr – 1650: AZK)

Black, Peter [† a. 1733?] (1690: APAp)

Bodkin, Peter (Cf – 1657: APA; Cf – 1690: APAp)

Brady, John (Fr, LPh, Uls –1650-1: Millett 135; 1653-4: Millett 137; Prov, VisP, LPhAs, LJ; LPh – 1656: APA; LTh – 1657: APA; 1669 G at Drogheda, Def – 1669-1672, MP – 1675-1678, Cf, Preach – 1678, G at Cavan – 1684-1687, Exam – 1689, PP – 1689, 1690, 1693, 1697: LL)

Brady, Patrick [† a. 1824] (LThA, Lit – 1765: Kuchařová/Pařez 195-196; Fr, LThA, CTD – 1768: Kelly 174; G at Carrickfergus – 1770, 1815, 1819, 1822, G at Dundalk – 1773, G at Elphin – 1793-1794, G at Derry – 1800, Def – 1801-1803, G at Bonamargy – 1804, 1806: LD)

Brady, Peter, the Elder (1770: Lists 75)

Brady, Peter, the Younger (Br, DT – 1780: Kuchařová/Pařez 219; STh – 1782: APA; LPh – 1784: APA)

Breen, Malachy see O'Brien, Malachy

Brimigam, Bonaventure (Bermingham) (Fr, Arr – after 1632: Hammerschmid 301)

Brinan, Hugh (Brennan) (LBr, Arr – after 1632: Hammerschmid 301; LBr, Lei – 1653-4: Millett 137)

Broden, Thomas (Bruodin?, Bradden?) [* c. 1705 Con] (Fr, GradTh, Join c. 1729 – 1737: APAp)

Brown, Francis [* c. 1712 Con] (Fr, S, Join c. 1735, Ord 22.9.1736 – 1737: APAp; Cf, Preach – 1741, G at Inisherkin – 1748, 1751, G in Roscrea – 1760: LD)

Brown, John (Broe) (L, Dep – 1763: Lists 72)

Brown, Martin [* c.1709 Mun – † a. 1742] (DT – 1735: NK 46 C 22; Fr, GradTh, Join c. 1730, Arr c. 1731, Ord 19.9.1733 – 1737: APAp; Fr, DT – 1736: Kuchařová/Pařez 209; Cf, Preach – 1736: LD)

Browne, James (Br, Arr – 1646: AZK; STh, Lei – 1653-4: Millett 137)

Browne, Valentine [† a. 1767] (Fr, DT, – 1727: Kelly 173; Cf, Preach – 1736, G at Kilcrea – 1738-1739, G at Bantry – 1742, G at Ennis – 1744-1745: LD)

Bruodin, Anthony [†7.5.1680] (Arr – 1649, incorporated into the Czech province – 1651: Mac-

Grath 338; LPhAs – 1656-7: Kuchařová/Pařez 196; Lit – Kuchařová/Pařez 196-198; Fr, G at the Virgin Mary of the Snows, at St. Bernardine's in Olomouc, at St. Catherine's in Jindřichův Hradec, LThAs 3x, LJ, LPrPh, LPrTh, Def of the Czech province: SIAS)

Bruodin, Bonaventure (Fr, LPh, Mun – 1650-1: Millett 136; LThAs, Lit – 1655-6: Kuchařová/Pařez 198; 1656-1659: APA; LPhAs, LThAs 15 years, died in prison in Dublin for his faith: SIAS)

Bruodin, Daniel [c. 1601-30.9.1687] (Fr, LTh, Con – 1650-1: Millett 135; LPhAs – 1643: AN; LThAs – 1644-45: AN; LThAs – 1646: VB; LJ – 1653-4: Millett 136; LJ – 1656: APA; 1657: APA; LJ: ŘF-SD; 1678-1665: APA; CVis, he taught 9 years in As: SIAS, Browne 360)

Bruodin, Simon [* c. 1714 Mun – † a. 1793] (Prof c. 1736, Ph – 1737: APApP; Cf, Preach – 1745: LD)

Bryan, Patrick [†1778] (O'Brien) (Cf, Preach – 1755: LD; LThA, CTD – 1766: Kuchařová/Pařez 217; L – 1770: Lists 75; LTh – 1773: APA; LThJ – 1776: LD)

Burke, Anthony see de Burgo, Anthony

Burke, Thomas (Br, Con – 1653-4: Millett 137)

Butler, James [† a. 1776] (S – 1770: Lists 75; Preach – 1772: LD; Cf – 1773: APA; Dep – 1775: Lists 73)

Cammius (1786: ČGP/2729)

Campbell, Anthony [* c. 1704 Uls – † a. 1748] (Fr, GradTh, Join c. 1726 – 1737: APApP)

Canavan, Anthony (SPh, Uls – 1650-1: Millett 135; SPh, Con [?!] – 1653-4: Millett 137)

Carolan, Philip (Dep – 1779: Lists 73)

Caron, Anthony (Carron) (Fr, Arr – after 1632: Hammerschmid 301; G at Elphin – 1639, G at Athlone – 1648-1650: LL)

Cassidy, Ambrose [† a. 1825] (1786: ČGP/2729; G at Derry – 1796, 1804, 1815, 1819, 1822, 1824, G at Bonamargy – 1800, 1801, 1803, Def – 1819: LD)

Cassidy, Maurice (G at Boulay – 1781: LD; 1782: Lists 82; G at Dundalk – 1791, 1793, G at Monaghan – 1815, G at Strabane – 1819, 1822, 1824: LD)

Cassidy, Peter (Dep – 1782: Lists 83; G at Monaghan – 1787, 1791, 1793, Cf, Preach – 1788, G at Downpatrick – 1794, 1796: LD)

Cavell, James (Cawell) (Fr, Arr – 1634: Hammerschmid 301; Fr, V, Cf, Preach, Dep to Silesia – 1641: AZK)

Chymanay, Eugene (Ph, Arr – after 1632: Hammerschmid 301)

Clancy, Bernardine (Clanchy) [c. 1612-5.5.1684] (LThAs – 1650: AN; Fr, LTh, Mun – 1650-1: Millett 136; CTD – 1658: Kelly 172; LPhAs, Lit – 1650 and LThAs, Lit – 1655-6, 1664-5, 1669, 1672, 1677: Kuchařová/Pařez 199-200; G – 1660: AZK; G – 1661: APA; G – 1674: AZK; G – 1675: NM; G 3x, CVis 2x, LJ, 27 years professor, LThAs and LPr 20 years: SIAS; LJ – 1678: LL; Browne 356)

Clancy, John (Clanchy) [c. 1630-19.10.1680] (LAs – 1678: APA; Fr, LPhAs, LThAs, LJ: SIAS; Browne 352)

Clancy, Patrick (Dep 1782: Lists 83)

Clancy, Thomas (LThA et em – 1782: APA; LThA, CTD, Lit – 1783: Kuchařová/Pařez 200; LPr – 1787: ČGP/2729; Ord Rome 1772, 41 years old – 1789: ČGP/2731; 1796 and 1789: APA; LJ – 1796: LD)

Clarke, Patrick (1773: APA)

Clary, Anthony (Ph, 1770: Lists 75; 1773: Lists 77)

Cleary, Thomas (1773: APA; Dep – 1773: Lists 73)

Clery, Daniel [†10.9.1657 Louvain] (Fr, SAs: SIAS; STL, V, G in Louvain: Browne 105)

Clinton, Arthur [* c. 1715 Uls] (Br, SPh – 1737: APApP; G at Monaghan – 1751, 1763, 1770, 1776, 1778, G at Downpatrick – 1754, G at Bonamargy – 1782, G at Carrickfergus – 1788, 1790: LD)

Coghlan, Anthony [† a. 1736] (Cf, Preach – 1683: LL; instructor of the young – 1690: APApP; G at Castledermot – 1693, G at Athlone – 1699-1700, G at Killeigh 1702, 1705, 1708. LL)

Coghlan, James (STh, Lei – 1650-1: Millett 136; LPh – 1653-4: Millett 137; LPh – 1656+1657: APA; G at Prague college – 1670, LJ, lector in Kladruby: SIAS, LL)

Coghlan, John (Fr, SAs, G in Athlone: SIAS; Cf, Preach – 1693: LL; G at Athlone – 1720: LD)

Coleman, Patrick (Coloman) (Br, N, Arr – 1633: Hammerschmid 301)

Colfer, Matthew [†30.3.1825 Wexford in the age of 75 years] (1773: APA; Dep – 1782: Lists 83; Browne 219)

Colfer, Thomas (Ph, N – 1770: Lists 76)

Colley, Peter (Kollius) (1690: APAp)

Collins, Anthony [† a. 1800] (Arr, STh – 1782: APA; LPh – 1784: APA; 1786: ČGP/2729; appointed LTh at Louvain – 1786, G at Ennis – 1788, Cf, Preach – 1788: LD)

Collins, James [* c. 1762] (Arr – 1782: Lists 83; STh – 1786: ČGP/2729)

Commins, John (V – 1782: APA; 1783: APA; IN at Boulay, Cf, Preach – 1787, V at Boulay – 1788, G at Ballymote – 1790: LD)

Connelly, Francis the Elder (Br, DT – 1772: Kuchařová/Pařez 202; Dep – 1782: Lists 82)

Connelly, Francis the Younger (1773+1786: APA; 1786: ČGP/2729)

Conney, Louis (Connaeus) [†14.4.1652 Prague] (Fr, LJ, LPhAs, 2x LTh at the Virgin Mary of the Snows: SIAS; LPhAs – 1643: AN; Browne 354)

Connin, Matthew [†9.6.1680] (Lists 63)

Connolly, Donat (Arr, Br, L? – 1633: AZK)

Connolly, James [† a. 1793] (Conolly) (Fr, DT – 1780: Kuchařová/Pařez 219; STh – 1782: APA; 1786: ČGP/2729; Cf, Preach – 1787, G at Boulay – 1787–1788: LD)

Connor, Anthony (Conor, O'Connor) (SPh, Con – 1650-1: Millett 135–6; V – 1653-4: Millett 136; G – 1656: APA, AZK; G – 1657: APA; Fr, SAs: SIAS; Cf, Preach, G at Elphin – 1672, CVis, LG – 1676: LL)

Connor, Bernardine [†1.9.1680] (Lists 63)

Connor, Bonaventure (O'Connor) (LJ – 1644: Kelly 172; LThAs, Lit – 1662-4: Kuchařová/Pařez 201: Fr, LTh, LJ: SIAS)

Connor, Francis (Conor) (Arr – 1673: AZK; Fr, SAs, fLTh, G in Rome: SIAS; Cf, Preach – 1687, G at Jamestown – 1693, 1697, G at Elphin – 1703, 1706, 1708, 1717: LL; J, G at Elphin – 1719: LD)

Connor, Thomas [† a. 1800] (Ph, 1770: Lists 75; 1773: Lists 78; 1782: Lists 82)

Conry, Francis (SPh, Mun – 1650-1: Millett 136; 1652: FA Harrach)

Conry, John (LPh at Nenagh – 1647, G at Cork – 1648, 1669–1670: LL; LTh – 1659: AZK; G at Kilcrea – 1661: LL)

Conry, Maurice (Fr, LTh, Mun – 1650-1: Millett 136; 1652: FA Harrach)

Considen, Daniel [† a. 1763] (chaplain to Count von Sporck – 1737: APAp; Cf, Preach – 1741, G at Quin – 1741, 1744, G at Ennis – 1746, 1751, 1753, 1760, 1761, Def – a. 1748: LD)

Contuly, John (Fr, SAs: SIAS)

Conway, Bonaventure (Fr, SAs, LPh: SIAS; SAs 1689-90: Ms. DD VI 6)

Conway, Patrick see also Guiney (Quonnay, Quameai, Quooney, Guameaus) (STh – 1786: ČGP/2729; Ph – 1786: APA)

Cooney, Michael (Connaeus) (Fr, Arr – 1681: AZK)

Cornen, Peter [† a. 1790] (LPh at Louvain, Cf, Preach – 1765: LD; Preach – 1770: Lists 75; LTh – 1773: APA; LJ – 1779: LD; Dep – 1780: Lists 73; G at Dungannon – 1782, G at Bonamargy – 1785, G at Dromore – 1787, Def – 1778: LD)

Cosgrave, Francis (Cosgrive) (Ph, 1770: Lists 75)

Cosgrave, Peter (Cosgrive) (1773: APA; LTh – 1782: APA; 1786: APA; fLPh, LTh, Prof 17 years – 1787: ČGP/2729)

Cosgrave, Philip (Cosgrive) (1770: Lists 75; Cf – 1773: APA; Cf, Preach – 1782: APA; 1786: APA + ČGP/2729)

Coskran, Anthony, (Cosgran, O'Cosgran) (Fr, DT – 1756: Kelly 173, Kuchařová/Pařez 216, Tříška 128; Cf, Preach – 1757, LPh at Louvain 1759: LD; LPhA, CTD – 1762: Kelly 174; LThA, CTD, Lit – 1764: Kuchařová/Pařez 201-202; L – 1770: Lists 75, LTh – 1773: Lists 77; 1786: ČGP/2729)

Costello, Thomas [† a. 1767] (Fr, DT – 1758: Kelly 173, Kuchařová/Pařez 217; Cf, Preach – 1760, 1763: LD)

Crowe, Laurence (Cro) [* c. 1701 Mun] (Fr, fSacr, Cf, Preach, Join c. 1717, Arr c. 1719 – 1737: APAp)

Crowley, Francis (Crouley) (1782: Lists 83; 1786: ČGP/2729; 1787+1788: APA)

Cusack, Joseph (Cusak, Kusak) (Fr, SAs: SIAS; SAs 1689-90: Ms. DD VI 6)

Dalton, Anthony (SPh, Lei – 1653-4: Millett 137; 1690: APAp)

Dalton, Laurence (Fr, DT – 1698: Kuchařová/Pařez 218; Cf, Preach – 1702, G at Killeigh – 1709, 1710, G at Athlone – 1717: LL; G at Athlone – 1719: LD)

Dalton, Nicholas [* c. 1700 Lei – † a. 1760] (Fr, LTh, Dis, Join c. 1719, LTh 1733, LPh 1733, Prae 1733, G 1734? – 1737: APAp; LThM at Louvain – 1733: LD; Fr, LThA, CTD – 1741: Kuchařová/Pařez 172; LTh, Dis – 1744: ŘF-SD; Cs – 1748–1751, LJ, Cf – 1748, G at Multyfarnham – 1751, 1753: LD)

Daly, Anthony [†15.12.1696 Louvain] (CC, Lei – 1653–4: Millett 137; Preach – 1656: APA; G at Louvain – 1659, G at Armagh – 1675, 1687, Exam – 1689: LL; STL – Browne 145)

Daly, Paul (STh, Con – 1653–4: Millett 137; Cf, Preach – 1697, G at Castledermot –1697, 1699: LL)

Davett, Anthony (Davitt) (Ph, 1770: Lists 75; 1773: APA)

Davett, Dominic [† a. 1791] (DT – 1752; Cf, Preach – 1755, G at Bunamargy – 1763, 1765, G at Donegal – 1767, 1770, 1779, Def – 1772, MP – 1776–1779, G at Boulay, PP – 1782: LD)

Davett, Francis [† a. 1757] (DT – 1750, 1752: Theses; Cf, Preach – 1755, LPh: LD)

de Burgo, Anthony, the Elder (Fr, LPh, Con – 1650-1: Millett 135; LTh – 1653–4: Millett 136LTh – 1656: APA; G – 1665: ŘF-SD; Fr, SAs: SIAS; G at Rosserilly – 1672, 1680–1681, LJ 1672, Def – 1675–1676, CVis, PraeC – 1678, MP – 1684–1687, Exam – 1689, PP – 1689–1690: LL)

de Burgo, Anthony, the Younger (Arr – 1673: AZK; Cf, 1690: APAp; Fr, G, Prov, VisP, LPhAs, LJ: SIAS)

de Burgo, Anthony, the Youngest (Fr, DT – 1759; Kelly 174; Dep – 1767: Lists 72)

de Burgo, Bonaventure, the Elder (Arr – 1673: AZK; LThAs – 1685, 1688, 1691: Kuchařová/Pařez 198–199; CTD – 1688: Kuchařová/Pařez 198–199; LTh – 1690: APAp; LTh – 1691: Tractatus; Lit – Kuchařová/Pařez 199; Fr, SAs, LPhAs 2x, LThAs 8 years, 1697 LThJ in St. Isidore's College in Rome, scriptor ordinis, V of Jerusalem, LThA in Bethlehem: SIAS)

de Burgo, Bonaventure, the Younger (1690: APAp)

de Burgo, Francis (G – 1689: NM; G – 1690: APAp; Fr, SAs, LTh: SIAS)

de Burgo, Francis Philippinus (LAs – 1678: APA; Fr, LThAs, LJ, CVis + G in Ireland: SIAS; PraesC – 1690: LL)

de Burgo, James [* c. 1702 Mun] (Fr, GradTh, Join c. 1726 – 1737: APAp)

de Collantes, Joseph (1641: APA)

Deady, Francis [* c. 1711 Mun – † a. 1763] (Fr, STh, Join c. 1730 – 1737: APAp; Cf, Preach – 1738, LPh at Boulay – 1738–1739, LJ – 1751, MP – 1754–1757, PP – 1760, 1761: LD)

Dean, Michael [†4.4.1697] (Fr, LPhAs and LThAs 2 years, fLTh, G in Louvain: SIAS; Cf, Preach, G at Louvain – 1687: LL, Browne 364)

Deleny, Anthony (Delany) [* c. 1710 Mun] (Join c. 1726: APAp; LPh at Louvain – 1733, Cf, Preach – 1735: LD; Dep 1737, Fr, PTh – 1737: APAp; G at Cashel – 1742, 1744: LD)

Dess, James (Dease ?) [* c. 1712 Con] (Br, Join c. 1735 – 1737: APAp; Cf, Preach – 1745: LD)

Devlin, Francis, the Younger (Dovlin) [† a. 1772] (1770: Lists 75)

Devlin, Joseph (Dowlin, Dowlen, Dowling) [† a. 1745] (Fr, G – 1712+1713: APA; fG 1714 – 1737: APAp; G at Nenagh – 1729, 1738, 1739, Cs – 1733–1735, J – 1742: LD)

Didacus ? [† a. 1779] (Ph, S – 1737: APAp)

Dillane, Anthony (Dillan) [† a. 1738] (1690: APAp; Cf, Preach – 1700, G at Boulay – 1714: LL; G at Louvain – 1724: LD)

Dillane, William (Dilanus) [* c. 1711 Con] (Fr, STh, Join c. 1729, Arr c. 1731 – 1737: APAp)

Dobson, John (Fr, DT – 1758: Kelly 173)

Dolan, Thomas (G – 1698: NM; G – 1699: APA)

Donell, Peter (Donellanus) (G – 1692: NM)

Donnelly, Anthony (Donelly, Donilly) (c. 1612–20.5.1682) (Fr, LTh, Uls – 1650-1: Millett 135; LPhAs – 1644-45: VB; LPhAs – 1646: AN; LThAs – 1651: AN; LTh – 1652-4: Millett 137, FA Harrach; LTh – 1658: APA; LTh, LJ – 1659: AZK; CVis – 1665: ŘF-SD; G, CVis 2x, LPhAs, LThAs, LJ: SIAS; LJ – 1670: LL)

Donnelly, Joseph (Donilly, O'Donnelly) [* c. 1703 Uls] (LThA – 1734: Quaestiones; LThA – 1734: NK 46 C 22; LThA – 1735: NK 46 C 20, De Deo uno; Fr, LTh, Join c. 1721 – 1737: APAp; LThA – 1738: NK 46 C 21)

Donnelly, Patrick [† a. 1806] (Ph, 1782: Lists 82; Cf, Preach – 1788: LD)

Donnergan, Patrick (Ph, 1770: Lists 75; Dep – 1782: Lists 83)

Donoghue, Francis (O'Donoghue) [† a. 1727] (Fr, SAs, LThA: SIAS; Cf, Preach – 1685, LTh at Louvain – 1685, ScP – 1697, G at Louvain – 1709: LL; LJ – 1710: Philosophia; G at Louvain – 1711: LL; Dis 1718 – 1737: APAp; LJ, NAp – 1719, 1720, G at Lislaghtin – 1724: LD)

Donoghue, Thomas (Fr, LPhA, CTD, Lit – 1770: Kuchařová/Pařez 219; LTh at Louvain – 1778, 1781: LD; Dep – 1782: Lists 83)

Doononne, Francis (LTh, Dis – 1722: AZK)

Dormer, Michael [† a. 1736] (Cf, Preach – 1714: LL; Fr, Dis 1714, 1718 – 1737: APAp, G – 1722: AZK; LTh em – 1724, G at Kilkenny – 1724, 1733, G at Clane – 1729: LD)

Dowdall, Andrew [† a. 1738] (Fr, SAs: SIAS; SAs 1689–90: Ms. DD VI 6; Cf, Preach – 1697, G at Drogheda – 1697, 1699: LL; G at Drogheda – 1724, Def – 1727–1729: LD)

Duffy, Francis [† a. 1778] (Ph, 1770: Lists 75; 1773: APA; Cf, Preach – 1776: LD)

Duigenan, Peter [* c. 1714 Lei] (Join c. 1735, Ph, SPh – 1737: APAp)

Duinn, Francis (Duin, Dunne) (Arr, Br – 1641 : AZK; Cf, Preach – 1647, G at Killeigh – 1658, 1659, 1672, G at Castledermot – 1669, 1670, Def – 1672: LL)

Dunne, Bonaventure (STh, Lei – 1653-4: Millett 137)

Dwyer, Peter (Dep – 1762: Lists 72; LTh – 1763, 1767, G at Kilconnell – 1763, 1767: LD)

Egan, Andrew (Fr, SAs, G 2x, Def: SIAS; Cf, Preach – 1676, G at Limerick – 1678, 1680, Def – 1681–1683, G at Roscrea – 1690, 1717 G at Nenagh – 1711, 1714, J – 1717: LL; G at Roscrea – 1719: LD)

Egan, Michael [*1761–†1814] (1786: ČGP/2729; Cf, Preach – 1787, 1793, G at Lislaghtin – 1787, G at Ennis – 1790, 1794, G at Roscrea – 1793, LTh – 1793, G at Castlelyons – 1796, 1800, 1801: LD; 1st Bishop of Philadelphia 1810 – Browne 253)

Fagan, Bartholomew [† a. 1791] (1770: Lists 75; Cf – 1770: LD; Fr, LPhA, CTD, Lit – 1772: Kuchařová/Pařez 202; LTh – 1773: APA; Dep – 1776: Lists 73; Cf, Preach – 1776, G at Killeigh – 1784, 1785, 1787: LD)

Fallon, Andrew (Fr, SAs: SIAS)

Fallon, Anthony (SAs 1689–90: Ms. DD VI 6)

Fallon, Malachy (he also used the surname Hanlan) [*Kilconnell, †9.1.1651] (1615 Fr, Preach, Cf, LTh in Louvain – 1629: IFD 178; LJ – 1637: AZK; 1646: APA; Fr, LJ, LPr, LThAs, Prae 2x: SIAS; G 2x – Browne 346)

Fallon, Thaddeus (LJ – 1675: LL; G – 1676: AZK; G – 1678: APA)

Farrell, Anthony (Ferall) [c. 1618–12.1.1681] (Arr – 1641: AZK; Lit, LPhAs – 1651, LTh, Lei – 1650-1: Millett 136; LTh – 1653-4: Millett 137; LTh – 1656–1657: APA; LThAs – 1662–1669, LThJ – 1665, CTD – 1665, LTh, LJ – 1665: ŘF-SD; 1669, 1674: Kuchařová/Pařez 202-205; LJ – 1678: LL; Vis – 1678: APA; Fr, G, CVis, LJ, LThAs 20 years and 9 years LPh: SIAS; period as G ended – 1660: AZK; LJ, LTh, LThAs – 1675: Armamentarium)

Farrell, Francis, the Elder (Ferall) (Fr, Arr – 1633: Hammerschmid 301, IFD 270; LThAs – 1636: VB; LTh – 1639; IFD 288; LThAs, Lit – 1637: Kuchařová/Pařez 206; LAs – 1638: APA; Fr, Prov, LPhAs, LThAs, LJ: SIAS; LPhAs – 1640-42: AN; G at Enniscorthy – 1645, Def – 1647-1648, LThJ – 1648, G at Multyfarnham – 1650, MP – 1655, G at Ballinasagart – 1658, 1659, 1661, PP – 1658: LL; Browne 353)

Farrell, Francis, the Younger (Farell) (escaped to Saxony – 1666: NM)

Farrell, James (Ferall, O'Ferral) [*c. 1728 Ardagh] (DT – 1766: Kuchařová/Pařez 217; V – 1786: APA, 1789: ČGP/2731; fV, 60 years old – 1788: ČGP/2730)

Farrell, John (Ferral) [* c. 1711 Lei – † a. 1772] (Fr, STh, Join c. 1731 – 1737: APAp; 1770: Lists 75)

Farrell, Peter (Ferall) (Fr, Def, Cs, VisP, G several times?, LPhAs, LTh: SIAS; G at Ballinasagart – 1675, 1676, 1678, 1680, 1684, 1685, 1699, 1700, 1706, 1708, 1717, Def – 1681-1683, IN at Athlone – 1687, G at Multyfarnham – 1693, G at Castledermot – 1705: LL)

Feargus, Francis [† a. 1806] (LThM at Louvain – 1781: LD; IN – 1782: Lists 81; G at Dromahaire – 1788, 1790, 1791, 1793, 1794, 1796, 1800, G at Ballymote – 1804: LD)

Fenell, Francis (LPhAs, Lit – 1655-6, 1659-60: Kuchařová/Pařez 202; Fr, LThAs 3x: SIAS; Cf, Preach – 1669: LL)

Field, Bonaventure [† a. 1800] (1786: ČGP/2729)

Finnegan, Patrick (Finigan) (STh – 1782: APA; Cf, Preach – 1784; G at Dundalk – 1785, 1787: LD)

Fitzgerald, Bartholomew (Fitz-Gerald) [* c. 1673 Lei] (Fr, Cf, Preach, Join c. 1703, Grad 1711 Rome, 19 years a missionary in Ireland, 3 years in Boulay, Lorraine – convent, Arr 1736 – 1737: APAp)

Fitzgerald, Bonaventure (SPh, Mun – 1650-1: Millett 136; 1652: FA Harrach; 1653-4: Millett 136)

Fitzgerald, Francis, the Elder (Br, Mun – 1650-1: Millett 136; 1652: FA Harrach)

Fitzgerald, Francis, the Younger (Br, Arr – 1782: APA; 1786: ČGP/2729)

Fitzgerald, James (Br, Lei – 1650-1: Millett 136; STh – 1653-4: Millett 137; Fr, LPhAs: SIAS; Cf, Preach – 1669, G at Kildare – 1670, 1675, 1678, 1680, 1683, G at Castledermot – 1672, 1676, 1684, 1685, 1689, Def – 1675-1676, G at Clane – 1681: LL)

Fitzgibbon, Francis, the Elder (Fitz-Gibbon, Gibbon) [† a. 1739] (Cf, Preach – 1699: LL; Fr, LTh – 1718: SbR; G – 1724: Origines; Dis 1714 – 1737: APAp)

Fitzgibbon, Francis, the Younger (Fitz Gibbon, Fitz-Gibbon) [* c. 1708 – † a. 1787] (Fr, STh, Join c. 1732 – 1737: APAp; DT – 1738: NK 46 C 21: Kuchařová/Pařez 210; G at Buttevant – 1751, 1754, 1755, G at Bantry – 1760, G at Kilcrea – 1761, G at Cork – 1767, G at Waterford – 1772, G at Inisherkin – 1779, J – 1781: LD)

Fitzpatrick, John (Fitz Patrick, Fitz-Patrick) [† a. 1819] (Cf, Preach – 1776, 1781, LPh at Boulay – 1776, 1778, 1779, LTh at Louvain – 1781: LD; LTh at Prague – 1785: APA; 1786: ČGP/2729; tutor to Count Marcolini – 1792: APA; 1799: APA)

Fitzsimon, Francis (1782: Lists 82; Cf, Preach – 1791, G at Clane – 1793, G at Dundalk – 1800, G at Armagh – 1801: LD)

Fitzsimon, Laurence (Fitz-Simon) [* c. 1717 Lei] (Join c. 1734, Ph, SPh – 1737: APAp; Cf, Preach – 1739: LD)

Fleming, Anthony (Dep – 1782: Lists 83)

Fleming, Christopher [† 1794] (Cf, Preach – 1755: LD; Fr, LPhA, CTD, Lit – 1756: Kuchařová/Pařez 206-207; Fr, LThA, CTD, Lit – 1756: Kuchařová/Pařez 206-207; Fr, LThA, CTD – 1758: Kelly 174; CTD – 1759: Kelly 174; G – 1760: Browne 252; 1760; Dep – 1762: Lists 72; Cf of Dublin sisters – 1763, 1765, 1767, LTh – 1765, G at Enniscorthy – 1765: LD, Browne 252; Def – 1766: Browne 25; 2Def – 1767: LD, MP – 1769: Browne 252, MP – a. 1772, 1776, 1778, 1779, 1781, 1782, 1784, 1785, 1788, 1791, CVis – 1785: LD, Browne 252)

Fleming, Christopher Patrick [17.4.1599 Lagan – 7.11.1631, Volešky near Votice] (biographical data: CE VI, Propugnaculum 734-758; 1631: AZK; Fr, Prae – 1631: Hammerschmid 300-1; LTh – 1631: IFD 213; Brown 337)

Fleming, Francis, the Elder (LPhAs – 1636: VB; LAs – 1638: APA; LTh – 1639: IFD 288; Fr, fLPhAs, fLThAs: SIAS)

Fleming, Francis, the Younger [† a. 1739] (LTh, Dis – 1722: AZK; LTh – 1724: Origines)

Fleming, Francis, the Youngest [* c. 1709 Lei – † a. 1763] (Fr, LTh, Join c. 1729 – 1737: APAp; Cf, Preach – 1735, LTh at Louvain – 1736, LJ – 1742, Cf and chaplain of Dublin sisters – 1744, LTh at Boulay – 1746, J – 1760, Def – a. 1760: LD)

Fleming, Patrick [† a. 1772] (Fr, DT – 1757: Kuchařová/Pařez 207; Fr, DT – 1758: Kelly 174; L – 1770: Lists 75)

Flynn, Anthony (Fr – 1673: AZK)

Flynn, Francis (Flinn) [* c. 1708 Con – † a. 1763] (Fr, STh, Join c. 1730, Arr c. 1732 – 1737: APAp; LPh at Boulay – 1741, LTh at Louvain – 1746, IN at Boulay – 1748, G at Rosserilly – 1753, 1754: LD)

Forestal, Bonaventure (Vorstall) (escaped to Saxony – 1666: NM)

Frain, Paul (Fr, Arr – 1633: Hammerschmid 301)

Frair, Paul (Fr, LPhAs: SIAS), see also probably Frain, Paul

Frame, Peter (Arr, Fr, L – 1633: AZK)

French, Anthony, the Elder (Cf, Preach – 1751, 1755: LD; Dep – 1756: Lists 72; LPh at Louvain – 1751, 1755, 1757, IN at Louvain – 1759, LTh at Louvain – 1759, Lib and Arch at Louvain – 1759, G at Galway – 1761, Cf of Galway sisters – 1761, Cs 1763-1765, G at Moyne – 1767, G at Ballymote – 1770, MP – 1772-1776: LD; Dep – 1774: Lists 73; PP – 1778, PraeC, CVis – 1779, J – 1796, J – 1801: LD)

Fullum, Michael [†1785] (S – 1770: Lists 75; Cf, Preach – 1772: LD; 1773: Lists 77; LThA et em – 1782: APA; G – 1783+1785: APA)

Fullum, Peter [* c. 1709 Lei, †1762 Prague] (S, Join c. 1731 – 1737: APAp; Cf, Preach – 1741, LPh at

Boulay – 1741: LD; LThA – 1754: Theologia; Fr, LThA, CTD, Lit – 1757: Kuchařová/Pařez 207: Dep – 1759: Lists 72; LJ – 1759, Vis, Cs a PraeC – 1760: LD)

Galaghan, Francis (Gualaghan) (Fr, SAs, LTh: SIAS)

Gallagher, Bernardine (1700: APA)

Gallagher, Francis (LThA – 1782: APA; 1786: ČGP/2729)

Gavan, Anthony (Fr, Arr – 1633: Hammerschmid 301; LThAs – 1640-2: Kuchařová/Pařez 207; Fr, LPh, missionary in Scotland: SIAS)

Gavan, Bernardine [†16.9.1701 Douai](CVis, PraeC – 1693, LJ – 1693, G at Louvain – 1693: LL; Fr, LPhAs, LThAs, LJ, CVis of the province appointed by the general, 1697 in Louvain: SIAS; G at Cavan – 1699: LL; Browne 152)

Gavely, Francis (Gawly?) (1690: APAp)

Gavoc, Bernardine (Cavoc) (LPhAs, Lit – 1639-1641, 1644-1645 + CTD – 1641: Kuchařová/Pařez 207-208; LThAs – 1646: VB; LThAs – 1648: AN; Fr, fLPhAs, fLThAs: SIAS)

Gearty, Nicholas (Gearly or Ganly according to Millett) (STh, Lei – 1650-1: Millett 136)

Geoghegan, Anthony (Geoghean) (Fr, SAs, LTh, Bishop of Clonmacnoise: SIAS)

Geoghegan, Peter (Fr, LPh, Lei – 1650-1: Millett 136; LPh – 1652: FA Harrach; LPh – 1653-4: Millett 137)

Geraghty, Anthony, the Elder (Geragoty) (1652: FA Harrach)

Geraghty, Anthony, the Younger (Br, STh – 1782: APA; 1786: ČGP/2729; Ord Prague 1783, 31 years – 1789: ČGP/2731; Cf, Preach – 1793, LTh at Louvain – 1793: LD)

Geraldin, Anthony (Br, Arr – 1650: AZK)

Geraldin, Bonaventure see Fitzgerald, Bonaventure

Geraldin, Francis see Fitzgerald, Francis

Geraldin, Gerald, the Elder (Fitz Gerald, Gerrott) (1631: AZK, Propugnaculum 738, IFD 198; G – 1638: APA; Dis – 1639: IFD 288)

Geraldin, Gerald, the Younger (G – 1696: APA)

Geraldin, James see Fitzgerald, James

Gernon, Anthony (Fr, SAs: SIAS; SAs 1689-90: Ms. DD VI 6)

Gossan, Francis [† a. 1788] (1773: APA; Dep – 1782: Lists 83; Cf, Preach – 1784, IN, V at Louvain – 1784: LD)

Grady, Bonaventure (Fr, Arr – 1692: AZK)

Gray, Hugh (Grajus) (Fr, Arr – 1644: AZK; Fr, SAs: SIAS)

Greefy, Mark (Fr, SAs: SIAS)

Griffin, James [* c. 1696 Mun, †1758 Prague] (Cf, Preach – 1724, G at Buttevant – 1724: LD; Fr, LTh, CTD – 1727: Kelly 173 ; CTD, LThA – 1732: NK 46 E 7; CTD, LThA – 1735: NK 46 C 22; CTD, fLThA – 1736: NK 46 C 20; Fr, LThA, Join c. 1713 – 1737: APAp; CTD, LThA – 1738: NK 46 C 21; LJ, Dis – 1744: ŘF-SD; LTh, CTD, Lit – 1732, 1735, 1736, 1738, 1739, 1741: Kelly 173, Kuchařová/Pařez 208-211; LJ – 1742: LD)

Guiney, Patrick see Conway, Patrick

Hackett, Patrick [† a. 1770] (LPh at Louvain – 1733, LThM at Louvain – 1735, G at Louvain – 1736, 1738, PNAp – 1738, G at Enniscorthy – 1741, G at Ballinasagart – 1744, IN at Boulay – 1746: LD; Lib – 1752: Catalogus librorum; LTh – 1754: Theologia)

Hanly, Eugene [† a. 1778] (Br, DT – 1750: Kuchařová/Pařez 216; Fr, DT – 1752: Kuchařová/Pařez 216; Cf, Preach – 1755, 1759, G at Elphin – 1760, 1761, G at Ballymote – 1772: LD)

Hanly, Francis [† a. 1724] (Br – 1673: AZK; G at Elphin – 1685, Cf, Preach – 1687, IN at Elphin – 1687, G at Aran – 1700: LL)

Harold, Francis [*Limerick – †16.3.1685 Rome](LThAs, Lit – 1645: Kuchařová/Pařez 211-212; Fr, LThAs 2x, LJ, annalist of OFM: SIAS; SPh in Prague, STh Austria – Browne 358)

Harran, Francis [†1680] (Lists 63)

Hart, Patrick (Harth) (1786: ČGP/2729; Cf, Preach – 1787, V at Boulay – 1787, G at Roscrea – 1790, G at Nenagh – 1791, 1793, 1794, 1796, 1800, 1801, 1803, 1804, 1806, G at Bantry – 1815: LD)

Heaffy, James (Fr, 1770: Lists 75)

Hease, Anthony (Br, 1770: Lists 76; 1773: Lists 77; Dep – 1782: Lists 82)

Hehir, Thaddeus (SPh, Mun – 1650-1: Millett 136)

Herbert, Jeremiah (G at Askeaton – 1645, 1647, 1648, 1670, 1675, 1676, 1681, 1683, 1687: LL; Br, Mun – 1650-1: Millett 136; 1652: FA Harrach; Fr – 1653-4: Millett 136; Def – 1650, 1678-1681, G at Adare – 1669, Exam – 1689: LL)

Hickey, Anthony (Hiquaeus) [* c. 1709 Mun – † a. 1778] (Fr, DT – 1736: NK 46 C 20; Fr, Join c. 1729, Arr c. 1731 – 1737: APAp; G at Bantry – 1751, 1753, G at Lislaghtin – 1763, 1765, G at Cashel – 1767, G at Quin – 1770, G at Askeaton – 1773: LD)

Higgin, Francis [* c. 1706 Uls – † a. 1772] (LThH – 1734: NK 46 C 22, Quaestiones; LThH – 1735: NK 46 C 20 † De Deo uno; Fr, LThH – 1737: APAp)

Higgins, Bernardine (Higgin) (Fr, Dep to Silesia – 1641: AZK; LPhAs – 1646: AN; LTh, Con – 1650-1: Millett 135; LTh – 1652: FA Harrach; LJ, LThAs, 13 years LTh in Plasy: SIAS; Lit – Kuchařová/Pařez 212; G at Rosserilly – 1669, 1670, LJ – 1670, G at Ballymote – 1672, Def 1678-1680: LL)

Higgins, Peter (Fr, LPh, Lei – 1650-1: Millett 136; LPh – 1653-4: Millett 137; G at Athlone – 1661: LL)

Hoar, Matthew (Hore, Hory) [*Dungarvan – †7.11.1631 Oleška, Bohemia](S at St Anthony, Louvain: Browne 338; about his death Propugnaculum 741-753; 1631: IFD 186-7; D – 1631: IFD 213)

Hogan, Daniel [† a. 1765] (Cf, Preach – 1757, 1763: LD; Dep – 1762: Lists 72; G at Inisherkin – 1763: LD)

Hogan, William [† a. 1760, Mun] (G – 1737-1739: APAp; G at Nenagh – 1744, 1746, 1748, 1751, 1753, 1755, Cs – 1757: LD)

Holtaghan, Philip (Fr, DT – 1735: Kuchařová/Pařez 209; LPh at Boulay – 1739, LPh at Louvain – 1741, LTh at Louvain – 1742, 1744, Cf, Preach – 1755, G at Dungannon – 1755, G at Drogheda – 1760, 1761, G at Downpatrick – 1765, Def – 1767: LD)

Hosey, John (Hosea) (Arr – 1713: APA)

Hughes, Benedict (STh, Uls – 1653-4: Millett 137)

Hughes, Peter (Hugonius) [† a. 1748] (1690: APAp; G at Multyfarnham – 1736, 1739, 1741, 1746: LD)

Jackson, Martin [† a. 1748] (V – 1712: APA; Cf, Preach – 1717, G at Castledermot – 1717: LL; G at Castledermot – 1719, G at Trim – 1727, 1742, 1744: LD)

Jennings, Thomas (Fr, V, Con – 1650-1: Millett 135; V – 1652: FA Harrach; Cf, Preach – 1672, LJ – 1672, G at Rosserilly – 1675, 1676: LL)

Jones, Peter (Junius) [* c. 1672 Lei] (Fr, SAs, LPh in Rome: SIAS; SAs 1689-90: Ms. DD VI 6; LTh – 1725: SbR; Fr, LJ, Dis, Join c. 1688, CVis, LJ 1735-1737: APAp)

Jordan, Francis (Fr, Arr – 1644: AZK; Cf – 1647: LL)

Jordan, Paul [* c. 1672] (Join c. 1703 in Louvain, Arr c. 1708, LBr – 1737: APAp)

Joyce, Joseph (Jois) [† a. 1830] (1786: ČGP/2729; Cf, Preach – 1787, G at Claregalway – 1787, 1788, G at Moyne – 1790, G at Dromahaire – 1819, 1822, 1824, 1825, 1827, 1828: LD)

Keally, Francis (Kealy) [† a. 1800] (Fr, DT – 1751: Kuchařová/Pařez 212; Cf, Preach – 1755: LD; Dep – 1758: Lists 72; G at Rosserilly – 1765, 1770, 1772, 1785, G at Rosserk – 1779, 1781, G at Aran – 1787, 1793, custos 1788-1790, CVis – 1791, G at Moyne – 1796: LD)

Kearney, Peter (Kearny) (G – 1684?: NM; Cf, Preach – 1689, Exam – 1689, G at Wexford – 1689, 1690, Cs – 1697-1700, G at Dublin – 1700, 1702: LL)

Kelly, Anthony, the Elder (Fr, SAs: SIAS)

Kelly, Bonaventure, the Elder (O'Kelly) (Br, Con – 1650-1: Millett 136; STh – 1653-4: Millett 137; LPhAs: SIAS; LPh – 1665: FA Harrach; Cf, Preach – 1669, 1681, G at Kilconnell – 1672, G at Meelick – 1683, 1684, 1685, 1687: LL)

Kelly, Martin (S – 1770: Lists 75)

Kelly, Peter, the Elder [† a. 1745] (SAs 1689-90: Ms. DD VI 6; 1690: APAp; Cf, Preach – 1699: LL; Cf, Preach – 1724, G at Dromore – 1733, 1735, G at Drogheda – 1738, 1744: LD)

Kennedy, John (LBr, Uls – 1653-4: Millett 137)

Keogh, Cornelius (Keoch) (Fr, Arr – after 1632: Hammerschmid 301)

Keogh, Michael [* c. 1709 Con] (Fr, LThM, Join c. 1727: APAp; DT – 1732: Kuchařová/Pařez 208-209, Kelly 173; G – 1754: Theologia; Fr, LThA, CTD – 1758: Kelly 173; LTh – 1760: LD)

Keoghy, Anthony (1690: APAp; Cf, Preach – 1699, V at Boulay – 1700, 1702, G at Boulay – 1709, 1711, G at Kilconnell – 1717: LL; G at Kilconnell – 1719, G at Boulay – 1727: LD)

Kernaghan, Laurence (Kennegan) (Preach, Lei – 1653-4: Millett 137)

Killdea, Bonaventure (Kildare?) (1773: APA; Cf, Preach – 1776, 1778, LThM at Boulay – 1776: LD; G – 1782+1783: APA; Dep – 1783: Lists 73)

Killilwelly, Bonaventure (Killikelly?) (1773: APA; Dep – 1773: Lists 73)

Kimmon, Simon (Kymon, Kimos) (SPh, Lei – 1653-4: Millett 137; Cf, Preach – 1661, G at Wicklow – 1675: LL)

Kinraghty, Anthony (Fr, Arr – 1650: AZK; SPh, Mun – 1650-1: Millett 136; 1653-4: Millett 136; Cf, Preach – 1678, G at Quin – 1678, 1680, 1684, 1685, 1689, G at Ennis – 1681, J – 1697: LL)

Kirwan, Andrew (Kiervan) [* c. 1718 Mun – † a. 1760] (Join c. 1735, Ph, SPh – 1737: APAp; Cf, Preach – 1746: LD)

Kirwan, Francis (Fr, DT – 1762: Kuchařová/Pařez 216-217; Cf, Preach – 1776, LPh at Louvain – 1776: LD)

Kirwan, James [† a. 1793] (IN at Louvain – 1778: LD; Dep – 1782: Lists 83; G at Castlelyons – 1787: LD)

Kullinan, Anthony (Ph, N – 1770: Lists 76)

Kullinan, Charles [† a. 1778] (V – 1770: Lists 75; V – 1773: Lists 77; LPh at Louvain – 1773, G at Limerick – 1776: LD)

Landy, Michael (Fr, SAs, LTh: SIAS; Cf, Preach – 1700: LL)

Lee, Thomas (1690: APAp)

Lewis, Francis [† a. 1782] (Cf, Preach – 1763, LPh at Boulay (appointed) – 1763: LD; Dep – 1764: Lists 72; LPh at Boulay – 1765, 1767, Lib at Boulay – 1778, 1779, LTh at Boulay – 1779: LD)

Lewis, Michael (Dep – 1782: Lists 83)

Lonnergan, Patrick (1773: APA; Cf, Preach – 1779, 1782, G at Kilcrea – 1782, 1784, 1785, 1787, G at Askeaton – 1793: LD)

Lorcan, Bernard [†29.1.1716 Meelick] (1690: APAp; Fr, SAs, LTh: SIAS; Cf, Preach – 1699, G at Ballymote – 1699, Def – 1700-1701, G at Meelick – 1703, 1705, 1714, 1716: LL; Browne 376)

Lorcan, John (Fr, SAs, LTh: SIAS)

Lorcan, Peter (Fr, Cf, Arr – 1649: AZK; incorporated into the Bohemian province – 1651: Mac-Grath 337)

Lorcan, Thomas (1786: ČGP/2729)

Lynch, Bernardine (Lynsius) (Ph, Arr – after 1632: Hammerschmid 302)

Lynch, John [† a. 1803] (Cf, Praech – 1778, LPh at Boulay (appointed) – 1781: LD; Dep – 1782: Lists 83; G at Bonamargy – 1787, G at Dromore – 1790, G at Donegal – 1793: LD)

Lynch, Patrick (LBr, Con – 1653-4: Millett 137)

Mac Caughwell, James (Fr, Uls – 1653-4: Millett 137)

Mac Guane, Anthony (Maguan) (STh – 1782: APA)

MacCaffrey, Anthony (SPh, Uls – 1653-4: Millett 137)

MacCullin, Anthony [* c. 1710 Lei, † c. 1782] (Fr, Join c. 1734, Ord c. 1736 – 1737: APAp; Fr, DT – 1739: Kuchařová/Pařez 210-211; Cf, Preach – 1760: LD; 1770: Lists 75; 1773: Lists 77)

MacCullin, Michael [†16.1.1734 Prague] (Fr, G, LThA – 1732: Tractatus theologicus; G – 1734, LTh – 1737: APAp)

MacCullin, Patrick [* c. 1712] (Fr, SPh, Join c. 1732, Arr c. 1733 – 1737: APAp)

MacDonell, Francis [† a. 1781] (1770: Lists 75; G at Cavan – 1773: LD)

MacGeoghegan, Peter see Geoghegan, Peter

MacGlaine, Peter (Mac Gloin?) (Ph, N – 1770: Lists 76; 1773: Lists 78; 1773: APA; Dep – 1782: Lists 83)

MacGrannell, Thaddeus (Mac Granell) (Fr, Cf, Con – 1650-1: Millett 135)

Machamius, Louis (Maugham?) (Fr, Arr – 1633: Hammerschmid 301)

Macher, Nicholas (Meagher?) [* c. 1707 Mun – † a. 1772] (Fr, Sacr, Join c. 1726, Arr 1736 – 1737: APAp; Cf, Preach – 1754: LD)

MacHugh, Anthony (MacHugo) [†1756 Meelick] (CVis 1714 – 1737: APAp; G at Aran – 1717, LTh – 1717: LL; G at Aran, Cf sisters of Galway – 1719, Def – 1720, MP – 1724-1727, G at Meelick – 1729, PP – 1733, 1734, 1736, 1738, 1741, 1742, 1748, 1751, J, LJ – 1748: LD; Browne 377)

MacHugh, Edmund (LPh – 1782: Lists 81)

MacHugh, Edward (L, Dep – 1765: Lists 72; Dep – 1783: Lists 73)

MacHugh, Francis, the Elder (MacHugo) [† a. 1742] (LThM at Louvain – 1707, LTh at Louvain – 1711: LL; LJ – 1724: Origines)

MacHugh, Francis, the Younger (Hughes) [† a. 1801] (S – 1770: Lists 75; LPh – 1782: APA; LTh – 1786, Cf, Preach – 1800, G at Ballymote – 1800: LD)

MacKenna, Francis (McKenna, Ma-Kenna) [c. 1645–19.10.1684] (Fr, LJ, LThAs 5 years: SIAS)

MacMahon, Anthony [† a. 1776] (DT – 1725: SbR; LTh – 1724: Origines; G at Dundalk – 1751, 1753, 1757, 1759, 1761, 1767, 1770, 1772, Def – 1763–1765: LD)

MacManus, Charles (Macmanus) [* c. 1706 Uls] (Fr, Join c. 1730 – 1737: APAp)

MacNamara, Anthony [† a. 1779] (Fr, DT – 1741: Kuchařová/Pařez 211; G at Quin – 1753, 1754, 1757, 1759, 1763, 1772, 1776, G at Ennis – 1767: LD)

MacNamara, Louis, the Elder (Mac-Namara) (Fr, G, SAs, LTh, LJ: SIAS; LJ – 1697: LL; LPh, LTh, CTD – 1698: Kuchařová/Pařez 218)

MacNamara, Louis, the Younger (Fr, LThA, CTD, Lit – 1751: Kuchařová/Pařez 212)

MacNamie, Louis (Arr, Fr, L – 1633: AZK)

MacVeigh, Andrew (Vitalis) (Fr, LPhAs, LTh in Rome, LJ: SIAS)

Madden, Francis, the Elder (Maddenus, Maddin) [* c. 1664 – †5.5.1728 Meelick] (1690: APAp; fLTh – Browne 383 Cf, Preach – 1699, G at Aran – 1709, 1711, G at Claregalway – 1714, G at Meelick – 1717: LL; G at Meelick – 1719: LD)

Madden, Francis, the Younger (Maddin) [* c. 1714 Con] (Join c. 1731, Br, S – 1737: APAp)

Madden, James (Maddin) [† a. 1753] (1700: APA; Cf, Preach – 1699, 1702, G at Aran – 1702, 1703, 1705, 1708, G at Meelick – 1709, 1711: LL; G at Meelick – 1727, 1738, 1739, G at Moyne – 1729, LJ – 1736: LD)

Magauran, Philip (N – 1773: Lists 78; Dep – 1780: Lists 73)

Magawly, Francis (Ma-Gauly) (Fr, SAs, LThA: SIAS; G at Drogheda – 1689, G at Bonamargy – 1690, Cf, Preach – 1700, Def – 1703–1706, G at Athlone – 1706, 1711, CVis, PraeC – 1709: LL)

Magdonon, Thomas [* c. 1708 Lei – † a. 1765] (Fr, Join c. 1730, Arr c. 1732, from 1736 chaplain to Count von Herberstein – 1737: APAp; Cf, Preach – 1736, G at Wicklow – 1751, 1761, G at Castledermot – 1753, G at Enniscorthy – 1757, 1759: LD)

Magennis, Anthony, the Elder (Magnesius) (1678: APA; Cf, Preach – 1684, G at Downpatrick – 1684, 1685 G at Dromore – 1690: LL)

Magennis, Anthony, the Younger (Magenis) [* c. 1709 Uls – † a. 1765] (DT – 1732: NK 46 C 7 + Kelly 173; Fr, LPh, Join c. 1726 – 1737: APAp; Cf, Preach – 1733: LD; LTh, Dis – 1744: ŘF-SD; LJ – 1751: Cs – 1754; LD; LJ, Dis – 1762: De divina revelatione)

Magennis, Francis (Magnesius, Magnetius) (Uls, Arr 1631: Propugnaculum 741, IFD 190; 1641: APA; 1650–1: Millett 135; 1652–4: Millett 137, FA Harrach; V – 1656: APA; Def – 1656: LL; 1657: APA; Fr, SAs, G 2x: SIAS)

Magoada, Benedict (SPh, Uls – 1650–1: Millett 135)

Magovan, Anthony (Dep – 1782: Lists 83)

Maguire, Denis (Bishop of Dromore and Kilmore) [† a. 1800] (LPh at Louvain – 1748, Cf, Preach – 1751, G at Louvain (appointed) – 1757: LD; Dep – 1758: Lists 72; LTh at Louvain – 1759, G at Lisgoole – 1761, 1765: LD)

Maguire, Francis [† a. 1782] (LThA, LPr 1731–1732: NK 46 E 7; Cf, Preach – 1735; G at Lisgoole – 1735, 1757, 1760, 1763, 1779, Def – 1736–1738, MP – 1739–1741, PP – 1745, CVis – 1757, primus PP – 1759, J – 1760, J – 1767: LD)

Mahony, Donat (Br, Arr – 1646: AZK; STh, Mun – 1650–1: Millett 136; G at Askeaton – 1672, G at Lislaghtin – 1675: LL)

Mahony, Thomas (SPh, Mun – 1650–1: Millett 136; 1652: FA Harrach; Cf, Preach – 1661: LL)

Malone, John [†8.4.1707 Louvain](Cf, Preach – 1700, G at Castledermot – 1700, G at Athlone – 1702: LL; PTh, CTD – 1703: Kelly 172; Fr, LTh, CTD, Lit – 1703: Kuchařová/Pařez 213; LTh at Louvain – 1705, 1706: LL; Browne 159)

Managhan, Bonaventure (Managan) (LPh, CTD – 1750: Theses)

Mannin, James (Mannene) (1690: APAp)

Marley, Patrick, the Elder (LBr, Uls – 1653–4: Millett 137)

Marley, Patrick, the Younger (Marly) [* c. 1706] (Fr, STh, Join c. 1731, Arr c. 1734 – 1737: APAp)

Martin, Denis [† a. 1788] (Cf, Preach – 1760, G at Kilcrea – 1760: LD; 1773: Lists 77; 1782: Lists 81; admitted to the Brothers of Mercy hospital – 1787: ČGP/2729)

Martin, James [† a. 1793] (1770: Lists 75; LPh at Boulay – 1770, LThM at Boulay – 1772, G at Aran – 1773, 1791, G at Galway – 1779, 1781, Cf of sisters – 1779: LD)

Martin, John (1773: APA; Dep – 1782: Lists 83)

McSweeney, Anthony (came from Lorraine to give lectures – 1786: ČPG/2729)

McSweeney, Francis (Sweiny) (Fr, SAs: SIAS)

McSweeney, Michael (Sweiny) [† a. 1724] (Fr, SAs: SIAS; Cf, Preach – 1714, G at Inisherkin – 1714, 1716, V at Louvain – 1714: LL; G at Timoleague – 1719, 1720: LD)

Mellaghlan, Francis [* Athlone – c. 1729] (LThJ, LTh at Cathedral Seminary of Imola: Browne 366)

Molloy, Anthony (SPh, Lei – 1650–1: Millett 136; STh – 1653–4: Millett 137; Fr, SAs: SIAS; Cf, Preach – 1669, G at Killeigh – 1669, 1670, 1681, 1683, 1684, 1685, G at New Ross – 1675, 1687, G at Wexford – 1676, 1678, 1693, 1699, 1700, Def – 1678–1681, Exam – 1689, J – 1697: LL)

Molloy, Bernard, the Elder (O'Molloy) [†c. 1733 Prague] (LThA – 1731: NK 46 E 7; LTh – 1732: Tractatus theologicus)

Molloy, Bernard, the Younger (Fr, LTh – 1737: APAp)

Molloy, Hugh (1636?: APA)

Molloy, John [† a. 1819] (Dep – 1776: Lists 73; Cf, Preach – 1779, G at Kildare – 1779, G at Trim – 1785, 1787, 1793, 1800, 1815, G at Castledermot – 1791, G at Monasteroris – 1794, 1796: LD)

Molloy, Laurence (1656: APA)

Molloy, Peter (Molloi) (Arr, Fr, L – 1633: AZK, Hammerschmid 301; G at Killeigh – 1647, 1648: LL)

Molloy, William (Moloy) [* c. 1708] (Fr, STh, Join c. 1730 – 1737: APAp; Cf, Preach – 1738, G at Slane – 1746, G at Dublin – 1748, 1751, 1754, 1755, 1763, 1765, Def – 1751–1753: LD)

Moran, Michael [† a. 1819] (Br – 1770: Lists 76; Cf, Preach – 1772, G at Kilkenny – 1776, 1778, G at Dublin – 1785, 1787, 1791, 1793, 1794, 1796, 1800, 1803, 1804, 1806, 1815, Def – 1788–1790, PraeC – 1815, J – 1815: LD)

Moran, Thomas (LPh – 1690: APAp; LJ – 1708: LL)

More, Francis (Moore, Morus) (1690: APAp; G – 1699: NM; Fr, Lit – 1700: Kuchařová/Pařez 214; G – 1700: APA; G – 1701: NM)

Moyne, Daniel (SPh, Con – 1653–4: Millett 137)

Mulligan, Michael (STh – 1782: APA)

Mulshinnoch, Francis (Fox, Mullsinoge) (SPh, Mun – 1650–1: Millett 136; 1652: FA Harrach; Cf, Preach – 1661: LL)

Murphy, Anthony, the Elder (Morphy) (LPhAs, Lit – 1688–9: Kuchařová/Pařez 214; LPhAs – 1689–90: Ms. DD VI 6; LTh – 1690: APAp; Fr, LPhAs 2x, fLTh: SIAS; Cf, Preach – 1697, G at Timoleague – 1697, 1699, G at Kilcrea – 1702, 1717, G at Bantry – 1703, 1705, 1709, 1711, 1714, Def – 1706–1708: LL; G at Bantry – 1719, G at Cork – 1724, 1727: LD)

Murphy, Anthony, the Younger [* c. 1695 Con, †1762 Prague] (Fr, LTh, Dis, Join c. 1720 – 1737: APAp; LTh, Dis – 1744: ŘF-SD; LTh, LJ, Lit – 1755: Kuchařová/Pařez 214–215; Cf, Preach – 1741, LJ – 1748: LD)

Murphy, Bernardine (Morphy) [† a. 1741] (DT – 1718: SbR; LJ – 1738: LD)

Murphy, James (1770: Lists 75; 1771–1773: APA; Dep – 1777: Lists 73)

Murry, Anthony (Fr, SAs: SIAS; SAs 1689–90: Ms. DD VI 6)

Murry, James (Cf, Preach – 1779, G at Castledermot – 1779: LD; Dep – 1782: Lists 83)

Murry, Peter Marian (Murray) [† c. 1697] (LThAs, Lit – 1691: Kuchařová/Pařez 215; LTh Waldsassen – 1695: NK 46 D 115; Fr, G, LThAs 9 years, lector in ethics there for 5 years, LJ, LTh in Waldsassen, LTh in Bologna 4 years: SIAS; LJ – 1697: LL, Browne)

Murtagh, Patrick (1773: APA; Cf, Preach – 1778: LD)

Neylan, Patrick [* c. 1714 Con – † a. 1787] (Br, D, Join c. 1731 – 1737: APAp; V – 1746: ČDK; Cf – 1748,

G at Claregalway – 1748, 1751, 1759, 1763, 1767, 1770, 1778, 1779, 1781, 1785, Def – 1751–1753, J – 1782: LD)

Nollet, Didacus (LBr, Arr – 1649: AZK)

Noulus, Matthew [* c. 1705] (Fr, STh, Join c. 1730, Arr c. 1733 – 1737: APAp)

O'Beirne, Francis (Beirne, Bern) (SPh, Con – 1650-1: Millett 135; LPh – 1653-4: Millett 136; LThAs, LPhAAs, CTD, Lit – 1660: Kuchařová/Pařez 215; LTh – 1657: APA; Cf – 1669, G at Elphin – 1669, 1670, 1675, 1680, 1683, 1684, Def – 1672, J – 1690: LL)

O'Brien, Anthony, the Elder (O'Bryne, Braen) (Fr, SAs: SIAS; SAs 1689-90: Ms. DD VI 6; 1690: APAp)

O'Brien, Anthony, the Younger (LPhA, CDT, Lit – 1750: Kuchařová/Pařez 216; LTh, CTD, Lit – 1752: Kuchařová/Pařez 216; LThA, CTD, Lit – 1756: Kuchařová/Pařez 216; LTh, CTD, Lit – 1762: Kuchařová/Pařez 216-217; L – 1770: Lists 75, 135; LJ – 1773: APA; LJ, LTh – 1782: APA; LJ, 72 years--old – 1786: ČGP/2729; Lib – 1786: ČGP/2729; 1786: APA)

O'Brien, Anthony, the Youngest [† a. 1793] (Ph, 1770: Lists 75; Fr, DT – 1772: Kuchařová/Pařez 202; 1773: Lists 77; 1782: Lists 82; 1786: ČGP/2729; Cf, Preach – 1787, G at Galbally 1787-1788, 1790-1791: LD)

O'Brien, Bonaventure [† June 1773 Cork] (Fr, LTh, CTD – 1756: Kelly 173; LPhA, CTD – 1758: Kelly 173; LPhA, CTD, Lit – 1758: Kuchařová/Pařez 217; G, fLTh – 1762: De divina revelatione; ex-G, Dep – 1766: Lists 72; ex-MP, G in Cork – 1773: Browne 180)

O'Brien, Joseph (Fr, SAs: SIAS; SAs 1689-90: Ms. DD VI 6; 1690: APAp)

O'Brien, Malachy (Fr, SAs, LTh: SIAS; Cf – 1693: LL)

O'Brien, William [* c. 1710 Lei – a. 1778] (Prof c. 1730, Arr 1736, Dep 1737, Fr, LPh – 1737: APAp; G at Bantry – 1748, LJ – 1751: LD)

O'Bruin, Laurence (Fr, Arr – 1634: Hammerschmid 301; G at Killeigh – 1639, G at Ballynabarny – 1647-1648, 1650, LTh – 1647, J – 1670; Def *subrogatus* – 1670; PrPS – 1672: LL)

O'Connor, John (Fr, Arr – 1650: AZK; STh, Lei – 1650-1: Millett 136)

O'Connor, Valentine (Cf, Preach – 1650: LL; Preach, Con – 1653-4: Millett 137)

O'Cornen, Thomas (insane – 1786: ČGP/2729)

O'Devlin, Francis, the Elder (Develin) [* Tyrone – † 1735] (SAs 1689-90: Ms. DD VI 6; Br, LPh, LJ – 1697: Kelly 172; LPh, CTD – 1697, LTh, CTD, Lit – 1698: Kuchařová/Pařez 217-219 + NK; LTh, CVis – 1704: SbR; LJ – 1711: LL; Br, LTh, LJ – 1713: Kelly 173; Fr, SAs, LTh, LTh in Waldsassen: SIAS; G at Dungannon – 1714, G at Drogheda – 1716, Cs – 1717: LL; G at Dungannon – 1720: LD, Browne 367)

O'Dolan, Anthony (1770: Lists 75; S, Cf – 1783+1786: APA; 1786: ČGP/2729)

O'Dolan, John (Cf, Sacr, fV – 1782: APA)

O'Dolan, Peter (1786: ČGP/2729)

O'Donell, Bonaventure (Dep – 1786: ČGP/2729)

O'Donell, John (Ph, 1770: Lists 75)

O'Donell, Michael [† a. 1791] (STh – 1782: Lists 80; Cf, Preach – 1784, G at Muckross – 1784, G at Bantry – 1787: LD)

O'Donnell, Anthony (1773: Lists 78)

O'Donnell, Louis (L, Dep – 1768: Lists 72)

O'Donoghue, Patrick (1786: ČGP/2729)

O'Flynn, Bonaventure (LPhAs – 1689-90: Ms. DD VI 6; LTh – 1690: APAp; Fr, LPhAs, LTh: SIAS)

O'Flynn, James, the Elder (V – 1690: APAp)

O'Flynn, James, the Younger [†21.4.1815 Kilkenny] (Fr, LPhA, CTD, Lit – 1780: Kuchařová/Pařez 219: Dep – 1781: Lists 73; Cf, Preach – 1781, 1790, G at Killeigh – 1781, 1782, LThM at Boulay – 1784, LTh at Louvain – 1790, G at Kildare – 1791, 1793, 1794, 1796, G at Drogheda – 1801, 1803, 1804, 1806, MP – July 1811: Browne 292)

O'Hagan, Francis [† a. 1793] (S – 1782: Lists 81; Cf, Preach – 1788, G at Monaghan – 1790, G at Dromore – 1791: LD)

O'Hogan, Denis [† a. 1815] (SPh – 1782: APA; Cf, Preach – 1785, G at Nenagh – 1787, 1788, 1790, G at Lislaghtin – 1791, G at Limerick – 1793, 1794, 1796, 1800, 1801, 1803, 1804, 1806, Cs 1796-1800: LD)

O'Hogan, Francis (Arr – 1782: Lists 83)

O'Hogan, Thomas [† a. 1803] (LPh – 1773: APA; fLThA – 1782: APA; 1783: APA; G, LJ – 1786: APA; 14th G – 1786: ČGP/2729; LJ – 1787: LD; 1796+1798: APA)

O'Kane (Ph, N – 1770: Lists 76)

O'Kelly, Anthony, the Younger (Dep – 1760: Lists 72; Sacr – 1773: APA)

O'Kelly, Anthony, the Youngest (Ph, SPh – 1782: APA)

O'Kelly, Bonaventure, the Younger [† a. 1815] (1770: Lists 75; LTh – 1773: APA)

O'Kelly, Edmund (Ph, SPh – 1782: APA)

O'Kelly, Francis [† a. 1785] (Cf, Preach – 1751, G at Clean – 1753, G at Kildare – 1754, G at Athlone – 1757, 1759: LD; Dep – 1782: Lists 83)

O'Kelly, James (Kelly) (Fr, DT – 1757: Kuchařová/Pařez 207; Ord Prague – 1754, 55 years old, 34 years in the college – 1786: ČGP/2729; Fr, DT – 1756+1760: Kuchařová/Pařez 206-207; LJ, LTh – 1782: APA; G – 1785+1786: APA)

O'Kelly, John, the Elder (DT, came from the family of O'Kellys "de Mullaghmore (north), Mulach (near Maynooth) et Raghlass" – 1732: Kelly 173)

O'Kelly, John, the Younger (Fr, DT – 1762: Kelly 174; 1770: Lists 75)

O'Kelly, Nicholas [† a. 1796] (1773: APA; Dep – 1774: Lists 73; Cf, Preach – 1776, G at Kilconnell – 1776: LD)

O'Kelly, Patrick [† a. 1733] (G – 1727-8: Autentika; LJ – 1729, G at Kilconnell – 1729: LD)

O'Kelly, Peter, the Younger (Kelly) [† a. 1790] (LJ – 1765: LD; L – 1770: Lists 75; LJ, fG – 1773: APA; LJ, LTh – 1782: APA; age over 60 – 1786: ČGP/2729; request for secularisation – 1786: APA)

O'Kennedy, James [† a. 1727] (Br, DT – 1697: Kelly 172; Cf, Preach – 1700, G at Downpatrick – 1716, G at Dromore – 1717: LL; Cf, Preach – 1720, G at Dromore – 1720: LD)

O'Madden, Thomas [† a. 1742] (O'Madden) (Fr, DT – 1735: Kuchařová/Pařez 209; Cf, Preach – 1739)

O'Mahony, Bernardine (Fr, DT – 1703: Kelly 172; Kuchařová/Pařez 213)

O'Neill, Anthony, the Elder (G – 1705: APS; G – 1707: ŘF-SD)

O'Neill, Anthony, the Eldest (G at Armagh – 1676, 1678, 1680, 1684, 1685, Def – 1681-1683, Exam – 1689, Cs – 1690, G at Drogheda – 1693, J – 1711: LL; Fr SAs, in Ireland Def, Cs, vice-CVis, G at Armagh 4x alternately: SIAS)

O'Neill, Anthony, the Younger [† a. 1772] (Fr, Join c. 1723 – 1737: APAp; G at Downpatrick – 1751, 1753, IN at Boulay – 1761, 1763: LD)

O'Neill, Bernard (O'Nellus) (G at Wieluń – 1650: LL; Fr, fG in Wieluń, Uls – 1653-4: Millett 137; LTh, V – 1665: ŘF-SD)

O'Neill, Francis, the Elder [c. 1645-31.1.1696] (Cf – 1670, LJ – 1681: LL; G – 1681: ŘF-SD; Cf, Preach – 1685: LL; MP – 1687-1690: LL, Browne 363; G – 1694: NM; Fr, G 2x, Prov, CVis in Louvain, LPhAs, LThAs, LJ: SIAS)

O'Neill, Francis, the Younger (1786: ČGP/2729; Cf, Preach – 1788, G at Dromore – 1788, G at Dungannon – 1790, 1793, 1794, 1796, 1800, 1801, 1803, 1804, 1806, 1815, G at Ardmagh – 1791, Def – a. 1815: LD)

O'Neill, Gabriel (1700: APA)

O'Neill, Louis (Cf, Preach – 1685: LL; Fr, LThAs 2x; LPh in Louvain 2x, CVis in Louvain, fLTh: SIAS; CVis – 1690: APAp; LTh – 1698: Gladius; LJ – 1703: LL; LJ – 1706: Philosophia; LJ, LTh – 1710: Philosophia)

O'Neill, Paul (Fr, SAs, G, Def: SIAS)

O'Neill, Peter (Fr, SAs: SIAS; SAs 1689-90: Ms. DD VI 6)

O'Neill, Rudolph [* c. 1679 Uls – † a. 1753] (LTh – 1710: Philosophia; LTh, Dis – 1722: AZK; LJ – 1724: LD; G – 1731, LJ – 1732: NK 46 E 7; LJ – 1732: Tractatus theologicus; LJ – 1734: Quaestiones; LThA – 1734: NK 46 C 22 + De Deo uno; LJ – 1735: NK 46 C 20; Fr, LJ, Dis, Join c. 1698, Dis 1714, G 1718 – 1737: APAp; LJ – 1738: NK 46 C 21; G – 1744: ŘF-SD; G – 1746: AZK; J – 1751: LD)

O'Reilly, Anthony, the Elder [† a. 1781] (Fr, DT – 1768: Kelly 174; 1770: Lists 75; Dep – 1778: Lists 73; Cf, Preach – 1778, 1779, G at Dundalk – 1779: LD)

O'Reilly, Anthony, the Younger (Dep – 1782: Lists 83; 1786: ČGP/2729)

O'Reilly, Eugene, the Elder (O'Reyl) [* c. 1704 Uls – † a. 1763] (Fr, LH, Join c. 1719 – 1737: APAp; LTh: LD)

O'Reilly, Eugene, the Younger [† a. 1790] (Fr, DT – 1765: Kuchařová/Pařez 195–196; G at Strabane – 1776, 1778, G at Cavan – 1781, 1785, 1787, Def – 1782–1784: LD)

O'Reilly, Francis, the Elder (Fr, Preach, Uls – 1653-4: Millett 137)

O'Reilly, Francis, the Younger (1773: Lists 78; Dep – 1778: Lists 73)

O'Reilly, James (Reilly) (LPh – 1773: APA; Dep – 1777: Lists 73)

O'Reilly, John (Fr, Dis 1714 – 1737: APAp)

O'Reilly, Philip, the Elder (Cf – 1629: LL; G – 1650-2: Millett 136, Browne 351; FA Harrach; G – 1653-4: Millett 137; 1656: APA; MP – 1656: LL, Browne 351)

O'Reilly, Philip, the Younger (O'Reily) [c. 1640-26.5.1680] (LAs – 1678: APA; LThAs, Lit – 1678-9: Kuchařová/Pařez 219; Fr, LPhAs, LThAs: SIAS; LJ, G: Browne 351)

O'Reilly, Philip, the Youngest [† a. 1781] (Dep – 1761: Lists 72; G at Monaghan – 1779: LD)

O'Reilly, Terence (V – 1715: ČDK)

O'Reilly, Thomas (Fr, 1770: Lists 75)

Patrick a S. Maria ? (G – 1641: APA)

Pettit, Patrick [* c. 1749 – † 30.11.1811 Wexford] (1773: APA; Cf, Preach – 1779, G at Enniscorthy: LD; Dep – 1782: Lists 82; G at Wexford – 1782, 1784, 1794, 1796, G at Killeigh – 1803: LD; Browne 216)

Phelan, Francis (Dep – 1783: Lists 73)

Phelan, James [* c. 1707, Lei – † a. 1759] ((Fr, SPh, Join c. 1730, Arr c. 1735 – 1737: APAp; SPh – 1737: Lists 68; Cf, Preach – 1739, G at Kilkenny – 1744, G at New Ross – 1746, 1754, 1755: LD)

Phelan, John (LPh – 1782: APA; Cf, Preach – 1784, LTh – 1784, G at Adare – 1784, Def – 1791-1793, G at Waterford – 1794, 1796)

Phelan, Patrick (S – 1782: Lists 81)

Plunkett, Bernardine (Fr, SAs, G 2x, Def: SIAS; Cf, Preach – 1681, G at Kilnalahal – 1681, 1683, Def – 1684-1685, G at Kilconnell – 1687, G at Wicklow – 1699, G at Boulay – 1700, 1702: LL)

Plunkett, James (1786: ČGP/2729; LPh – 1786, LThM at Boulay – 1788: LD)

Prendergast, John (DT – 1762; Dep – 1765: Lists 72; V at Louvain – 1767, V at Boulay – 1776, 1785, IN at Louvain – 1781, 1790, 1791, 1793, LTh at Louvain – 1781, 1790, 1791, 1793, Arch at Louvain – 1781, 1790, 1791, G at Castledermot – 1784, IN at Boulay – 1785, LTh at Boulay – 1785: LD)

Purfield, James (STh – 1782: APA; Cf, Preach – 1785, G at Wicklow – 1790, 1791, 1793, G at Monasteroris – 1804, 1806, G at Castledermot – 1815: LD)

Quin, James (Fr, SAs: SIAS; Cf, Preach – 1699, G at Quin – 1700, 1702: LL)

Ranilly, Bonaventure (Ranillus) (LTh – 1657: APA)

Ranilly, Thaddaeus (1656+1657: APA)

Ravell, Francis (Br, Arr – 1640: AZK)

Ravell, Peter (Fr, Preach, Cf, Arr – 1663: AZK)

Rea, Matthias [* c. 1708 Mun – † a. 1763] (Fr, STh, Join c. 1732 – 1737: APAp; Cf, Preach – 1738, G at Buttevant – 1741, 1757, G at Galbally – 1742, 1746, 1751, 1753, 1755, G at Lislaghtin – 1745, G at Cork – 1760, 1761: LD)

Reilly, Bernardine (Reili) [* c. 1705 – † a. 1781] (Fr, STh, Join c. 1730, Arr c. 1734 – 1737: APAp; Cf, Preach – 1738, LPh at Boulay – 1738, LThM at Louvain – 1739, Cf, Preach – 1742, G at Cavan – 1744, 1754, 1760, 1772, 1776, Def – 1745-1747, G at Derry – 1751, MP – 1751-1754, PP – 1757: LD)

Reynolds, John [† a. 1822] (Dep – 1782: Lists 83; G at Jamestown – 1804, 1806: LD)

Roch ? (Rochus) (Ph, Arr – 1634: Hammerschmid 301)

Roddy, Francis [† a. 1815] (1773: APA; Cf, Preach – 1779, G at Ballinasagart – 1781, 1782, G at Clane – 1791: LD)

Roddy, Philip (Dep – 1782: Lists 82)

Rooney, Edward (Roony) [* c. 1707 Lei – † a. 1773] (Fr, SPh, Join c. 1731 – 1737: APAp; 1770: Lists 75)

Ruane, John (Rouan, Ronan) (Br, SPh – 1782: APA)

Ryan, Louis, the Elder (Fr, DT – 1689: Kuchařová/Pařez 218; Cf, Preach – 1693: LL)

Ryan, Louis, the Younger (DT – 1698: NK; Cf, Preach – 1699, G at Roscrea – 1699: LL)

Scallan, Ambrose (Br – 1770: Lists 76; Cf, Preach – 1772, G at Enniscorthy – 1776, 1782: LD)

Scallan, James (Dep – 1765: Lists 72)

Scot, John (Cf, Preach – 1685: LL; LThAs, Lit – 1688-9: Kuchařová/Pařez 220; LPhAs – 1689-90: Ms. DD VI 6; LTh – 1698: Gladius; LJ – 1703: LL; LTh, LJ, fLThA – 1710: Philosophia; Fr, Dis 1714, 1718 – 1737: APAp; G – 1715: ČDK; LTh, Dis – 1722: AZK; LJ – 1724: Origines; Prae or G – 1728: AZK; Fr, LPhAs 1x, LPh in Louvain 2x, fLTh in Rome and Prague: SIAS)

Sheenan (?), Anthony (Dep – 1764: Lists 72)

Sheenan, James [† a. 1852] (1770: Lists 75; G at Limerick – 1772, G at Lislaghtin – 1773, G at Ardfert – 1776, 1779 G at Inisherkin – 1778, G at Buttevant – 1781, 1785, 1790, 1791, 1793, 1794, 1796, 1800, 1801, 1803, 1804, 1806, 1815, 1819, G at Ennis – 1784, G at Adare – 1787, J – 1815, G at Kilcrea – 1824: LD)

Shiel, James (Cf, Preach – 1687, 1697: LL; 1690: APAp; G at Dundalk – 1697, 1699, G at Downpatrick – 1703, 1705, 1706, 1708, 1714, 1717, G at Dromore 1709, 1711: LL)

Simon, ? (Fr, Arr – 1634: Hammerschmid 301)

Skerrett, Bartholomew, the Elder (Br, Con – 1650-1: Millett 136; STh – 1653-4: Millett 137; Cf, Preach – 1669, G at Claregalway – 1670: LL)

Skerrett, Bartholomew, the Younger [† a. 1742] (Fr, SAs: SIAS; SAs 1689-90: Ms. DD VI 6; 1690: APAp; Cf, Preach – 1699: LL)

Smith, Bonaventure (Fr, DT – 1783: Kuchařová/Pařez 200; 1786: ČPG/2729)

Smith, Laurence (SPh – 1782: APA)

Stuart, Francis, Bishop of Down [† a. 1751] (Dis 1718 – 1737: APAp; MP – 1727-1729, CVis – 1733, PP – 1735: LD)

Suind, James (Arr, Fr, Cf – 1635: AZK)

Taaffe, Denis [† a. 1815] (Br, SPh – 1782: APA; Cf, Preach – 1788, G at Dundalk – 1788: LD. See also Browne 257 where a lot of information does not match)

Taaffe, James [* c. 1623 or 1624 – † 7.12.1681] (Br, Con – 1650-1: Millett 136; STh – 1653-4: Millett 137; Fr, SAs, LJ, apostolic nuncio /not strictly speaking; he was sent on a special mission by Rome/ in Ireland: SIAS)

Taaffe, Nicholas (Br, Uls – 1650-1: Millett 135; SPh – 1653-4: Millett 137)

Taaffe, Patrick, the Elder (Propugnaculum 741, 747; 1631: AZK, IFD 230; G at Drogheda – 1645, G – 1647: LL; 1649: APA; Fr, Cf, Preach, Uls – 1653-4: Millett 137)

Taaffe, Patrick, the Younger [* c. 1681 Lei – † a. 1751] (Fr, V, Join c. 1711 – 1737: APAp)

Thally (?), Patrick (fLTh – 1773: Lists 77; G at Drogheda – 1776, 1778: LD; Dep – 1778: Lists 73; custos – 1779-1781, G at Carrickfergus – 1782, 1784, 1785, 1794, 1796 G at Downpatrick – 1787, Lisgoole – 1790, 1791: LD)

Tighe, Edmund (STh, Con – 1650-1: Millett 136)

Tipper, Michael [* c. 1733 Kildare – †8.10.1801 Trim?] (Fr, DT – 1758: Kelly 173; L, Dep – 1768: Lists 72; G – 1773: APA; Dep – 1774: Lists 73; Cf, Preach – 1776, LThem – 1776, G at Kildare – 1776, 1778, Def – 1779-1781, G at Trim – 1784, 1790, 1791, 1794, 1796, 1801, G at Killeigh – 1793, PraeC, CVis of the chapter – 1801, J – 1801: LD; parish priest of Moimet, vicar forane of Rathmullan district: Browne 265)

Toole, Daniel (Toole) (Cf, Preach – 1735, G at Muckross – 1736: LD; CVis – 1743: ŘF-SD)

Tuite, Anthony (Tuit) (Br, DT – 1697: Kuchařová/Pařez 217-218; Cf, Preach – 1702: LL)

Tuite, James (Br, Lei – 1650-1: Millett 136; STh – 1653-4: Millett 137)

Tunny, Francis (Tunney) [† before 1781] (Ph, 1770: Lists 75; 1773: APA; Cf, Preach – 1778, LTh at Boulay – 1779: LD)

Tyrrell, Edward (Tyrell) (Fr, LPh, Arr – 1634: IFD 277; LThAs – 1646: VB; LThAs – 1648: AN; G – 1641-2: AZK, FA Harrach; Fr, G, LJ, LPhAs, LThAs: SIAS)

Wall, Edmund (Arr – 1713: APA)

Wallis, Anthony (Walsh) [* c. 1709 Mun – † a. 1776] (Fr, LPh, Join c. 1726 – 1737: APAp; LTh at Louvain – 1754, 1755, 1757, G at Killeigh – 1759, 1761, 1765, 1767: LD)

Walsh, Francis (Wallis) (Fr, G, SAs, LTh, G and Def in Apulia: SIAS; Lit – 1713: CIL 379)

Ward, Francis [†19.1.1683 Louvain](Fr, LPh, Arr – 1640: AZK; LTh – 1640: AZK; Fr, Lit, LThAs – 1640–1, LPhAs – 1642: Kuchařová/Pařez 220–221; LPhAs 2x alternately: SIAS; LTh in Louvain: Browne [133])

Ward, Hugh [* Donegal – † 18.11.1635 Louvain](G at Louvain – 1626–1629: LL, Browne 340; Fr, LTh – appointed 1630: IFD 180–1; Browne 92, 340)

Ward, Patrick, the Elder (Arr – after 1632: Hammerschmid 301; Lit, LPhAs – 1636, LAs – 1638: APA; LPhAs – 1640–42: AN; Fr, Th, Con – 1650–1: Millett 135; LPh – 1653–4: Millett 136; 1656+1657: APA; LPhAs, LThAs, LJ: SIAS)

Ward, Patrick, the Younger [c. 1622–1678] (LPh – 1665: FA Harrach; LThAs – 1672–3, 1676–7, LTh, LJ, CTD – 1677: Kuchařová/Pařez 221–222; LTh, LJ, LThAs – 1675: Armamentarium; Fr, LPhAs and LThAs 14 years, LJ: SIAS)

Ward, Paul (Wardaeus) (LPh – 1690: APAp; G – 1702: NM; Preach – 1703: NM; G – 1704: APA; Fr, SAs, LTh: SIAS)

Warren, Peter (Varren) (Vis – c. 1697: NM; PraeC – 1697, G at Dublin – 1697, 1699, 1700, Def – 1700–1702, 1714–1716, VisP – 1700, G at Multyfarnham – 1703, 1705, 1716, MP – 1706–1709, PP – 1714: LL; G at Multyfarnham – 1720, 1724: LD)

Weldon, John (Veldon) (V – 1699–1700: NM)

Weldon, Juniper (LBr, Arr – 1649: AZK)

Whelan, James see Phelan, James

Whelan, Patrick (Fr, DT – 1770: Kuchařová/Pařez 219, Lists 75)

Wyse, Stephen (Fr, DT – 1750: Kuchařová/Pařez 215–216: DT – 1752: Kuchařová/Pařez 216; Cf, Preach – 1755: LD; G at Boulay – 1772: LD; 1773: Lists 78)

Yore, Anthony (Dep – 1782: Lists 83)

Authors' note

We based the identification of Irish names mainly on the reference works by Edward MacLysaght, *Irish Families, Their Names, Arms & Origins*, Blackrock 1991 and by Ida Grehan, *Irish Family Histories*, Schull 1993. We would like to thank the Embassy of Ireland in Prague for their willingness to lend them to us.

If it was not possible to identify the original form of the name, we recorded them in the form of spelling which we found in the sources.

bold form of the name = the form of spelling recorded by us
(name in brackets) = a possible form
[data in square brackets] = identified dates of birth and death

Abbreviations used in the list of Franciscans

46 C 20	*Tractatus theologicus de Deo uno ... Pragae 1736*
46 C 22	*Tractatus theologicus expendens quaestiones prologeticas ... Pragae 1735*
46 D 115	*Disputationes theologicae ... 1695*
46 E 7	*Tractatus theologicus de tribus naturae humanae ... Pragae 1732*
AN	Anály Norbertina [The Annals of Norbertinum]
APA	Archiv pražského arcibiskupství [Archives of the Prague Archbishopric], archive group in NA
APAp	Archiv pražského arcibiskupství, visitační protokol [Archives of the Prague Archbishopric, visitation protocol]
Armamentarium	A. Bruodin, *Armamentarium theologicum*, Pragae 1676
Autentika	Certificate of authenticity drawn up by Simone Gritti, Bishop of Ferentino, on 12 April 1727, in Ferentino for Patrick O'Kelly. The original is held in the private collection of Mr Ladislav Záparka of Prague.
AZK	Archivy zrušených klášterů [Archives of the Abolished Religious Institutes], archive group in NA

Browne	Maelísa Ó Huallacháin, *Notebook 36 of Father Laurence Browne, O.F.M.*, Collectanea hibernica 44–45, 2002–2003, pp. 246–311. Numbers refer to the numbers of persons.
ČDK	Česká dvorská kancelář, kart. č. 387 [Bohemian Court Chamber, cart No. 387], archive group in NA
ČG Publ/(+ number)	České gubernium publicum [Bohemian Regional Governorate - Publicum/carton number], archive group in NA
CIL	Oxford Concise Companion to Irish Literature, ed. R. Welch, Oxford, 2000
De Deo uno	J. Griffin, *Tractatus theologicus de Deo uno*, Pragae 1736
De divina revelatione	Anthony O'Brien, *De divina revelatione ... tractatus*, Pragae 1762
FA Harrach	Familienarchiv Harrach, Allgemeines Verwaltungsarchiv, Österreichisches Staatsarchiv Wien
Gladius	F. O'Devlin, *Gladius spiritus*, Pragae 1698
Hammerschid	J.F. Hammerschmid, *Prodromus gloriae Pragaenae*, Pragae 1723
IFD	B. Jennings (ed.), *Irish Franciscan documents*. Prague I., Archivium Hibernicum or Irish Historical Records. Volume IX., Maynooth 1942
Kelly	R.J. Kelly, *The Irish Franciscans in Prague (1629–1786): Their Literary Labours*, JRSAI 52, 1922
Kuchařová/Pařez	H. Kuchařová and J. Pařez, *On the trail of Irish émigrés in the collections of the Strahov Abbey Library in Prague*, In: The Ulster Earls and Baroque Europe. Refashioning Irish Identities, 1600–1800, eds. Thomas O'Connor and Mary Ann Lyons, Dublin 2010, pp. 183–222
LD	Anselm Faulkner (ed.), *Liber Dubliniensis. Chapter documents of the Irish Franciscans 1719–1875*, Killiney 1978
Lists	Benignus Millett, *Some lists of Irish Franciscans in Prague, 1656–1791*, Collectanea hibernica 36–37, 1994–5, pp. 57–84
LL	Cathaldus Giblin (ed.), *Liber Lovaniensis*, Dublin 1956
MacGrath	K. MacGrath, *The Bruodins in Bohemia*, The Irish Ecclesiastical Record, 5th series 77, 1952
Millett	B. Millett, *The Irish Franciscans 1651–1665*, Analecta Gregoriana vol. 129, Rome 1964
Ms. DD VI 6	*Disputationes viginti de logica*, manuscript in the Strahov library classified under ref. no. DD VI 6, 1689–90
NM	Nová manipulace [New Handling], archive group in NA
SbR	Sbírka rytin [Engraving Collection], saved in NA
Origines	M. A. Franck von Franckenstein, *Origines Magawlyanae*, Pragae 1736
Philosophia	F. O'Devlin, *Philosophia scoto-aristotelico universa*, Norimbergae 1710
Propugnaculum	A. Bruodin, *Propugnaculum catholicae veritatis*, Pragae 1669
ŘF	Řád františkánů [Order of Franciscans Statuta domestica, book no. 14, or carton no. 22], archive group in NA
Quaestiones	J. Griffin, *Tractatus theologicus expendens quaestiones prologeticas*, Pragae 1735
Schmid I.	L. Schmid, *Irská emigrace do střední Evropy v 17. a 18. století, I. část* [L. Schmid, *Irish Emigration to Central Europe in the Seventeenth and Eighteenth Centuries. Part I*], SH 32, 1985
Schmid II.	L. Schmid, *Irská emigrace do střední Evropy v 17. a 18. století, II. část* [L. Schmid, *Irish Emigration to Central Europe in the Seventeenth and Eighteenth Centuries. Part II*], SH 33, 1986
SIAS	Soupis Irů na arcibiskupském semináři [List of Irishmen at the archiepiscopal seminary]: Quartum quod incedit feliciter seu numerus quaternarius, celeberrimo collegio archi-episcopali Pragensi, felix, faustus, et fortunatus, discursu panegyrico deductus, [Pragae] 1697

Theologia	A. Murphy, *Theologica dogmatica*, Pragae 1755
Theses	*Theses philosophicae*, Pragae 1750
Tractatus	B. Baron, *Tractatus catholicus de divino opificio*, Pragae 1744
Tractatus theologicus	J. Griffin, *Tractatus theologicus de ultimo fine hominis*, Pragae 1732
Tříška	J. Tříška, *Disertace pražské university 16.–18. století* [*The Dissertations of Prague University in the Sixteenth to Eighteenth Centuries*], Praha 1977
VB	Vyšší Brod – manuscripts of lectures preserved in the monastery library in Vyšší Brod. Lists of the manuscripts and old prints before 1800 in the State Scientific Library in České Budějovice, compiled by Bohumil Ryba, České Budějovice 1980

GUARDIANS OF THE FRANCISCAN COLLEGE OF THE IMMACULATE CONCEPTION OF THE VIRGIN MARY IN PRAGUE (1629–1786)

1630	Patrick Fleming
1638	Gerald Geraldin
1641	Patrick a S. Maria
1641–1642	Edward Tyrell
1647	Patrick Taaffe
1647	Bernardine Clancy
1650	Mallachy Fallon (only as praeses)
1651–1651	Philip O'Reilly
1653–1654	Philip O'Reilly
1656–1657	Anthony Connor
Until 1660	Anthony Farrell
1660–1661	Bernardine Clancy
1664–1665	Anthony Burke
1670–	James Coghlan
1673–1675	Bernardine Clancy
1676, 1678	Thaddeus Fallon
1681	Francis O'Neill
1684?	Peter Kearney
1689–1690	Francis Burke
1692	Peter Donell
1694	Francis O'Neill
1696	Gerald Geraldin
1698–1699	Thomas Dolan
1699–1701	Francis More
1702–1704	Paul Warde
1705, 1707	Anthony O'Neill
1712–1713	Joseph Devlin
1718	Rudolph O'Neill
1722	Michael Dormer
1724	Francis Fitzgibbon
1727–1728	Patrick O'Kelly
1728	John Scot (guardian or praeses)
1731	Rudolph O'Neill
1732–1734	Michael MacCullin
1734	Nicholas Dalton
1737, 1739	William Hogan
1744, 1746	Rudolph O'Neill
1754	Michael Keogh
1760	Christoph Fleming
1762	Bonaventure O'Brien
1770	Peter Cornen
1773	Michael Tipper
1782–1783	Bonaventure Killdea

1783–1785	Michael Fullum
1785–1786	James O'Kelly
1786	Thomas O'Hogan

Guardians with no precise dates
Anthony Donnelly (until 1682)
Anthony Burke the Younger
Andrew Egan (twice)
Peter Farrell
Louis MacNamara the Elder
Peter Marian Murry
Paul O'Neil
Bernardine Plunkett (twice)

ABBREVIATIONS

AUC	Acta Universitatis Carolinae
AUC-HUCP	Acta Universitatis Carolinae – Historia Universitatis Carolinae Pragensis
BS	Bibliotheca Strahoviensis
CE	The Catholic Encyclopedia, Online Edition 1999
ČKD	Časopis katolického duchovenstva [Journal of the Catholic Clergy]
DP	Documenta Pragensia
HaG	Heraldika a genealogie [Heraldry and Genealogy]
HG	Historická geografie [Historical Geography]
JSH	Jihočeský sborník historický [South Bohemian Historical Review]
MS	manuscript
NA	Národní archiv [National Archives]
NA, 1. odd.	Národní archiv, 1. oddělení [National Archives, Department 1]

Archive groups

	APA	Archiv pražského arcibiskupství [Archives of the Prague Archbishopric]
	AZK	Archivy zrušených klášterů [Archives of dissolved monasteries]
	ČG Publ	České gubernium – Publicum [Bohemian Regional Governorate – Publicum]
	ČSÚ	Česká státní účtárna [Bohemian State Exchequer]
	NM	Nová manipulace [New Handling]
	ŘF	Řád františkánů [Order of Franciscans]
	ŘHyb Praha	Řád hybernů Praha [Order of Irish Franciscans Prague]
	ŘHyb sA	Řád hybernů sv. Ambrož [Order of Irish Franciscans by St. Ambrose]
	L 2, ŘHyb sA	Listiny 2, řád hybernů sv. Ambrož [Documents 2, Order of Irish Franciscans by St. Ambrose]
	SM	Stará manipulace [Old Handling]
	SbR	Sbírka rytin [Engraving Collection]
	SbT	Sbírka typářů [Seal Matrix Collection]

NK	Národní knihovna České republiky [National Library of the Czech Republic]
NPÚ	Národní památkový ústav [National Heritage Institute]
ÖSW, FA Harrach	Familienarchiv Harrach, Allgemeines Verwaltungsarchiv, Österreichisches Staatsarchiv Wien
PA	Památky archeologické (a místopisné) [Archaeological (and Topographical) Monuments]
PSH	Pražský sborník historický [Prague Historical Review]
SH	Sborník historický [Historical Review]
SHK	Sborník historického kroužku [Review of the Historical Circle]
SK	Strahovská knihovna [Strahov Library – the library of the Royal Canonry of Premonstratensians at Strahov, Prague]
Zprávy AUK	Zprávy Archivu Univerzity Karlovy [Newsletter of Charles University Archives]

INDEX

JAN PAŘEZ
HEDVIKA KUCHAŘOVÁ

THE IRISH FRANCISCANS
IN PRAGUE 1629-1786
HISTORY OF THE FRANCISCAN COLLEGE
OF THE IMMACULATE CONCEPTION
OF THE VIRGIN MARY IN PRAGUE

From the Czech original *Hyberni v Praze – Dějiny františkánské koleje
Neposkvrněného početí Panny Marie v Praze (1629–1786)*,
Prague: 2001, English translation by Jana Stoddart and Michael Stoddart

Published by Charles University in Prague,
Karolinum Press
Ovocný trh 3-5, 116 36 Prague 1, Czech Republic
Prague 2016
Vice-Rector-Editor Prof. PhDr. Ing. Jan Royt, Ph.D.
Edited by Jan Sušer, Martin Světlík and Linda Jayne Turner
Proofreading Peter Kirk Jensen
Cover and layout by Jan Šerých
Typeset by DTP Karolinum Press
Printed by Karolinum Press
First English edition, First reprint

ISBN 978-80-246-2676-5
ISBN 978-80-246-2709-0 (online: pdf)